CULTURE CENTERS IN HIGHER EDUCATION

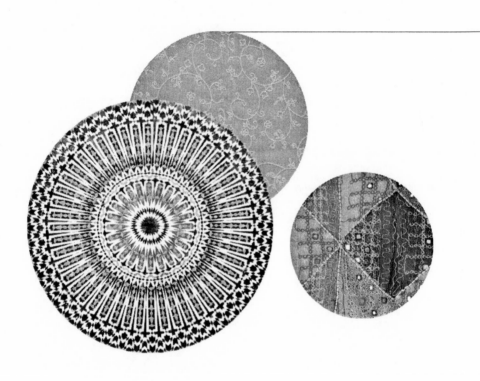

CULTURE CENTERS IN
HIGHER EDUCATION

Perspectives on Identity, Theory, and Practice

Edited by Lori D. Patton

Foreword by Gloria Ladson-Billings

STERLING, VIRGINIA

Sty/us

COPYRIGHT © 2010 BY STYLUS PUBLISHING, LLC.

Published by Stylus Publishing, LLC
22883 Quicksilver Drive
Sterling, Virginia 20166–2102

Library of Congress Cataloging-in-Publication-Data
Culture centers in higher education : perspectives on identity, theory, and practice / edited by Lori Patton ; foreword by Gloria Ladson-Billings.
    1st ed.
      p.   cm.
Includes index.
ISBN 978-1-57922-231-4 (cloth : alk. paper)
ISBN 978-1-57922-232-1 (pbk. : alk. paper)
1. Minority college students—United States—Social
conditions.   2. Education, Higher—Social
aspects—United States.   3. Multiculturalism—United
States.   4. Group identity—United States.   5. United
States—Race relations.   6. United States—Ethnic
relations.
I. Patton, Lori D.
LC3731.C845   2010
378.1'982—dc22   2009042237

13-digit ISBN: 978-1-57922-231-4 (cloth)
13-digit ISBN: 978-1-57922-232-1 (paper)

Printed in the United States of América

All first editions printed on acid free paper
that meets the American National Standards Institute
Z39–48 Standard.

Bulk Purchases

Quantity discounts are available for use in workshops and for staff development.
Call 1–800–232–0223

First Edition, 2010

10   9   8   7   6   5   4   3   2   1

To my parents,
who, no matter what,
consistently encourage me
to pursue my dreams

CONTENTS

ACKNOWLEDGMENTS

A number of individuals made significant contributions to the completion of this book. I would like to thank my partner, Tobias Davis, for his continuous support, for listening when I needed to vent, and for providing the necessary time and space for me to work on this project. I am also thankful to Dr. Mary Howard-Hamilton for serving as my dissertation chair and encouraging me to continue to write about culture centers as an aspect of my research agenda. I am also grateful to her for encouraging me to pursue this book project. I also acknowledge Dr. Shaun Harper, Dr. Michelle McClure, Dr. Ontario Wooden, and Chayla Haynes for their constant support as colleagues and dear friends. I would also like to thank my graduate assistant, Natasha Croom, for providing feedback, keeping materials organized, maintaining contact with the contributors, proofreading, and assisting me with pulling the book together in its final stages. Lastly, this book would not have been possible without the wonderful perspectives and insights shared by the contributors. I appreciate each of these individuals for remaining patient and dedicated for the duration of this project.

My interest in campus culture centers stems from my own place in the historical unfolding of such centers. At the ripe old age of 17, I made the decision to attend a historically Black college. Having attended an integrated high school and grown up in a northern city where race was never far from the thoughts of most adults I encountered, I hoped for a college experience that might allow me to place race "on the shelf" for a few years. Of course, the idea of not dealing with race in the United States is a fiction. It is particularly unfeasible for an African American. However, my participation in protests and social change took place in the safety of an almost all-Black college community. We marched on city hall, we protested the war in Vietnam, and we stood in vigil over the death of Dr. Martin Luther King Jr. However, we never had to worry about racism on campus. We did not need a separate place to congregate to talk about how race and culture were affecting our lives. We could have those conversations any-where—in our dormitories, in the dining hall, on the quad, or in the student center.

When I went to graduate school on the West Coast, I began to see how important these culture centers were (and are) to the intellectual and social growth of the students who access them. The establishment of the Black Community Services Center at my graduate school was a result of the 1968 assassination of Dr. Martin Luther King Jr. It, along with some theme houses, provided a place of refuge and a place of service for Black students. Today, that center provides services to 35 Black volunteer service organiza-tions along with advising, training, and social networking. Its services extend beyond graduation in coordination with the Black alumni organization.

Why do students need culture centers in the 21st century? Haven't we moved past the need to divide into separate racial and ethnic groups? With all that we know about the spurious nature of race as a category, why are we continuing to use the category as a basis for organizing into separate and distinct groups? The answer to this question lies in the reality of life in the United States and on our college campuses. Despite advertising themselves as open and democratic spaces where the marketplace of ideas allows for different and divergent viewpoints, many college and university campuses remain difficult places for students of color to negotiate.

One of the organizations at the Student Associations Fair on a campus in the Southwest recently had a table with a sign proclaiming: "Catch an Illegal Immigrant—Get $100K." Students from the organization wore bright orange T-shirts with the words "Illegal Immigrant" written across the back. One of these students would take off running, and the participant was prompted to chase and retrieve him or her. Upon returning the student to the table, the successful "border agent" received a 100 Grand candy bar. This occurred on a campus where 12.7% of the student population is Latina/o.

Perusing the newspapers, we can find numerous incidents of racial harassment and intimidation. These places that we believe should be safe havens often are not. Students of color often report feeling isolated and misunderstood on the campuses of predominately White institutions. They are less likely to use conventional university services like academic advisors, counseling centers, or mainstream student organizations to deal with their feelings and concerns. Thus the student culture center becomes a source of support and comfort.

In addition to providing social and psychological support for students of color, well-developed centers also serve as an important educational corrective. These centers support lectures, artistic exhibits, workshops, performing arts, and library collections beyond the typical campus offerings. They are places where members of the mainstream and members of a variety of cultural groups can learn about the history, culture, and experiences of others.

Given what we know about the origins and history of student culture centers, a volume that looks at a variety of perspectives regarding cultural centers and asks hard questions about their utility, viability, and sustainability in difficult economic times seems appropriate. As editor, Lori Patton has assembled an outstanding group of scholars who bring multiple lenses to the question of the place of racial/ethnic culture centers on the 21st-century campus. This is a collection that should find a warm welcome on the shelves of college and university administrators and higher education scholars alike.

Gloria Ladson-Billings
University of Wisconsin–Madison

A CALL TO ACTION

Historical and Contemporary Reflections on the Relevance of Campus Culture Centers in Higher Education

Lori D. Patton

In hard times, it is especially important to create homeplaces: safe places among trusted friends to seek refuge and dress wounds of battle and places for hard conversations, where differences can be aired and strategy mapped, where we can struggle with and affirm one another.

—Charles R. Lawrence III, 2002

I n 2004, I completed the first dissertation to focus on the significance of Black culture centers (BCCs) in higher education. As I endeavored to complete the study, it became abundantly clear that the information on culture centers was limited and that there was a need for more research on this particular topic. Much of what I found was historical and focused on the student protests of the 1960s and 1970s. As I read, I realized that the historical literature on BCCs consistently characterized administrators and higher education institutions in general as resistant to change. However, I would argue that another form of resistance was taking place on campuses across the country. Black students were resistant to the discrimination and isolation they felt at predominantly White institutions (PWIs). They were resistant to the lack of change and extremely active during this period of unrest. In order to practice resistance, they galvanized to form coalitions and identified spaces where they could continue resistance.

As I conceptualized this volume, I searched for a quote that encapsulated why I envision culture centers as spaces of resistance. The epigraph eloquently captures the sense of culture centers as counterspaces, a home away from home, and a haven in a hostile territory. The history of culture centers is rooted in a struggle for students to hold institutions of higher education accountable. They made a host of demands to ensure that their experiences were represented and supported in the cultural, academic, and social contexts of the university. BCCs have existed on college campuses dating back to the Black student movement of the late 1960s and early 1970s. They served as the impetus for the establishment of multicultural centers and culture centers representing various racial/ethnic populations. Although they boast a 40-year history, much remains to be learned about their historical roots, current status, and future presence on college campuses. Moreover, the various culture center models and the role that such centers play in the experiences of students are minimally represented in the current literature.

The purpose of this book is to offer an in-depth understanding of culture centers and their role in higher education. This volume is designed to provide readers with multiple perspectives on campus culture centers at PWIs. The chapters in this book provide theoretical lenses through which readers can view culture centers, as well as scholarship that identifies the issues and challenges associated with culture centers.

My hope is that this book will fill a significant void in the literature on culture centers. Despite their significant history, there is only one book on the topic, and it focuses specifically on BCCs. Fred Hord's *Black Culture Centers: Politics of Survival and Identity* is a pioneering work, the first of its kind to address historical and contemporary perspectives regarding BCCs. There remains a need to examine the landscape of culture centers in higher education. As a result of the huge gap in the literature, very little is known about these facilities, which leaves room for erroneous assumptions and criticisms about their value in the absence of substantial evidence. *Culture Centers in Higher Education* sheds light on the genesis of culture centers at PWIs and their current contributions. Quite often, culture centers are viewed as promoting segregation and separatism from the larger campus body. The perspectives offered in this volume clarify the mission of the centers, explain their leadership role and programmatic initiatives, and describe the services they provide to students. Knowledge of these diverse perspectives is essential to recognizing the larger mission of culture centers; a mission rooted in bringing voice, support, and celebration to college students, particularly those from racially underrepresented populations. This book is also designed to provide insight into students' experiences at PWIs, where culture centers are disproportionately represented.

This book can serve several purposes. For administrators and researchers who are unfamiliar with these facilities, we hope its insights will lead to increased support for ethnic minority student populations on campuses. This book can be beneficial in providing information that will help universities improve the experiences of their students—even those institutions with no culture center and no plans to establish one. For campuses that host culture centers, this book will reinforce their importance and role on campus.

Audiences

This book is intended for several audiences, first and foremost those who serve as leaders of culture centers and similar facilities. As a result of the tightening of institutional budgets, administrators of culture centers are under increasing pressure to make a sound case for continued or additional funding. This book provides evidence justifying the continued existence of culture centers on campus. It is a valuable tool for assessing their viability, improving their functioning, and ensuring their future relevance. Moreover, it is a practical resource that can be utilized to inform decisions about sustaining a culture center.

This book is useful for institutions considering the creation of a culture center or similar facility on campus. The contributors provide recommendations and describe models from which other institutions might generate ideas. This book can also be used in the classroom. Faculty who teach student affairs courses will find this book to be a great resource for courses that focus on the campus environment, and courses concerned with diversity and multiculturalism in higher education. This book also contributes to the work of researchers who are interested in investigating the role of culture centers in higher education.

Organization of the Book

This book is divided into three parts. Part One provides perspectives on culture centers from the point of view of various racial/ethnic identity groups.

In chapter 1, Adele Lozano discusses the role that campus environments play in the persistence and retention of Latina/o college students, as well as the ways in which Latina/o culture centers can be positioned to mediate campus environments that often devalue Latina/o culture. In chapter 2, William Ming Liu, Michael J. Cuyjet, and Sunny Lee discuss the impact of culture centers on Asian American college students. Specifically, they highlight the cultural needs of Asian American students and examine how culture center initiatives can foster supportive and safe environments for this population of students. The authors of chapter 3 envision American Indian culture centers as "islands of sanctuary" that can address many of the challenges that these students face while attending college. Heather J. Shotton, Star Yellowfish, and Rosa Cintrón situate their examination of American Indian student experiences within the context of the University of Oklahoma culture center and offer recommendations for supporting American Indian college students. In chapter 4, I move beyond the rhetoric regarding culture center "extinction" and describe the research-driven efforts of two Black culture centers to support and validate the experiences of African American students.

Part Two describes three theoretical perspectives that frame the role of culture centers. In chapter 5, Tara J. Yosso and Corina Benavides Lopez use critical race theory as a framework through which culture centers are viewed as counterspaces. They consider how culture centers operate as transformative sites of resistance for students of color. Mary F. Howard-Hamilton, Kandace G. Hinton, and Robin L. Hughes examine the impact of culture centers through a student development theoretical lens in chapter 6. They offer examples of how culture center programs and outreach can translate theory into practice. In chapter 7, Michael Benitez Jr. suggests that although culture centers have mainly served students of color, now is the time to broaden how culture centers are conceptualized. Using a social justice theoretical framework, he examines the role that culture centers can play in helping White students acknowledge White racism and privilege, while maintaining their mission of serving students of color.

Part Three focuses specifically on administrative and practice-oriented issues related to culture centers. In chapter 8, Toby S. Jenkins describes the tri-sector practitioners model as a framework guiding culture center practitioners in program development, organizational management, and student programming and advising. E. Michael Sutton and Phyllis McCluskey-Titus address the career typecasting of professionals who work in and lead culture centers in chapter 9. They examine career mobility and institutional racism in the lives of culture center professionals. In chapter 10, Salvador B. Mena examines the administrative decisions that must be made to establish or maintain multicultural and identity-based culture centers.

Culture Centers in Higher Education presents a cogent argument for the continued relevance of culture centers in higher education. Although some progress has been made, literature over the past few decades has consistently confirmed that students of color face discrimination and feelings of isolation within predominantly White collegiate spaces, whether the classroom, the residence hall, or the student union. Their daily interactions with peers, faculty, and administrators in these diverse settings are often clear reminders that as students of color, their experiences, culture, and mere presence are often dismissed, unacknowledged, or treated as invisible. Such situations warrant culture centers, where students' feelings, ideas, cultures, and experiences not only matter but receive validation and support.

PART ONE

RACIAL/ETHNIC GROUP–SPECIFIC CULTURE CENTERS

LATINA/O CULTURE CENTERS

Providing a Sense of Belonging
and Promoting Student Success

Adele Lozano

I n 2003 tremendous media coverage was devoted to the fact that Latinas/os had achieved the status of the largest racial/ethnic minority group in the United States. Unfortunately, very little national attention was focused on the significant disparities between the educational attainment of the Latina/o population and that of other groups, particularly in higher education. The U.S. Census Bureau (2003) reported that 37.4 million Latinas/os were living in the United States in 2002, comprising 12.6% of the total population. That number is projected to increase to 15.5% of the total population by the year 2010 (U.S. Census Bureau, 2004b). It has been estimated that by the year 2050, Latinas/os will comprise 24.4% of the population, meaning nearly one in four people in the United States will be of Latina/o or Hispanic origin (U.S. Census Bureau, 2004b).

A closer look at the demographics shows that the educational attainment of Latinas/os has lagged far behind their population growth. In 2003 only 57% of the Latina/o population over 25 years of age had attained a high school diploma, compared to 89.4% of the White population (U.S. Census Bureau, 2004a). The number of Latinas/os over age 25 with a bachelor's degree was only 11%—lower than that of non-Latino Whites, Blacks, and Asians (U.S. Census Bureau, 2004a). Significantly, a critical discrepancy exists between enrollment and graduation rates for Latina/o college students. Although Latinas/os are enrolling in two- and four-year colleges at a higher rate than most other major ethnic groups, they fall behind all other groups in attaining undergraduate degrees (Fry, 2002). This disparity between enrollment rates and graduation rates underscores the importance of addressing retention issues for Latina/o college students, particularly those factors that have a positive impact on retention.

Given that Latinas/os are disproportionately enrolled in two-year colleges (Fry, 2002) and are often first-generation students, it is important to understand how to better serve this population. Factors such as the immigration backlash currently sweeping across the nation, a surge in racial stereotype–themed campus activities (such as the "catch an illegal immigrant" game, Bannerji, 2006), and the increasing number of college-bound undocumented Latina/o high school students signal a need for change in campus environments. College administrators, faculty, and staff must recognize the importance of empowering Latina/o students to create space and build community so they can thrive in an environment in which social, cultural, and academic capital is held mainly by the majority population.

The purpose of this chapter is to examine the role that environment plays in the persistence and retention of Latina/o students. A brief overview of retention as it relates to institutional environments is followed by a consideration of the role that culture centers can play in mediating the effects of a campus environment that not only devalues Latina/o culture but often fosters a climate hostile to non-White students. Current challenges facing Latina/o culture centers, particularly as they relate to organizational models, are also examined. Finally, the chapter considers the future of Latina/o culture centers at predominantly White institutions (PWIs) and discusses the need for empirical research to shed light on the impact they have on Latina/o college students' sense of belonging and thus on retention.

Although the literature on the experience of Latina/o college students has grown in the past 10 years, research on racial/ethnic minority culture centers, especially as it relates to retention and campus climate, is virtually nonexistent. A literature search in ERIC using the key words "cultural center," "ethnic," and "higher education" yields only six results, two of which are empirical studies. These two studies do not focus exclusively on culture centers but rather include them as one of many factors affecting racial/ethnic minority students' college experiences. As a result of the lack of empirical research on culture centers, I rely on my own knowledge base and extensive experience working with Latina/o culture centers and collaborating with colleagues who support culture centers (African American, Latina/o, Native American, and Asian American) at PWIs.

The Importance of Institutional Environment

Institutional environment and student-environment interaction have been used to study student development, student retention, and student withdrawal. Astin (1993) developed the input-environment-output model as a guide to study college student development. This model defines input as student characteristics upon college entry; environment as "various programs, policies, faculty, peers, and educational experiences to which the student is exposed" (Astin, 1993, p. 7); and outcome as characteristics of students after they have been exposed to the institutional environment. On the basis of his study, which analyzed the effects of 135 college environmental factors and 57 student involvement measures on over 80 outcomes, Astin (1993) found that retention was "significantly affected by more environmental variables than almost any other outcome measure" (p. 195).

Pascarella and Terenzini (1991) identified theoretical models of student retention that support the common premise that persistence is a function of a student's fit with the institutional environment. They posited that the fit or match is evident in a student's interactions with the institution's academic and social systems, and that the factors that affect those interactions are many. Those factors that enhance college persistence include an ethic of care, participation in college-sponsored activities, an emphasis on support services, and a peer culture where close on-campus friendships are developed (Pascarella & Terenzini, 1991). They also suggested that because of differences between the academic, social, and psychological spheres occupied by White and non-White students on predominantly White campuses, non-White students are likely to have significantly different experiences and outcomes than White students.

The "domains" that students inhabit in higher education affect student persistence. Pascarella and Terenzini (1991) refer to these domains as the "academic, social and psychological worlds" (p. 644). Others have emphasized similar domains, particularly in terms of how they affect the persistence of Latina/o students. González (2002) referred to the "social, physical, and epistemological worlds" in his study of Chicano student persistence. Similarly, Attinasi (1989) referred to three different "geographies": the physical, social, and academic/cognitive geographies. Gloria (1999) identified four domains in which cultural ambiance and community commitment occur for Chicano students: the general university environment, the student training and learning environment, the classroom and curricular environment, and the faculty environment. Hurtado, Milem, Clayton-Pedersen, and Allen (1998) described the four "dimensions of campus climate" that affect Latina/o students: an institution's historical legacy of exclusion or inclusion, structural diversity, the psychological dimension, and the behavioral dimension. It is helpful to keep these dimensions in mind in consideration of Latina/o student retention and the role of Latina/o culture centers at PWIs.

Retention Models and Latina/o Students

Several college student retention models have emerged over the past three decades. One of the most comprehensive and widely used models of student retention is Vincent Tinto's theory of student departure (1993). Tinto's theory, which he revised several times, featured a student integration model that described and explained the longitudinal process by which individuals leave institutions of higher education. He suggested that student departure serves as "a barometer of the social and intellectual health of institutional life" (Tinto, 1993, p. 5). Tinto also argued that social and intellectual integration are essential to college student persistence and that the individual student and the institution are continually interacting with each other, and these interactions affect student persistence/withdrawal.

Tinto revised his model of student retention several times in response to the criticism and studies of other researchers who identified omissions in his model. Much of the criticism focused on problems in applying the model to students of various ethnic/racial backgrounds. In his revised model, Tinto admitted that student participation in college life does not necessarily indicate actual integration in social and academic systems. Tinto (1993) pointed out, "The mere occurrence of interactions between the individual and others within the institution will not insure that integration occurs" (p. 136). This is an important distinction, because despite the fact that racial/ethnic minority students may participate in the social and academic life of an institution, it is possible that because of historic, structural, and institutional racism, they may not feel a sense of belonging or integration in the life of the institution.

However, the concept of integration and the underlying assumption of acculturation continue to be problematic. Students from underrepresented populations that have been historically marginalized in higher education may have a different understanding of the meaning of integration (Hurtado & Carter, 1997). Underlying the concept of acculturation is the assumption that students from racial/ethnic minority backgrounds should adopt the values and beliefs of the dominant culture in order to succeed in higher education. Tinto's measures of social integration exclude certain forms of affiliation utilized by Latina/o students, such as involvement in racial/ethnic minority student organizations, church activities, and community activism (Hurtado & Carter, 1997).

Moving away from Tinto's model of student departure, González (2000) developed a grounded conceptual framework for understanding Chicano student participation and persistence in PWIs. His framework examines cultural survival and cultural transformation within the domains of the social, physical, and epistemological worlds. He found that students act as "cultural workers" to transform their environments and fight marginalization while seeking "cultural nourishment" from family, friends, and cultural symbols. The students are empowered through their own actions, which lead to the transformation of the campus environment as they seek a synthesis between their own culture and that of the university. This framework provides insight into the forms of alienation and marginalization experienced within these domains and how they affect Latina/o students.

Latina/o Students' Sense of Belonging

Most theories and models of college student retention include a person-environment fit or match as a key ingredient of student persistence. Student-institution fit is often measured in different ways (integration, membership, participation, inclusion); however, the main point is that it is important for all students to feel they are part of the campus community—to have what Hurtado and Carter (1996) described as a sense of belonging. As an increasing number of students from underrepresented groups began enrolling in institutions of higher education, many researchers began to reexamine these models to assess how well they apply to racial/ethnic minority students.

More recently, researchers have begun focusing on the unique factors affecting the persistence of Latina/o college students. Their research often utilizes qualitative methods to examine and understand the multiple realities and complex cultural realms of minority racial/ethnic student populations (Hernandez, 2000).

Traditional models of college student persistence and retention often ignore unique pre-college characteristics of Latina/o college students. Part of that uniqueness stems from the fact that the Latina/o population is so diverse. The U.S. Census Bureau (2000) recognized that Latinas/os (Hispanics) may be of any race and defined members of this group as having Mexican, Puerto Rican, Cuban, Central or South American, or other similar origins. There are also generational status differences regarding residency in the United States, as some students are first-generation immigrants, and others come from families who have lived in the United States for several generations. This is likely to affect a student's degree of biculturalism and bilingualism (Torres, 1999). Moreover, because only 11% of Latinas/os over age 25 have a bachelor's degree, many Latina/o students are first-generation college students. Velásquez (1996) argued that a history of sociopolitical subordination in the United States, combined with strong elements of resistance, and a bicultural identity are unique characteristics that must be considered when one is addressing persistence issues for these students. Thus, a complex combination of pre-entry characteristics and campus environment characteristics may influence the persistence decisions of Latina/o students.

For student affairs practitioners, the important piece of the retention puzzle is identifying and addressing environmental factors that promote or hinder college persistence for Latina/o students. Campus culture is a salient characteristic of higher education that influences the social and academic climate. Kuh and Whitt (1988) defined culture in higher education as:

> The collective, mutually shaping patterns, norms, practices, beliefs, and assumptions that guide the behavior of individuals and groups in an institute of higher education and provide a frame of reference within which to interpret the meaning of events and actions on and off campus. (pp. 12–13)

This definition stresses the interactions between people on and off campus as well as shared underlying beliefs. Traditional retention models assume entering students must conform to the campus culture in order to be success-ful. However, Latina/o students often enter institutions with a set of cultural beliefs and assumptions that are different from those of the dominant culture (Torres, 2003). In order to counter the normative interpretation of Tinto's model, researchers have begun to expand his framework and connect it to other theories addressing the persistence of racial/ethnic minority students, particularly Latinas/os.

González (2000) stressed the importance of "cultural nourishment" for Chicano students in fighting feelings of marginalization and alienation on campus. Sources of cultural nourishment include family, friends, language, role models, and existing cultural works (music, art, etc.). In an exploratory study conducted with Chicano students attending a university in the South-west, Velásquez (1996) found that although students did not perceive the overall institutional environment as supportive and enabling, their strong bicultural background characteristics helped facilitate their integration into the environment. In her national study of how talented Latina/o students perceived institutional receptivity to a Latina/o presence on campus, Hur-tado (1994) found that despite their strong backgrounds of achievement prior to enrolling, Latina/o students experienced discrimination on college cam-puses. Their experiences in the campus environment led to perceptions that students belonging to the dominant culture knew very little about Latina/o students and that they viewed them as "special admits."

Gloria (1999) argued that colleges and universities must expand their learning environments to encompass the multicultural and multicontextual perspectives of racial/ethnic minority students. She posited that two factors positively affect Chicano student retention: (1) an inclusive and validating environment and (2) the commitment and efforts of individuals within that environment. The first factor, which Gloria called "cultural ambiance," occurs within four domains: the general university environment, the student training and learning environment, the classroom and curricular environ-ment, and the faculty environment. The second factor, which Gloria called "community commitment," is a requirement if cultural ambiance is to occur at an institution.

Subcultures and Ethnic Enclaves

Recently more researchers have been examining the concept of ethnic "sub-cultures" within the university environment. A subculture is a "sociological construct that denotes groups within an organization whose members share patterns of norms and values that differ from those of other groups" (Kuh, 2001, p. 26). On the basis of their qualitative study of Latina/o and Native American students at a large southwestern university, Murguia, Padilla, and Pavel (1991) found that ethnic enclaves can play an important role in the social integration of Latina/o students. They proposed that ethnicity can be a critical conditioning agent in the social integration process. Their study demonstrated that ethnicity can limit access to majority enclaves and that when that happens, students may engage primarily in ethnic enclaves. These ethnic enclaves or subcommunities then play an important role in the social integration of the student. Therefore in studies of the social integration of Latina/o students it is important to use ethnic enclaves as a measurement and to include in data analysis (Murguia et al., 1991).

It is possible for racial/ethnic minority students to be well integrated into their own ethnic subcultures while feeling alienated from the larger institutional environment (Loo & Rolison, 1986). Ironically, White students often view these ethnic enclaves as constituting segregation, whereas racial/ethnic minority students perceive them as safe havens from White cultural domination. On the basis of their study of racial/ethnic minority students at a PWI within the University of California system, Loo and Rolison (1986) concluded that racial/ethnic minority students experienced greater sociocultural alienation than White students and that those experiences stemmed from feelings of cultural domination and ethnic isolation. They also found that regardless of how satisfied racial/ethnic minority students are with their academic experience, they may still experience alienation within the campus environment.

Villalpando (2003) argued that "racial balkanization"—the self-segregation of students of color from the predominantly White student population—is a myth and is unsubstantiated by empirical research. In his national longitudinal study of Chicano college students, Villalpando used quantitative data and qualitative data in the form of "counterstories" to understand the students' experiences. Counterstories, used to tell the stories of marginalized populations, are a tool for analyzing and challenging the dominant perceptions of race and White privilege. The study revealed that ethnic subcommunities enabled Chicano students to draw on cultural resources to mitigate challenges and obstacles faced in a predominantly White institutional environment. Furthermore, his study indicated that affiliation with ethnic enclaves increased Chicano students' social consciousness and involvement in community service activities. On the basis of her study of intentional communities among female students of color at a PWI, Aleman (1998) argued, "Separation and integration are not antithetical but sympathetic operational positions" (p. 4). In other words, by participating in intentional communities with other women of color, the students in her study gained a gendered and raced subjectivity that helped them to more effectively navigate the dominant White institutional environment.

The Role of Latina/o Culture Centers at PWIs

When culture centers were established in the late 1960s and early 1970s, they served as a haven for racial/ethnic minority students who were searching for a support system. They often served as a launching pad for discussion of the pressing social and political issues faced by underrepresented students (Hefner, 2002). Over the years, the role of culture centers at PWIs has evolved and there is no single model. Many culture centers continue to promote community outreach and social justice. Some centers have added an academic emphasis on student retention, and others are struggling to survive. Some culture centers have gained credibility in the eyes of administrators and constituents, whereas others face criticism as the campus community, including racial/ethnic minority students, questions their relevance (Hefner, 2002).

Throughout a 30-plus-year struggle for resources and sustainability, Latina/o culture centers have provided a unique and empowering space for Latina/o students to experience college life. A culture center is often the only space on campus to offer a holistic learning experience allowing Latina/o students to explore racial/ethnic identity development and engage in social justice activism, political education, community outreach, academic mentoring and support, leadership development, social and professional networking, and alumni outreach. Within an ethnic enclave, each of these activities can have an impact on a student's sense of belonging while strengthening the student's leadership skills and academic self-confidence. Whether this will then lead to a greater sense of connection to the institution depends on the campus environment as a whole. Institutions must recognize the value of culture centers and the many ways in which they affect college student life, which are discussed in the following pages.

Racial/ethnic identity development among Latina/o students is complex and involves issues of language, bicultural identity, biracial identity, ethnic background, generational residency status, indigenous identity, sexual orientation, gender roles, and internalized oppression. Latina/o culture centers offer a safe space where students are supported as they resist labels that come with being a racial/ethnic minority student on a predominantly White campus while being challenged to think critically about race and society. Culture center staff members often work collaboratively with other units on campus such as the counseling center, the LGBT center, women's programs, the African American culture center, and the Native American culture center to coordinate programs that address racial/ethnic identity development for Latina/o students. Culture centers also play an important role in making the larger campus aware of the vast diversity within the Latina/o population, thus counteracting the tendency to view all Latina/o students as a single homogenous group.

Students founded many culture centers as part of a wave of social justice activism in the late 1960s and early 1970s. During that period, Latina/o students at PWIs found that they comprised only a handful of the student population and were compelled to fight for resources to force the institutions to recruit and enroll more Latina/o students. Among their demands were the hiring of bilingual admissions staff to focus on Latina/o recruitment, establishment of Latina/o studies programs, development of support services to serve underrepresented students, and the creation of Latina/o culture centers. Once Latina/o culture centers were established, Latina/o students had a home base from which to coordinate culturally relevant programs addressing educational, cultural, and community issues.

Another outcome of social justice activism was the creation of student-run alternative publications. Taking the form of newsletters, bulletins, and literary journals, these publications were often housed at Latina/o culture centers, where students taught each other the basics of journalistic reporting and writing. Some students used publications as a means to voice their opinions about current issues through creative writing. Student publications provided students with a media outlet that may not have been available through traditional student newspapers. Often written in both English and Spanish, these publications serve as valuable resources for anyone interested in researching Latina/o culture centers and Latina/o experiences at PWIs.

Latina/o culture centers continue to serve as a resource for students interested in journalism, creative writing, and other forms of media. However, many culture centers lack the resources necessary for the state-of-the-art equipment expected by today's students. Typewriters and mimeograph machines of the late 1960s have given way to desktop graphic programs, digital equipment, and web technology in the 21st century.

Social justice activism, political education, and community outreach often occur simultaneously at Latina/o culture centers. At the University of Iowa in the 1970s, the Latino and Native American Cultural Center (LNACC) created a prison visitation program in which the students traveled to the state prison once a month to interact with the Latino and Native American prisoners, provide them with books, and discuss issues affecting the prisoners. Students involved with the LNACC also established a Latina/o "teacher core" that created a free preschool program, La Escuelita, to work with migrant children in a nearby community. During that period, the students also regularly visited the Meskwaki Settlement (Sac and Fox Tribe of the Mississippi) located an hour from the university to build a supportive relationship between the Meskwaki Tribe and the culture center.

Social justice activism continues to be an important component of Latina/o culture centers. Current Latina/o students are active in issues ranging from immigration rights and voting rights to labor issues, educational access, media representation, affirmative action, and the prison system. Recently a wave of racially offensive parties and activities promoting negative stereotypes of Latina/o and African American students has swept across campuses throughout the United States (Rogers, 2007). With themes like "pimps and hos" and "tacos and tequila," these activities perpetuate an environment where racial stereotypes and White privilege are the norm. Amid a climate of distrust and intolerance, Latina/o culture centers serve as a safe space where students can vent their anger in group discussions, strategize future actions, and provide emotional support as they balance academic responsibilities with active resistance to social injustices. Latina/o culture centers can also be an important link in institutional efforts to reach out and work with Latina/o students to improve campus climate.

Community and family outreach has traditionally been an important component of Latina/o culture centers. Beginning with students in the early 1970s who traveled to Latina/o communities to speak to parents in Spanish regarding access to college (essentially doing the job of an admissions counselor) and continuing with students who offer informational workshops on immigration rights and tutor Latina/o youths, Latina/o culture centers have served to connect students with Latina/o communities. These programs are a way for Latina/o college students to give back to the community in a way that is culturally congruent with their own experiences, values, and beliefs.

Academic mentoring and support programs fulfill a core mission of many Latina/o culture centers. These programs take various forms, including peer mentoring, peer tutoring, faculty-student mentoring, and alumni-student mentoring. The structures of the programs also vary from formal mentoring programs with contracts and scheduled activities to loosely run programs where participants meet informally and work at their own pace. In some cases, a culture center may not have a mentoring program per se, but mentoring occurs intrinsically as students have meaningful interactions with student, faculty, and staff role models. Latina/o culture center staff may seek to collaborate with faculty from a Latina/o studies program to promote graduate studies to undergraduate students. Academic support is also provided through a culture center's connections with other units on campus. At the University of Illinois at Urbana-Champaign, the career center staffs a satellite office at La Casa Cultural Latina once a week where students can drop in to have their resumes critiqued. La Casa also offers regular workshops on topics such as study skills, choosing a major, time management, and test anxiety. Latina/o culture centers can play a role in reaching out to students who might be reluctant to approach traditional support services for help.

Latina/o alumni outreach is becoming more important as culture centers struggle to survive in an era of limited resources and funding for higher education. Latina/o alumni, especially those from the 1970s who still feel a deep connection to a culture center (and in some cases were directly involved in the founding of a center) are at a point in their lives where they are ready to give back. However, they are not necessarily enticed by the requests from traditional alumni associations. Latina/o alumni are often more interested in giving their time and resources in a way that is culturally relevant and meaningful to them. Whereas traditional alumni associations may not recognize the value of outreach to Latina/o alumni, some institutions (often at the urging of Latina/o culture center staff and students) have formed Latina/o alumni associations. Institutions in the Midwest, including the Indiana University Bloomington and Purdue University, have formed Latina/o alumni organizations in the past 5 years. Others such as the University of Illinois at Chicago formed organizations 20 years ago. Regardless of when they were established, one of the main functions of a Latina/o alumni organization is connecting current Latina/o students with alumni who can provide networking opportunities and advice to students who are looking forward to becoming new professionals.

Leadership development is inherent in each of the activities that takes place at Latina/o culture centers. Although many campuses have leadership centers, they do not necessarily embrace leadership styles outside the corporate business model, leading Latina/o students to look for alternative leadership opportunities. Latina/o culture centers offer myriad opportunities for leadership development, from student organization meetings where first-year students can learn from older students how to form networks and navigate the university system to coalitions formed by graduate students with undergraduates to address racial inequities and hostile campus climates. Latina/o student organizations often use culture centers as a home base for meetings, programming, and study sessions. Latina/o culture center staff members play a key role in encouraging collaboration among groups and empowering students to use their knowledge and experience to create positive change.

In their review of programs designed to support the college transition for Latina/o students, González, Olivas, and Calleroz (2004) found the following themes: creation of community, collaboration with other groups, community service, and validation of students. The various programs and activities offered at Latina/o culture centers serve to promote the concept of *comunidad* (community), which enhances a sense of belonging for Latina/o students. They also address the physical, social, and academic/cognitive domains that have an impact on Latina/o student retention. The number of programs offered at a Latina/o culture center and their effectiveness in creating a sense of belonging among Latina/o students is greatly affected by the center's organizational and administrative model.

Organizational Models

Latina/o culture centers operate under various organizational models depending on the historical, social, political, and cultural context of an institution at the time the center was established, as well as how the center has evolved within the institutional environment. One of the main differences between culture centers models involves the reporting line for the center. Some centers, such as those at the University of Illinois in Urbana-Champaign and the University of Iowa, report to a student affairs/student services office. Others such as the Latina/o culture centers at Purdue University and the University of Illinois at Chicago report to the office of the provost. Each model has advantages and disadvantages. The office of the provost may have considerably more funding and resources than a student affairs office. However, the student affairs division may have a deeper understanding of student development and the concerns of underrepresented students. Whether under the auspices of academic affairs or student affairs, culture center staff often find themselves competing with other units for funding and resources in a political environment that may only give lip service to the value of diversity.

Another main difference between organizational models concerns the staffing of culture centers. When Latina/o culture centers were first established at PWIs in the Midwest, staff often consisted of graduate and undergraduate students, which produced an environment with high staff turnover and inconsistency in programming. As these centers became established and gained support from administrators, full-time professionals were hired as directors, assistant directors, and program coordinators. Students were employed as assistants to help with programming. Unfortunately, not all centers received adequate funding to meet staffing needs.

An institution that does not provide sufficient funding and resources for a culture center is setting the center up for failure. At the University of Iowa, students managed the Latino and Native American Cultural Center for over 30 years with minimal funding for programming. Although students can serve as passionate and motivated staff, they have limited time to devote to the center and limited experience compared to professional full-time student affairs staff members. Without full-time staff, a culture center cannot serve the needs of the students and will not become a vital part of the institution. Hours of operation will necessarily be limited, especially during the evening, when students are more likely to utilize a center. A lack of full-time staff will also lead to instability in programming and lack of student participation. If a Latina/o culture center is viewed as ineffective, idle, and outdated, it becomes vulnerable to budget cuts and possible elimination to make room for more "relevant" facilities or possibly a new multicultural center.

By contrast, not only has the University of Illinois at Urbana-Champaign provided its culture centers with resources for full-time professional staff, student staff, and programming, but the directors of the culture centers also serve as assistant deans. This model promotes an environment where culture center directors have credibility as valued members of student affairs, as opposed to being marginalized and pigeonholed. The presence of a full-time director and sufficient support staff increases the effectiveness, leadership, and sustainability of culture centers at PWIs.

The physical structure of a culture center also affects its ability to serve students and promote an inclusive environment at PWIs. Many culture centers founded in the late 1960s and early 1970s were set up in separate facilities, often in older two-story houses on campus. Other centers are located in a suite of offices within a student services building. These facilities tend to be somewhat more formal but often include a common area with comfortable seating, meeting space, and programming space. Whether a center is located in an older house or suite offices, its vitality is affected by the centrality or remoteness of its location on campus. Culture centers that are accessible and located in or near the heart of campus have an opportunity to attract larger and more diverse groups of students.

Even though it does not directly affect the organizational structure of a culture center, the name that is chosen for a center can send a strong message to the campus community. This is particularly true for Latina/o culture centers. At the University of Iowa, the Latino and Native American Cultural Center was originally named the Chicano–Indian American Cultural Center. The name was changed in the 1980s to reflect the diversity of the Latina/o population. This center is also unique in that Chicano and American Indian students, recognizing their shared history of oppression and small numbers on campus, demanded a joint center in the early 1970s. As both populations grew on campus, the American Indian students began to feel the need for a separate facility. Many Latina/o culture centers use the phrase "La Casa" in their titles. This underscores the importance of a safe haven or second home for Latina/o students.

Future Trends and Suggestions for Research

In the late 1960s and early 1970s the establishment of racial/ethnic minority culture centers began to change the landscape of PWIs in the Midwest.

Latina/o culture centers were originally established as safe havens where culturally relevant activities and programs were created to serve Latina/o students at PWIs. As enrollment of Latinas/os increased, some centers evolved to address retention issues through programs such as peer mentoring, tutoring, and academic skills workshops. The Latina/o student population also grew more diverse as larger numbers of students with Puerto Rican, Central American, South American, and Caribbean backgrounds enrolled in PWIs. Latina/o studies programs were also developed at some institutions, creating more knowledge and awareness of Latina/o issues. Meanwhile, the financial well-being of universities, particularly public institutions, grew increasingly uncertain as state funding decreased. This confluence of factors greatly influenced the manner in which Latina/o culture centers thrived or struggled on their perspective campuses.

As ethnic culture centers on predominantly White campuses fight to maintain relevancy, they must reexamine their role and purpose within the institution. It is essential for these centers to support the overall mission of the institution while being responsive to the needs of particular student groups. They must find ways to contribute seamlessly to both the academic and student affairs components of the institution. Latina/o culture centers must open their doors to Latina/o students from diverse ethnic, racial, social, and political backgrounds as well as to non-Latina/o students who are interested in working with Latina/o students to improve the campus environment. Latina/o culture centers should be at the forefront of addressing issues of retention, campus climate, and social justice while serving as a beacon for community building.

The extant literature on racial/ethnic minority culture centers is minimal, even though many culture centers have been in existence for over 30 years. As a result, student affairs professionals lack a body of empirical research on which to base decisions regarding best practices and best organizational models. Activity in several areas of research, beginning with a historical analysis, will enhance the future success of Latina/o culture centers. In a search for historical research on Latino culture centers, only one document was found. *Creando una Casa: Embracing Space, Containing Space in the Definition of a Latina/o Community at the University of Illinois at Urbana-Champaign* (Esquivel, 2001) documents the history of the culture center and the struggle of Latina/o students at the university. This type of historical research enhances our understanding of the complex dynamics that led to the creation of Latina/o culture centers at PWIs. Hurtado et al. (1998) emphasized that "acknowledging a past history of exclusion implies an institutional willingness to actively shed its exclusionary past" (p. 283). Villalpando (2004) advocated a focus on historical context in order to "gain a deeper understanding of the historical factors that have affected and continue to affect their [Latina/o students'] lives and educational experiences" (p. 47). Obstacles to conducting historical research on culture centers include a lack of sufficient archival documents and a lack of funding for personal interviews.

Research on the impact of Latina/o culture centers on recruitment and retention of students is nonexistent. Culture center directors are aware, through anecdotal evidence, that Latina/o students who participate in center activities and programs are positively affected in myriad ways. However, quantitative and qualitative studies must be conducted to provide evidence that Latina/o culture centers improve student involvement on campus, increase a sense of belonging, and increase student retention.

Accountability is becoming increasingly important as institutions seek to fund programs that increase diversity and cultural understanding on campus. Latina/o culture centers can provide quality programming by establishing learning outcomes and assessing programs regularly. This will require staff members who are experienced in conducting focus groups, developing survey instruments, and analyzing data. It also presents an excellent opportunity for Latina/o culture centers to partner with academic departments to provide graduate students with research projects.

Finally, a comprehensive survey of organizational models must be conducted to determine the current landscape for Latina/o culture centers at PWIs. This will open the door to the discovery of best practices for the retention of Latina/o students. Knowledge of organizational models combined with empirical research on best practices and a deep understanding of their own institutional history will empower Latina/o staff and students to create a vision for their culture centers. In order to survive and thrive, Latina/o culture centers must build on their past legacies while taking a central role in shaping the campus environment to increase cultural understanding among current and future students. (See Appendix 1.1 for a partial list of Latina/o culture centers.)

The campus environment is complex and multidimensional. For Latina/o students who attend PWIs, the issues of race, class, and privilege permeate everyday experiences. Student affairs practitioners must investigate emerging models of student retention in order gain a deeper understanding of the factors affecting the persistence of Latina/o students. Latina/o culture centers can serve as critical resources to increase student retention. By recognizing the diversity of Latina/o college students, understanding how background characteristics can be mediated by the campus environment, and using current models to inform practice, student affairs professionals will be better prepared to change the institutional environment to support Latina/o student success.

References

Aleman, A. M. (1998, November). *Intentional communities: Do they foster integration or separation?* Paper presented at the Annual Meeting of the Association for the Study of Higher Education, Miami, FL.

Astin, A. W. (1993). *What matters in college? Four critical years revisited.* San Francisco: Jossey-Bass.

Attinasi, L. C., Jr. (1989). Getting in: Mexican Americans' perceptions of university attendance and the implications for freshman year persistence. *Journal of Higher Education, 60*(3), 247–277.

Banerji, S. (Sept. 16, 2006). "Minority Groups Protest 'Catch an Illegal Immigrant Day' on Michigan Campus." http://diverseeducation.com/article/6371/

Esquivel, A. (2001). *Creando una casa: Embracing space, containing space in the definition of a Latina/o community at the University of Illinois at Urbana-Champaign.* Unpublished master's thesis, University of Illinois at Urbana-Champaign.

Fry, R. (2002). *Latinos in higher education: Many enroll, too few graduate.* Retrieved on February 15, 2007, from http://pewhispanic.org/files/reports/11.pdf

Gloria, A. M. (1999). *Comunidad: Promoting the educational persistence and success of Chicana/o college students* (JSRI Occasional Paper No. 48, Latino Studies Series). Retrieved on March 1, 2007, from http://www.jsri.msu.edu/RandS/research/ops/oc48abs.html

González, K. P. (2000). Toward a theory of minority student participation in predominantly White colleges and universities. *Journal of College Student Retention, 2*(1), 69–91.

González, K. P. (2002). Campus culture and the experiences of Chicano students in a predominantly White university. *Urban Education, 37*(2), 193–218.

González, K. P., Olivas, L., & Calleroz, M. (2004). Transforming the post-secondary experiences of Latinos. In L. I. Rendón, M. García, & D. Person (Eds.), *Transforming the first-year of college for students of color* (Monograph No. 38, pp.

23–35). Columbia: University of South Carolina, National Resource Center for the First-Year Experience and Students in Transition.

Hefner, D. (2002). Black cultural centers: Standing on shaky ground? *Black Issues in Higher Education, 18*(26), 22–29.

Hernandez, J. C. (2000). Understanding the retention of Latino college students. *Journal of College Student Development, 41*(6), 575–588.

Hurtado, S. (1994). The institutional climate for talented Latino students. *Research in Higher Education, 35*(1), 21–41.

Hurtado, S., & Carter, D. F. (1996). Latino students' sense of belonging in the college community: Rethinking the concept of integration on campus. In F. K. Stage, G. L. Anaya, J. P. Bean, D. Hossler, & G. D. Kuh (Eds.), *College students: The evolving nature of research* (pp. 123–136). Needham Heights, MA: Simon & Schuster.

Hurtado, S., & Carter, D. F. (1997). Effects of college transition and perceptions of the campus racial climate on Latino college students' sense of belonging. *Sociology of Education, 70*, 324–345.

Hurtado, S., Milem, J. F., Clayton-Pedersen, A. R., & Allen, W. R. (1998). Enhancing campus climates for racial/ethnic diversity: Educational policy and practice. *The Review of Higher Education, 21*(3), 279–302.

Kuh, G. D. (2001). Organizational culture and student persistence: Prospects and puzzles. *Journal of College Student Retention, 3*(1), 23–39.

Kuh, G. D., & Whitt, E. J. (1988). *The invisible tapestry: Culture in American colleges and universities* (ASHE-ERIC Higher Education, Report No. 1). College Station, TX: Association for the Study of Higher Education.

Loo, C. M., & Rolison, G. (1986). Alienation of ethnic minority students at a predominantly White university. *Journal of Higher Education, 57*(1), 58–77.

Murguia, E., Padilla, R. V., & Pavel, M. (1991). Ethnicity and the concept of social integration in Tinto's model of institutional departure. *Journal of College Student Development, 32*, 433–439.

Pascarella, E. T., & Terenzini, P. T. (1991). *How college affects students: Findings and insights from twenty years of research.* San Francisco: Jossey-Bass.

Rogers, I. (2007). Students stand up against racially offensive parties. *Diverse: Issues in Higher Education.* Retrieved on February 15, 2007, from http://www.diverse education.com/artman/publish/article_7056.sht ml

Tinto, V. (1993). *Leaving college: Rethinking the causes and cures of student attrition* (2nd ed.). Chicago: University of Chicago Press.

Torres, V. (1999). Validation of a bicultural orientation model for Hispanic college students. *Journal of College Student Development, 40*(3), 285–298.

Torres, V. (2003). Mi Casa is not exactly like your house. *About Campus, 8*(2), 2–7.

U.S. Census Bureau. (2000). *Our diverse population: Race and Hispanic origin, 2000.* Retrieved on March 1, 2007, from http://www.census.gov/population/pop-pro file/2000/chap16.pdf

U.S. Census Bureau. (2003). *The Hispanic population in the United States: March 2002.* Retrieved on March 1, 2007, from http://www.census.gov/prod/2003pubs/p20–545.pdf

U.S. Census Bureau. (2004a). *Educational attainment in the United States: 2003.* Retrieved on March 1, 2007, from http://www.census.gov/prod/2004pubs/p20–550.pdf

U.S. Census Bureau. (2004b). *Table 1a. Projected population of the United States, by race and Hispanic origin: 2000 to 2050.* Retrieved on March 1, 2007, from http://www.census.gov/ipc/www/usinterimproj/natprojtab01a.pdf

Velásquez, P. M. (1996, October). *Resisting the normative implications of Tinto: Student and institutional characteristics supporting the persistence of Chicanos in higher education.* Paper presented at the Annual Meeting of the Association for the Study of Higher Education, Memphis, TN.

Villalpando, O. (2003). Self-segregation or self-preservation? A critical race theory and Latina/o critical theory analysis of a study of Chicana/o college students. *Qualitative Studies in Education, 16*(5), 619–646.

Villalpando, O. (2004). Practical considerations of critical race theory and Latino critical theory for Latino college students. In A. M. Ortiz (Ed.), *Addressing the unique needs of Latino American students* (New Directions for Student Services No. 105, pp. 41–50). San Francisco: Jossey-Bass.

LATINA/O CULTURAL CENTERS

El Centro
Northeastern University—Chicago, IL
Established 1969

The Centro Cultural de la Raza
University of California—Berkeley, CA
Established 1970

Latino/Native American Cultural Center
University of Iowa—Iowa City, IA
Established 1971

The Centro Cultural César Chávez
Oregon State University—Corvallis, OR
Established 1972

Puerto Rican/Latin American Cultural Center
University of Connecticut—Storrs, CT
Established 1972

Casa Latina Cultural Center
Western Illinois University—Macomb, IL
Established 1973

La Casa Latino Cultural Center
Indiana University—Bloomington, IN
Established 1973

La Casa Cultural Latina
University of Illinois—Urbana, IL
Established 1974

Rafael Cintron-Ortiz Latino Cultural Center
University of Illinois at Chicago—Chicago, IL
Established 1976

La Casa Cultural
Yale University—New Haven, CT
Established 1977

El Centro Chicano
Stanford University—Palo Alto, CA
Established 1978

Latino Resource Center
Northern Illinois University—DeKalb, IL
Established 1978

Chicano Center
San Jose State University—San Jose, CA
Established 1982

The Cesar Chavez Cultural Center
University of Northern Colorado—Greeley, CO
Established 1985

The Center for Latino Arts and Culture
Rutgers University—New Brunswick, NJ
Established 1992

The Latino Center
Tufts University—Medford, MA
Established 1993

Casa Latina Culture Center
Knox College—Galesburg, IL
Established 1994

The Institute of Hispanic-Latino Cultures
University of Florida—Gainesville, FL
Established 1994

Eliana Ortega Cultural Center
Mt. Holyoke College—South Hadley, MA
Established 1995

La Casa del Sol
Carleton College—Northfield, Rice, MN
Established 1996

The Latino/a Student Cultural Center (LSCC)
Northeastern University—Boston, MA
Established 1997

La Casa Latina
University of Pennsylvania—Philadelphia, PA
Established 1999

Hanna Street Cultural Center
DePauw University—Greencastle, IN
Established 2001

Hispanic/Latino Cultural Center
State University of New York Old Westbury—Old Westbury, NY
Established 2003

Latino Cultural Center
Purdue University—West Lafayette, IN
Established 2003

Latino and Multicultural Center
Northern Kentucky University—Highland Hts., KY
Established 2005

The Casa Latina Cultural and Heritage House
Washington State University—Pullman, WA
Established 2005

2

ASIAN AMERICAN STUDENT INVOLVEMENT IN ASIAN AMERICAN CULTURE CENTERS

William Ming Liu, Michael J. Cuyjet, and Sunny Lee

African American or Black cultural centers took root in American higher educational institutions during the 1970s and served as the model for other racial/ethnic culture centers (i.e., Asian American, Latina/o, and American Indian). Originally, many of the centers provided a safe haven and a programming resource for African American students (Wei, 1993). However, as campus demographics changed, certain campuses experienced an increase of students from other racial/ethnic communities. Concomitant to the increasing racial/ethnic diversity was the growing activism and voice of these communities. Since the mid-1980s, campuses have responded to the increasing needs of Asian and Pacific Islander American, Latina/o, and American Indian students by providing facilities and programming agencies that address their particular cultural cocurricular needs (Gupta, 1998; Hurtado, Milem, Clayton-Pedersen, & Allen, 1998).

This chapter examines the use of culture centers by Asian American students and the role these centers play in their lives. We examine some of the cultural needs of Asian American students and how several of the important issues confronting them can be addressed in the programming and activities occurring in culture centers. Of particular importance are the relationships that need to be supported among students, faculty, and administrators and the significance of providing a place for Asian American students to feel comfortable and safe on campus. We also examine ways in which such culture centers contribute to the overall mission of the institution.

Asian American Students

The U.S. Census Bureau (2003) reported that in 2003 there were approximately 13 million Asian Americans in the United States. One important distinction made in the 2000 census was the disaggregation of the group Asian and Pacific Islander. Previous to the 2000 census, Asian and Pacific Islanders were considered one group, but now there are two groups (1) Asian Americans and (2) Native Hawaiians and Pacific Islanders (U.S. Census Bureau, 2003). This disaggregation is meant to ensure better counts and representation of Pacific Islanders in terms of education, housing, and economics.

Although there are officially two terms used to categorize Asian Americans and Pacific Islanders, and an acculturative difference between Asians (i.e., typically new immigrants with low acculturation to the dominant culture) and Asian Americans, we choose to use the term "Asian American" to describe all Asians with similar phenotypes and cultural heritage. Sue and Sue (1990) broadly delineated 11 ethnic groups among Asian and Pacific Islander Americans (APIAs): Asian Indians, Chinese, Filipinos, Japanese, Koreans, Cambodians, Laotians, Vietnamese, Hawaiians, Guamanians, and Samoans. Sandhu, Kaur, and Tewari (1999) have indicated that APIAs encompass "more than 40 disparate cultural groups" (p. 3). Although we do allude to these ethnic differences within the Asian American community, we focus specifically on the racialized term "Asian American." The reason for using one term is that in the dominant American society, wherein ethnic variations are minimized and similarities are exaggerated (E. Lee, 2005; Liu, 2002), an individual's personal ethnic identification is often unrecognized (Kim, 2001).

In many colleges and universities, there has been a steady enrollment increase among Asian Americans. Between 1993 and 2003, the number of Asian Americans enrolled in institutions of higher education increased 44% (American Council on Education, 2006). During the same period of time, Asian Americans had high persistence in higher education (64%) and the highest rate of bachelor's degrees conferred (American Council on Education, 2006). Reports from the American Council on Education (2006) revealed that 987,000 of the almost 15 million U.S. college students identified themselves as Asian, although Asians represented only about 4.4% of the U.S. population (U.S. Census Bureau, 2003). This represents approximately 6.4% of the college population, compared to American Indians (1%), Blacks or African Americans (11.5%), Hispanics or Latinas/os (9.2%), and Whites (69.4%; Almanac, 2001). In 1998, Asian Americans had the highest graduation rate (66%), exceeding the graduation rate for Whites (American Council on Education, 2001). The American Council on Education (2006) report also shows that Asian Americans obtained bachelor's degrees (62.3%) at a higher rate than both African Americans and Hispanics.

These aggregate enrollment numbers suggest that Asian American students are a relatively small but viable and important component of U.S. higher education. Because the presence of Asian American students can range from negligible Asian American populations at small schools to large numerical majorities on college campuses, the importance of Asian American cultures and their visible presence in the campus community vary from institution to institution.

Cultural Needs of Asian American College Students

It should not be a surprise that student demands for culture centers have been precursors of, simultaneous with, or immediately subsequent to movements to establish Asian American studies programs (Umemoto, 1989; Wei, 1993). As intellectual and cognitive space is devoted to identity and culture, physical space is sought for the psychosocial and personal development and exploration of students (Young, 1991). Hence, in serving multiple foci for students, faculty, and staff, the culture center or cultural space for Asian Americans not only is celebratory but also serves as a physical space of resistance and activism, networking, and student development (Chew & Ogi, 1987; Krantz, 2001).

Asian Americans represent a diverse array of ethnicities (Yeh & Hwang, 2000), acculturation levels (Liu, Pope-Davis, Nevitt, & Toporek, 1999), nationalities, history, and community coherence. Thus, race-specific culture centers may not always be the most advantageous use of resources. For instance, in some schools, Asian American culture centers were products of student activism (i.e., the yellow power movement) during the height of civil rights and human rights protests in the late 1960s and early 1970s (Wei, 1993). As such, these culture centers were products of a certain era that made them a symbol of resistance, activism, visibility, and institutional recognition when Asian American invisibility was being fought. This issue of invisibility may still be salient for some Asian American students in areas of the nation where they are the minority and where these issues remain prevalent. For instance, as a result of the model minority image, which promotes the belief that because many Asian Americans perform well academically, they are not perceived by non-Asians as in need of any services or attention, the establishment of a specific Asian American culture center (i.e., building, floor, office) may not be seen by non–Asian Americans as a necessity. On the other hand, the needs of some Asian Americans and their communities can be met through cultural space within a larger culture center rather than an Asian American culture center. These cultural spaces may again be products of a particular era and a locale where multiple racial/ethnic minority groups exist, and where a larger culture center with cultural space allocated to various groups is a better use of resources. Such culture centers facilitate intergroup relationships, community participation, and campus involvement in potentially different ways than an Asian American culture center and differ from each other based on campus-specific variables that include institutional history, population size and density, and commitment to various racial/ethnic minority populations within the student body.

Uses of Culture Centers

To address some of the cultural needs of Asian American students examined in the preceding section, Asian American students and the faculty, administrators, and staff who support them can use cultural center facilities to abet the students' social, academic, and developmental needs in a variety of important ways.

Promoting Asian American Culture and Asian American/ Ethnic Studies

An Asian American culture center/space (AACC/S) can serve multiple purposes on campus, the most observable of which is promoting the recognition of Asian American culture. Appendix 2.1 provides a list of Asian American culture centers and other student service agencies located at colleges and universities in the United States. The list consists of several centers that have at least one professional staff member dedicated to Asian American student development. The recognition afforded by physical accommodations, staffing, and resources far outweighs the cursory acknowledgement achieved by food fairs, cultural festivals, and campus performances (Cuyjet & Liu,

1999). The AACC/S allows for these activities to continue but also may facilitate the creation of other forms of observable Asian American culture such as Asian American political groups, community-focused organizations, increased intergroup activities, and student leadership activities. The implication is that through the establishment of an AACC/S, a concerted and strategic effort can be made to fulfill the short- and long-term student development and cultural needs of students, which otherwise may not happen because of space restrictions. The AACC/S thus can provide a location where students may seek Asian American cultural knowledge within the campus community. Additionally, the AACC/S can serve as a recognizable point of entry for student development for both Asian and non–Asian Americans as well as a consistent source of community activity for the campus.

But the success of an AACC/S does not usually occur in isolation. AACC/Ss and Asian American studies programs and departments (AASP/Ds) can operate congruently to meet the intellectual and developmental needs of Asian American students. This curricular/cocurricular relationship ruptures the academic/psychosocial boundary between academic pursuits and student affairs. Student development can occur in the AACC/S but also in Asian American studies classes (Alvarez & Liu, 2002). Students can take away from their participation in both the classroom and student activities an understanding of how Asian Americans are perceived, examined, researched, and taught (Alvarez & Liu, 2002). A well-developed relationship between culture centers and the ethnic studies program provides an environment for holistic student learning, promoting both academic and interpersonal development.

Fostering Sensitivity Among and Collaboration With Faculty, Staff, and Administrators

Because the explicit mission of the university and college is the intellectual development of its students, faculty plays an important role in campus governance, resource allocation, and student development. Research on Asian American and other racial/ethnic minority students has shown that faculty relationships are sought and valued and have an impact on self-efficacy and perceived academic success (Anaya & Cole, 2001; Liu, 1995; Okutsu, 1989). Yet not all faculty may recognize this desire among Asian American students, and not all faculty may be aware of how to mentor and nurture Asian American students. Thus, the AACC/S can be a catalyst for the development of sensitivity among faculty and can expose them to the specific needs of various Asian American groups, their career and academic concerns (Cheng, Leong, & Geist, 1993; Park & Harrison, 1995), cultural issues (Chew & Ogi, 1987; Minatoya & Sedlacek, 1981), and the cultural differences and similarities between Asian Americans and other cultural groups (Kwon, 1995). In essence, the AACC/S can be a resource for faculty multicultural competency development.

Similarly, the AACC/S can provide many of the same resources toward student development and student affairs personnel to help build their multicultural competencies with Asian American students (Pope & Reynolds, 1997). Student affairs personnel may learn about how to reduce feelings of alienation through social contact (Nicassio, 1983), about the specific issues faced by Asian American gay men and lesbians (Chan, 1989; Hom, 1994), and about those Asian Americans struggling with multiple identities (Jones & McEwen, 2000) and how social class may affect ethnic identity (Miyamoto, Hishinuma, Nishimura, Nahulu, Andrade, & Goebert, 2000).

Asian American culture centers can provide various academic resources that support the intellectual development of the student. One such way is for the center to house a library consisting of print and video (both DVDs and on-line) materials relevant to Asian American experiences. Such a library can offer practical support to students by providing texts and reference materials used in courses in the Asian American studies or ethnic studies department. Besides academic texts, journals, and literature, libraries can also offer Asian American newspapers and magazines covering the news and experiences of both the pan–Asian American culture and specific ethnic groups. Because the main campus library may not carry such a collection of books, journals, newspapers, and DVDs, it is important that centers invest in these materials so that students have access to information that reflects their histories as well as their contemporary experiences.

Centers should also provide programs that are sensitive to the need for both academic enrichment (i.e., Asian American studies) and student development (Alvarez & Liu, 2002). Examples of such programs are events with speakers and workshops related to Asian American studies. These programs can be particularly powerful on campuses that do not offer Asian American studies classes. Besides these one-time activities, centers can install faculty-in-residence programs that encourage Asian American faculty members to teach courses in the center itself and serve as role models. The center can also sponsor study circles that can be led by any member of the campus or community. Such study groups can be offered to supplement existing Asian American studies courses or to generate interest in organizing a class or program. Centers can also offer mentoring programs that bring together students and faculty and staff members or upper-class students to facilitate academic support.

In addition to providing academic resources, centers can also assist in the career development of the student, often in collaboration with the career development center. Centers may disseminate information to students about fellowships, scholarships, internships, and research opportunities that are relevant to students of color. Regardless of whether this is achieved through websites, e-mail lists, or informational workshops and panels, students can be exposed to a variety of academic fields and careers in areas outside those that are perceived to bring financial security and stability (e.g., sciences, business). In addition, student affairs staff and counselors can also work with students on how to find a compromise between strong parental pressure (Leong, 1995) and their personal interests.

Challenging Stereotypes and Racism on Campus

As a visible racial/ethnic minority, Asian Americans are often stereotyped in one fashion or another. One common and pernicious stereotype that has plagued Asian Americans since the 1960s is that of the model minority (S. J. Lee, 1994; Sue & Okazaki, 1990; Toupin & Son, 1991). The model minority stereotype essentially focuses on a few indices of success achieved by some Asian Americans, such as income, education, and occupational attainment, and then generalizes this success to members of the entire population regardless of an individual's ethnicity, acculturation, economic status, or generation. Such an ahistorical application of a stereotype connotes an innate "Asian" cultural value system underlying their success, and their adherence to the upward mobility ideology of America (S. J. Lee, 1994; Sue & Okazaki, 1990; Toupin & Son, 1991). Consequently, those who do not subscribe to the success ideology are deemed deficient (i.e., an individual dispositional problem), and social changes and inequality are left unexamined (S. J. Lee, 1994). The broad application of this stereotype results in failure to recognize that some segments of the Asian American population are suffering from identifiable social and economic hardships for which remedies may be available. Problematically, intergroup resentment and conflict also arise as the achievements of African American and Latina/o communities are compared to the stereotypical Asian American success (S. J. Lee, 1994; Wei, 1993).

University and college campuses mirror the larger society with regard to politics and race; hence Asian American students are stereotyped in contextually congruent ways. That is, on campus, Asian Americans are typified as nerds (Goto, 1997; Iwamoto & Liu, 2009; Liu & Chang, 2006), men are seen as asexual and lacking masculinity, and women are sexualized or exoticized. Thus, not only is combating stereotypes and racism a psychosocial developmental concern, but these issues are related to academic success. Being able to identify and cope with racism is imperative for Asian American students to achieve academic success (Alvarez & Helms, 2001; Fuertes, Sedlacek, & Liu, 1994). The problem with these stereotypes is the futility of refuting them because, regardless of what is done, a new stereotype is waiting to attach itself to Asian Americans. Stereotypes founded on lack of experience and ignorance can be corrected by ongoing exposure to the spectrum of Asian cultures. Therefore, a concerted and strategic effort aimed at prejudice reduction that coordinates curricular and cocurricular resources in a long-term endeavor is needed. Such activities can only be accomplished if staff and resources are available over a period of time, as in a viable AACC/S.

These efforts may also galvanize Asian American students. Activities directed at increasing campus and community involvement and development can actualize students' leadership and community interests and skills (Cress, Astin, Zimmerman-Oster, & Burkhardt, 2001; Ting, 2000). However, this may also entail an examination of how leadership and involvement are defined traditionally (Liu & Sedlacek, 1996; Solberg, Choi, Ritsma, & Jolly, 1994), as some Asian American students may not identify with the "leader" label or may not be comfortable engaging in traditionally defined leadership behaviors (e.g., public speaking, charismatic leadership; Liu & Sedlacek, 1996, 1999). An AACC/S can offer opportunities for leadership experiences and training focusing on Asian American students and culture that can affirm their ways of leading while showing them how to become bicultural leaders. The AACC/S affords students the opportunity to explore both their strengths and areas in which they can grow and develop within a supportive and confidence-building atmosphere without being compared to non–Asian American student leaders. For instance, many Asian Americans are raised to defer to authority. Asian American student leaders can be supported in developing ways in which they might talk to and disagree with faculty and/or staff that incorporate their cultural values. When these cultural leadership styles are compared with those of non–Asian Americans, Asian American students might be perceived as quiet and acquiescent, but for Asian American students, this can have long-lasting consequences, such as future community involvement and activism (Sinha, 1998).

Although the AACC/S can be an affirmational space for Asian Americans (see, e.g., Chow, 1987; Gupta, 1998), the creation of such a space is not without controversy. Resistance to an AACC/S typically revolves around the notion that the "spacializing" of Asian Americans, along with Asian American studies, reinforces a kind of "Asiacentrism" (Wong, Manvi, & Wong, 1995) that is no better than other forms of racism. That is, Asiacentrism, much like other ethnocentrisms, posits a binary view of the world wherein Asian concerns are paramount and Asian culture is always correct and anything non-Asian is deviant or deficient. But what may appear to be a form of Asiacentrism is rather a safe space wherein Asian American–related discourse can occur outside Eurocentric critique (Okutsu, 1989).

Providing Role Modeling, Mentorship, and Leadership Development

The beneficial effects of campus and community involvement do not occur without the leadership and support of staff and faculty. Research has suggested that the presence of a strong support person as a role model on campus is related to Asian American educational success and achievement (Fuertes et al., 1994). These important relationships do not occur spontaneously through one interaction but instead need to be nurtured as part of a developmental process. Additionally, staff and faculty's continual involvement in campus activities can help students identify individuals who may be sources of guidance or mentors in the future.

AACC/Ss can allow students to take part in leadership opportunities in settings more comfortable than the larger campus community. Internships allow students not only to assist in the daily operations of the center but also to play an integral role in developing programs and services for the campus. With the mentorship of student affairs staff, students can actualize their ideas into tangible projects that serve social, educational, or political goals. Such opportunities also allow students to be visible role models to other Asian American students on campus.

A mentorship program can also promote leadership among Asian Americans in a cultural context. Students who mentor other students, particularly new students, should be trained to deal with issues of adjustment related to Asian American culture and racial identity. For example, new students may be coming from diverse or homogeneous hometowns to a campus that is demographically very different from what they find familiar. This can lead to adjustment issues that affect their academic success and overall psychosocial development (Kodama, McEwen, Liang, & Lee, 2001). Having peer mentors who are prepared to understand these concerns can help make new students' adjustments successful.

An AACC/S can also provide a variety of leadership development programs that prepare students to be multiculturally competent leaders. Such activities and trainings should focus on helping students understand various aspects of their own identity and culture (race, gender, sexual orientation, socioeconomic status, etc.) in leadership. For example, students can have the opportunity to explore the dissonance of traditional Asian cultural values and respected leadership traits in Western societies. Through increased awareness of the relationship between culture and leadership, Asian American students may feel more empowered to view themselves as qualified for leadership and take on more positional roles either in Asian American–specific groups or in the larger campus community (Liang, Lee, & Ting, 2002).

Creating Intragroup Relationships and Activities

Although one of the outcomes of an AACC/S is increased intergroup interactions and contact, which ease future interactions (Kohatsu, Dulay, Lam, Concepcion, Perez, et al., 2000; Tsai, Ying, & Lee, 2001), the AACC/S can also facilitate intragroup interactions and contact. Specifically, the AACC/S can sponsor, support, and nurture interactions among Asian American students and other cultural groups that vary in terms of acculturation level. On many campuses the Asian American cultural groups may be clumped into service, religious, professional, political, and cultural organizations. The cultural organizations can be further divided into groups that tend to attract Asian Americans who are either high or low in acculturation. We have observed a tendency among these two groups to stereotype and practice internalized racism toward each other. The Americanized or highly acculturated Asian American student organization may only speak and conduct meetings in English and perceive the "other" group of Asian Americans as too Asian affiliated, or derogatorily as "fresh off the boat." The more Asian-affiliated organizations may hold social and group meetings in their native languages and perceive the other organization as "White people inside Asian skin" or "Twinkies and bananas" (White on the inside and yellow on the outside). They both may perceive the other as having a different agenda and function without much overlap or need to interact.

Intragroup interactions are as important as intergroup interactions in reducing anxiety in relationships and communication and enhancing future encounters. Different Asian American groups may perceive each other in some prejudicial way that produces discriminatory behavior and reduces contact. The AACC/S can serve administratively as the site where multiple types of student organizations are financed and advised. From here, various groups can be supported in cosponsoring events and activities that focus on understanding the other groups but also, and more important, understanding the biases and prejudices each has against the others. If an Asian American studies faculty member is available to facilitate discussion, groups can tie together how these prejudices feed societal racism and prejudices, and discussions can ensue about how best to combat them.

Serving as a Social Gathering Place

Asian American culture centers provide a physical location where students can find social support from both peers and student affairs staff. Such support is necessary for Asian American college students, who often report feelings of alienation, isolation, and dissatisfaction with their social relationships, which affect their overall college satisfaction (Bennett & Okinaka, 1990; Loo & Rolison, 1986). Alienation is compounded for students who are first-generation immigrants to the United States, who also face issues related to language and cultural adjustment (Kiang, 1992). Building social relationships and having a sense of social support are important factors in a student's overall satisfaction with campus life (Benjamin & Hollings, 1997). Centers often become a safe space where Asian Americans can find other students from similar ethnic and racial backgrounds who share similar cultural values. Such a space can quickly become a hangout where students come to build relationships on a casual and informal basis. Such a social gathering place, whether it is a lounge, lobby, or office, combats social withdrawal and feelings of isolation. Such a location also provides an important source of support for commuter students, who experience additional marginality on campus (Kodama, 2002). The physical location not only serves as a focal point of social interaction but is also a symbol of psychological and institutionalized commitment to campus diversity (Hurtado et al., 1998).

In addition to serving as gathering places for students to establish peer groups, physical centers where students can gather in an informal manner also provide opportunities for intraethnic interactions. In an AACC/S, students can begin relationships with members of ethnic backgrounds different from their own. Such interactions can trigger a sense of panethnic identity, which is important for understanding oneself as a racialized being (Espiritu, 1992). Even though not all students spend a great deal of time together, students can become familiar with leaders and members of various organizations and constituencies. Such a common social gathering place makes it easier for different Asian ethnic groups to work together on programs or to build coalitions for political and advocacy goals. The social aspect of a panethnic culture center can also make Asian American students feel more comfortable and at ease exploring questions about race, identity, and culture. It can lead students to address larger questions of race relations, which is an important process for developing racial identity (Alvarez, 2002). Students may interact not only across different ethnic backgrounds but also across other identities beyond race, including social class, religion, political beliefs, sexual orientation, and generational status.

The Intersection of Culture and Community

In addition to the numerous purposes that culture centers provide to Asian American students on college campuses, culture centers offer a place for the campus community to encounter and inform the larger community outside the campus boundaries. One benefit that culture centers provide is that they help students understand perceptions of Asians and Asian Americans in the country and the world and how they can have a positive impact on those opinions. This can enhance both the campus and its surrounding community and facilitate the process of both communities learning about each other.

A Source of Cultural Development

AACC/S programs and resources can expose students to the use of culture to challenge the dominant society's racialized and gendered stereotypes of

Asians and Asian Americans. Through the arts, speakers, and workshops, students can explore the complexities of Asian American identity and culture. In planning such activities, staff of culture centers can play an important role in programming. Such activities as heritage celebrations that are nonthreatening to both Asian American and non–Asian American populations can serve to bring in audiences for educational purposes. For example, events with Asian food and dancing, which are often popular and attract a large number of participants, can expose both Asian American and non–Asian American audiences to keynote speakers who address the importance of political and community involvement by Asian Americans. Culture center staff can ensure that such celebrations not only involve entertainment (Alvarez & Liu, 2002; Cuyjet & Liu, 1999) but provide educational content that increases awareness and sociopolitical consciousness of Asian America.

Centers can also act as a place of inquiry, exploration, and support of various cultural identities. Multiracial students often struggle with identity issues as a result of monoethnic Asian groupings and ethnic identification (Root, 1997) and should be able to find social support and resources at an Asian American culture center. Another group that culture centers should serve is Asian American lesbian, gay, bisexual, and transgender (LGBT) students, who experience issues involving coming out in a culture that places great emphasis on preserving family heritage and passing on the family name and where sexuality is rarely discussed (Aoki, 1997). Students often find peer support by forming organizations that address their multiple identities or Asian American LGBT groups. Asian American culture centers need to encourage and proactively support the formation of such groups and work closely with sister centers such as LGBT centers, if they exist. Centers should also ensure that resources and programs do not simply reflect the ethnic diversity of the Asian American population but also address various forms of oppression in a cultural context. Examples include sexism, homophobia, ethnocentrism, and classism both in and outside the Asian American community.

Cultural dialogue and programs should also address race relations between Asian Americans and other racial/ethnic minority groups in the United States and among Asian ethnic groups. Asian American culture centers must work with other racial/ethnic culture centers to cosponsor programs that not only address issues faced by all people of color but also look at race relations among communities of color.

Community Support and Stability

The center's student affairs staff can also provide advising and consultation services to student organizations with a variety of missions. Staff with longevity on campus can provide institutional memory that helps them support student groups. These groups can include social and cultural clubs, religious groups, and activist and political organizations. Staff can work closely with the leaders of these organizations to address general leadership issues such as leadership style, officer transitions, and event planning. More important, staff can attempt to keep student organizations accountable to the larger Asian American community by not perpetuating racial and cultural stereotypes through their events (exoticized fashion shows, overemphasis on food and martial arts, etc.). For student affairs staff to be effective in working with Asian American student groups and leaders, a sense of trust and rapport must be developed before advice can be "dropped" (Cuyjet & Liu, 1999). This makes the consistency of staffing at culture centers important. Asian American student organizations can play a vital role in fostering a sense of ethnic awareness and understanding (Inkelas, 2004), and consistent staffing and a sense of place can support such groups in being active and engaging.

In geographic settings where external ethnic Asian American communities exist, the AACC/S can serve as the locus of the linkage between the campus population and local communities. In those settings where there is no such viable external ethnic Asian community, the AACC/S can welcome non–Asian American students and foster interaction and collaboration with the off-campus non–Asian American communities. The AACC/S can also act as a clearinghouse for information on internships and volunteer opportunities in the external community that are relevant to Asian Americans. Centers can also provide a space where students can organize efforts to reach out to high school students in recruiting Asian Americans to the campus. Such activities that are planned and facilitated by college students give them the opportunity to actualize their leadership skills in organizing programs that affect their community.

Conclusion

This chapter has examined the importance of the college or university culture center in enriching the lives of Asian American students. The AACC/S, whether as a stand-alone facility or part of an entity that serves as a cultural support for multiple groups of students on the campus, acts as a clearly identifiable agency performing some essential roles. Among these roles, the AACC/S serves to convey to the students that the institution values their culture in daily campus life. The center also serves as a repository for materials and as a location for activities that promote the cultures of the broad spectrum of ethnic groups that fall under the "Asian" umbrella.

The AACC/S serves the entire campus community as a source of information about Asian American cultures, disseminating knowledge to the general student body, faculty, staff, and administrators, such that greater understanding enhances their day-to-day interactions with Asian American students. In this role the AACC/S can also work to combat stereotypes about Asian Americans among people on campus and in the community surrounding it. The center and its staff can also help non–Asian Americans understand the wide diversity of cultures and ethnic groups included under the general label of Asian American.

The AACC/S also serves Asian American students directly as a social gathering place, as a non-Eurocentric cultural refuge on campus, as a place where they can learn about ethnic cultures besides their own (particularly in multicultural centers), and as a source of leadership development activities targeted at their needs and interests. Clearly, any campus with even the smallest population of Asian American students needs to ensure that this kind of facility exists for the benefit of Asian American students as well as for the benefit of the entire campus population.

References

Almanac. (2001, August 31). *The Chronicle of Higher Education, 48*(1).

Alvarez, A. N. (2002). Racial identity and Asian Americans: Supports and challenges. In M. K. McEwen, A. N. Alvarez, S. Lee, & C. Liang (Eds.), *Working with Asian American students* (New Directions for Student Services No. 97, pp. 3–44). San Francisco: Jossey Bass.

Alvarez, A. N., & Helms, J. E. (2001). Racial identity and reflected appraisals as influences on Asian Americans' racial adjustment. *Cultural Diversity and Ethnic Minority Psychology, 7,* 217–231.

Alvarez, A. N., & Liu, W. M. (2002). Student affairs and Asian American studies: An integrationist perspective. In M. K. McEwen, A. N. Alvarez, S. Lee, & C.

Liang (Eds.), *Working with Asian American students* (New Directions for Student Services, No. 97, pp. 73–80). San Francisco: Jossey-Bass.

American Council on Education. (2001). *Minorities in higher education, 2000–2001: Eighteenth annual status report.* Washington, DC: Author.

American Council on Education. (2006). *Minorities in higher education: Twenty-second annual status report.* Washington, DC: Author.

Anaya, G., & Cole, D. G. (2001). Latina/o student achievement: Exploring the influence of student-faculty interactions on college grades. *Journal of College Student Development, 42,* 3–14.

Aoki, B. K. (1997). Gay and lesbian Asian Americans in psychotherapy. In F. Lee (Ed.), *Working with Asian Americans: A guide for clinicians* (pp. 411–419). New York: Guilford Press.

Benjamin, M., & Hollings, A. (1997). Student satisfaction: Test of an ecological model. *Journal of College Student Development, 38,* 213–228.

Bennett, C., & Okinaka, A. M. (1990). Factors related to persistence among Asian, Black, Hispanic, and White undergraduates at a predominantly White university: Comparison between first and fourth year cohorts. *The Urban Review, 22*(3), 3–60.

Chan, C. S. (1989). Issues of identity development among Asian-American lesbians and gay men. *Journal of Counseling and Development, 68,* 16–20.

Cheng, D., Leong, F. T. L., & Geist, R. (1993). Cultural differences in psychological distress between Asian and Caucasian American college students. *Journal of Multicultural Counseling and Development, 21,* 182–190.

Chew, C. A., & Ogi, A. Y. (1987). Asian American college student perspectives. In D. J. Wright (Ed.), *Responding to the needs of today's minority students* (New Directions for Student Services No. 38, pp. 39–48). San Francisco: Jossey-Bass.

Chow, E. N. L. (1987). The development of feminist consciousness among Asian American women. *Gender and Society, 1,* 284–299.

Cress, C. M., Astin, H. S., Zimmerman-Oster, K., & Burkhardt, J. C. (2001). Developmental outcomes of college students' involvement in leadership activities. *Journal of College Student Development, 42,* 15–27.

Cuyjet, M. J., & Liu, W. M. (1999). Counseling Asian and Pacific Islander Americans in the college/university environment. In D. S. Sandhu (Ed.), *Asian and Pacific Islander Americans: Issues and concerns for counseling and psychotherapy* (pp. 151–166). Commack, NY: Nova Science.

Espiritu, Y. L. (1992). *Asian American panethnicity: Bridging institutions and identities.* Philadelphia: Temple University Press.

Fuertes, J. N., Sedlacek, W. E., & Liu, W. M. (1994). Using the SAT and noncognitive variables to predict the grades and retention of Asian American university students. *Measurement and Evaluation in Counseling and Development, 27,* 74–84.

Goto, S. T. (1997). Nerds, normal people, and homeboys: Accommodation and resistance among Chinese American students. *Anthropology & Education Quarterly, 28,* 70–84.

Gupta, A. (1998). At the crossroads: College activism and its impact on Asian American identity formation. In L. Shankar & R. Srikanth (Eds.), *A part, yet apart: South Asians in Asian America* (pp. 127–145). Philadelphia: Temple University Press.

Hom, A. Y. (1994). Stories from the homefront: Perspectives of Asian American parents with lesbian daughters and gay sons. *Amerasia Journal, 20*(1), 19–32.

Hurtado, S., Milem, J. F., Clayton-Pedersen, A. R., & Allen, W. R. (1998). Enhancing campus climates for racial/ethnic diversity: Educational policy and practice. *The Review of Higher Education, 21,* 279–302.

Inkelas, K. K. (2004). Does participation in ethnic co-curricular activities facilitate a sense of ethnic awareness and understanding? A study of Asian Pacific American undergraduates. *Journal of College Student Development, 45,* 285–302.

Iwamoto, D., & Liu, W. M. (2009). Asian American men and Asianized attribution: Intersections of masculinity, race, and sexuality. In N. Tewari & A. Alvarez (Eds.), *Asian American psychology: Current perspectives* (pp. 211–232). New York: Lawrence Erlbaum.

Jones, S. R., & McEwen, M. K. (2000). A conceptual model of multiple dimensions of identity. *Journal of College Student Development, 41,* 405–413.

Kiang, P. N. (1992). Issues of curriculum and community of first-generation Asian Americans in college. In L. S. Zwerling & H. B. London (Eds.), *First-generation students: Confronting the cultural issues* (New Directions for Community Colleges No. 80, pp. 97–112). San Francisco: Jossey-Bass.

Kim, J. (2001). Asian American identity development theory. In C. L. Wijeyesinghe & B. Jackson III (Eds.), *New perspectives on racial identity development: A theoretical and practical anthology* (pp. 67–90). New York: New York University Press.

Kodama, C. M. (2002). Marginality of transfer commuter students. *NASPA Journal, 39,* 233–250.

Kodama, C. M., McEwen, M. K., Liang, C. T. H., & Lee, S. (2001). A theoretical examination of psychosocial issues for Asian Pacific American students. *NASPA Journal, 38,* 411–437.

Kohatsu, E. L., Dulay, M., Lam, C., Concepcion, W., Perez, P., Lopez, C., & Euler, J. (2000). Using racial identity theory to explore racial mistrust and interracial contact among Asian Americans. *Journal of Counseling and Development, 78,* 334–342.

Krantz, C. (2001, August 14). Students fight plan for centers. *The Des Moines Register,* pp. B1, B2.

Kwon, P. (1995). Applications of social cognition principles to treatment recommendations for ethnic minority clients: The case of Asian Americans. *Clinical Psychology Review, 15*, 613–629.

Lee, E. (2005). Orientalisms in the Americas: A hemispheric approach to Asian American history. *Journal of Asian American Studies, 8*(3), 235–256.

Lee, S. J. (1994). Behind the model-minority stereotype: Voices of high- and low-achieving Asian American students. *Anthropology & Education Quarterly, 25*, 413–429.

Leong, F. T. L. (Ed.). (1995). *Career development and vocational behavior of racial and ethnic minorities.* Mahwah, NJ: Lawrence Erlbaum.

Liang, C. T. H., Lee, S., & Ting, M. (2002). Developing Asian American leaders. In M. K. McEwen, C. M. Kodama, A. N. Alvarez, S. Lee, & C. T. H. Liang (Eds.), *Working with Asian American college students* (New Directions for Student Services No. 97, pp. 81–90). San Francisco: Jossey-Bass.

Liu, W. M. (1995). *The fastest growing populations in the United States: Comparing the participation, opinions, and satisfaction between Asian Americans and Hispanic/Latino/Chicano students on a predominantly White university.* Unpublished master's thesis, University of Maryland, College Park.

Liu, W. M. (2002). Exploring the lives of Asian American men: Racial identity, male role norms, gender role conflict, and prejudicial attitudes. *Psychology of Men and Masculinity, 3*, 107–118.

Liu, W. M., & Chang, T. (2006). Asian American men and masculinity. In F. Leong, A. Inman, A. Ebreo, L. Yang, L. Kinoshita, & M. Fu (Eds.), *Handbook of Asian American psychology* (2nd ed., pp. 197–212). Thousand Oaks, CA: Sage.

Liu, W. M., Pope-Davis, D., Nevitt, J., & Toporek, R. L. (1999). Understanding the function of acculturation and prejudicial attitudes among Asian Americans. *Cultural Diversity and Ethnic Minority Psychology, 5*, 317–328.

Liu, W. M., & Sedlacek, W. E. (1996). *Perceptions of co-curricular involvement and counseling use among Asian Pacific and Latino American college students* (Counseling Center Report No. 7–96). College Park, MD: University of Maryland, Counseling Center.

Liu, W. M., & Sedlacek, W. E. (1999). Differences in leadership and co-curricular perception among entering male and female Asian-Pacific-American college students. *Journal of the First-Year Experience, 11*(2), 93–114.

Loo, C. M., & Rolison, G. (1986). Alienation of ethnic minority students at a predominantly White university. *Journal of Higher Education, 57*, 58–77.

Minatoya, L. Y., & Sedlacek, W. E. (1981). Another look at the melting pot: Perceptions of Asian-American undergraduates. *Journal of College Student Personnel, 22*, 328–336.

Miyamoto, R. H., Hishinuma, E. S., Nishimura, S. T., Nahulu, L. B., Andrade, N. N., & Goebert, D. A. (2000). Variation in self-esteem among adolescents in an Asian/Pacific-Islander sample. *Personality and Individual Differences, 29,* 13–25.

Nicassio, P. M. (1983). Psychosocial correlates of alienation: Study of a sample of Indochinese refugees. *Journal of Cross-Cultural Psychology, 14,* 337–351.

Okutsu, J. K. (1989). Pedagogic "hegemonicide" and the Asian American student. *Amerasia Journal, 15*(1), 233–242.

Park, S. E., & Harrison, A. A. (1995). Career-related interests and values, perceived control, and acculturation of Asian-American and Caucasian-American college students. *Journal of Applied Social Psychology, 25,* 1184–1203.

Pope, R. L., & Reynolds, A. L. (1997). Student affairs core competencies: Integrating multicultural awareness, knowledge, and skills. *Journal of College Student Development, 38,* 266–277.

Root, M. P. P. (1997). Multiracial Asians: Models of ethnic identification. *Amerasia Journal, 23*(1), 29–41.

Sandhu, D. S., Kaur, K. P., & Tewari, N. (1999). Acculturative experiences of Asian and Pacific Islander Americans: Considerations for counseling and psychotherapy. In D. S. Sandhu (Ed.), *Asian and Pacific Islander Americans: Issues and concerns for counseling and psychotherapy* (pp. 3–19). Commack, NY: Nova Science.

Sinha, S. T. (1998). From campus to community politics in Asian America. In L. D. Shankar & R. Srikanth (Eds.), *A part, yet apart: South Asians in Asian America* (pp. 146–167). Philadelphia: Temple University Press.

Solberg, V. S., Choi, K. H., Ritsma, S., & Jolly, A. (1994). Asian-American college students: It is time to reach out. *Journal of College Student Development, 35,* 296–301.

Sue, S., & Okazaki, S. (1990). Asian American educational achievements: A phenomenon in search of an explanation. *American Psychologist, 45*(9), 913–920.

Sue, D. W., & Sue, D. (1990). *Counseling the culturally different: Theory and practice* (2nd ed.). New York: Wiley.

Ting, S. M. R. (2000). Predicting Asian Americans' academic performance in the first year of college: An approach combining SAT scores and noncognitive variables. *Journal of College Student Development, 41,* 442–449.

Toupin, E. S. W. A., & Son, L. (1991). Preliminary findings on Asian Americans: "The model minority" in a small private east coast college. *Journal of Cross-Cultural Psychology 22,* 403–417.

Tsai, J. L., Ying, Y. W., & Lee, P. A. (2001). Cultural predictors of self-esteem: A study of Chinese American female and male young adults. *Cultural Diversity and Ethnic Minority Psychology, 7,* 284–297.

Umemoto, K. (1989). "On strike!" San Francisco State College strike, 1968–69: The role of Asian American students. *Amerasia Journal, 15*(1), 2–42.

U.S. Census Bureau. (2003). *The Asian and Pacific Islander population in the United States: Population characteristics* (Department of Commerce, Economics and Statistical Division Publication No. P20–540). Washington, DC: U.S. Government Printing Office.

Wei, W. (1993). *The Asian American movement*. Philadelphia: Temple University Press.

Wong, P., Manvi, M., & Wong, T. H. (1995). Asiacentrism and Asian American studies? *Amerasia Journal, 21*(1–2), 137–147.

Yeh, C. J., & Hwang, M. Y. (2000). Interdependence in ethnic identity and self: Implications for theory and practice. *Journal of Counseling and Development, 78,* 420–429.

Young, L. W., Jr. (1991). The minority cultural center on a predominantly White campus. In H. E. Cheatham (Ed.), *Cultural pluralism on campus* (pp. 41–53). Alexandria, VA: American College Personnel Association.

ASIAN AMERICAN CULTURAL CENTERS

Asian American Studies Center
University of California, Los Angeles—Los Angeles, CA
Established 1969

Asian American Activities Center
Stanford University—Palo Alto, CA
Established 1972

Asian Pacific Student Services
Loyola Marymount University—Los Angeles, CA
Established 1980

Asian American Cultural Center (AACC)
Yale University—New Haven, CT
Established 1981

Asian Pacific American Student Services
University of Southern California—Los Angeles, CA
Established 1982

The Asian American Center
Tufts University—Medford, MA
Established 1983

Asian/Pacific American Student Services
Colorado State University—Fort Collins, CO
Established 1984

Asian/American Center
Queens College—New York, NY
Established 1987

Asian American Student Life
University of Oklahoma—Norman, OK
Established 1988

Asian Pacific Student Programs
University of California, Riverside—Riverside, CA
Established 1990

Asian & Pacific Cultural Center
Oregon State University—Corvallis, OR
Established 1991

Asian American Resource Center
Pomona College—Claremont, CA
Established 1991

Asian American Cultural Center
University of Connecticut—Storrs, CT
Established 1993

Asian/Pacific American Student Services – Kohl House
University of Northern Colorado—Greeley, CO
Established 1995

ASIA House
Carleton College—Northfield, Carleton College-Northfield, MN
Established 1996

Asian and Asian-American Student Services
Brown University—Providence, RI
Established 1996

Asian & Pacific Islander Student Center
California State Polytechnic University, Pomona—Pomona, CA
Established 1998

Asian Culture Center
Indiana University—Bloomington, IN
Established 1998

Asian American Cultural Center
Rutgers University—New Brunswick, NJ
Established 1999

Asian American/Pacific Islander Resource Center
University of California, Santa Cruz—Santa Cruz, CA
Established 1999

Pan-Asian American Community House
University of Pennsylvania—Philadelphia, PA
Established 2000

Hanna Street Cultural Center
DePauw University—Greencastle, IN
Established 2001

Center for Asian Pacific American Students
Pitzer College—Claremont, CA
Established 2002

Charles B. Wang Asian American/Asian Cultural Center
State University of New York, Stony Brook—Stony Brook, NY
Established 2002

Asian Pacific American Cultural Center (APACC)
University of Iowa—Iowa City, IA
Established 2003

Asian American Center
Northern Illinois University—DeKalb, IL
Established 2004

The Asian American Center
Northeastern University—Boston, MA
Established 2005

Asian American Cultural Center
University of Illinois—Urbana, IL
Established 2005

Asian American Resource and Cultural Center
University of Illinois at Chicago—Chicago, IL
Established 2005

Asian Pacific American Student Services and Advocacy
University of Maryland—College Park, MD
Established 2006

3

ISLAND OF SANCTUARY

The Role of an American Indian Culture Center

Heather J. Shotton, Star Yellowfish, and Rosa Cintrón

sanc.tu.ar.y:
A space in which individuals seek solace and
  refuge
A place of comfort and protection from a
  potential or real threat

(Dictionary.com, n.d.)

T he relationship between American Indians and higher education has a long and troubled history. Since the founding of this nation's first universities, American Indian people have struggled to find their place within institutions of higher education. Some of our first colleges (Harvard, College of William & Mary, and Dartmouth to name a few) were founded with educating American Indians as a part of their original missions (Carney, 1999). However, these efforts failed miserably (American Indian Higher Education Consortium, 2000; Belgarde, 1996; Wright, 1996). It has been argued that the conflicting cultural values of American Indian tribes and postsecondary institutions played a large role in the failure of this mission. American Indians viewed the Euro-American education offered by these institutions as providing nothing of value to tribes. Moreover, this type of education, which was centered on the goal of assimilation of American Indians, was perceived to undermine traditional tribal skills and values (American Indian Higher Education Consortium, 2000; Noriega, 1992; Thelin, 2003). Cultural conflict continues to be an issue today.

Since then, there has existed a debate over the suitability of education of American Indians at predominantly White institutions, where assimilation and cultural conflict remain an issue. Empirical evidence indicates that the variable of ethnicity and culture plays a significant role in the completion or non-completion of higher education among American Indian students (Deloria, 1978; Garcia & Goldenstein Ahler, 1992; Garrett, 1995; Huffman, 2001; Pottinger, 1989; Swisher & Deyhle, 1989). American Indian students, and other students of color, often experience isolation, alienation, dissatisfaction, and overt racism in American institutions of higher education (Pascarella & Terenzini, 2005).

To counter these devastating realities, many programs and services have been established to provide support to American Indian students, including American Indian studies programs, academic enrichment programs, American Indian/multicultural student services offices, and American Indian culture centers. When American Indian students sacrifice the comfort and familiarity of their close-knit tribal communities to attend predominately White institutions, the experience is often traumatic (Reyhner & Eder, 2004). American Indian culture centers serve as one way to address these traumatic experiences by providing community and reinforcing American Indian values.

American Indian Student Needs

American Indians constitute one of the most underrepresented student groups in postsecondary institutions in the United States. Over the last four decades, American Indian enrollment in institutions of higher education has fluctuated (Woodcock & Alawiye, 2001). Official figures indicate that the matriculation of American Indian students in institutions of higher education has more than doubled over the last 25 years, increasing from approximately 76,000 in 1976 to over 176,000 in 2005 (U.S. Department of Education, 2006). However, American Indians continue to remain grossly underrepresented, accounting for only 1% of the total postsecondary student population (Snyder, Tan, & Hoffman, 2004).

The attrition of American Indian students has caused further concern for institutions of higher education. American Indian students graduate at a significantly lower rate than does the general population (Jackson, Smith, & Hill, 2003). Data indicate that the 6-year persistence-to-graduation rate for American Indian students is 36%, compared to 56% for the general population (U.S. Department of Education, 1998). The American Indian college graduation rate is among the lowest for ethnic minority student populations (Reddy, 1993; U.S. Department of Education, 1998).

A number of scholars have attempted to address the issue of attrition among American Indian students. Key factors that they have identified include inadequate academic preparation, financial difficulties, personal or family problems, lack of academic motivation, low self-esteem, insufficient parental support, cultural conflict, and difficulty adjusting to university life (Deyhle, 1992; Falk & Aitken, 1984; Huffman, 1993, 1999, 2001; Huffman, Sill, & Brokenleg, 1986; Jackson et al., 2003; Lin, 1985; Lin, LaCounte, & Eder, 1988; Scott, 1986; Wells, 1997). Jackson et al. (2003) categorized the factors associated with attrition as sociocultural factors, academic factors, and personal factors. Isolation has been identified as a key sociocultural factor associated with attrition (Day, 1999; Jackson et al., 2003). Day (1999) explained that when American Indian students perceive an institutional climate to be nonreceptive to cultural diversity, they often develop feelings of isolation. Other researchers have suggested that feelings of isolation arise among American Indian students as a result of their perception that a campus is hostile to them (Lin et al., 1988) or fails to accommodate their culture (Benjamin, Chambers, & Reiterman, 1993).

Because feelings of isolation have an impact on the success of American Indian students in higher education, several researchers have suggested that structured support systems and cultural reinforcement may be important factors that should be considered in attempts to address their issues of isolation, and thus increase their academic success. Jackson et al. (2003) explained that support programs are critical in aiding American Indian students with the transition to, and survival in, university settings. Brown and Robinson Kurpius (1997) suggested that social integration with peers and faculty can be crucial to the persistence of American Indian students. In accordance with this view, Murguia, Padilla, and Pavel (1991) posited that if integration can be achieved with a subunit population of minority students of a similar ethnicity, then the disintegrative effects of attending a large university can be eased for American Indian students. A clear sense of ethnic identity and strong identification with American Indian culture have also been identified as key factors in the academic success of American Indian students (Benjamin et al., 1993; Huffman, 1993, 1995, 2001; Jackson et al., 2003; Willeto, 1999).

Because culture is a key factor in the success of American Indian students, it is vital to understand the cultural nuances and values of this population. While each tribe is distinctly different (there are approximately 562 federally recognized tribes in the United States) and it is difficult to generalize a single American Indian culture, some commonalties do exist across tribal cultures. In particular, notions of kinship, community, and cooperation are central values in many American Indian communities. American Indian identity is tied to family (including extended family), kinship, or clan affiliation (Horse, 2001). That is, the identity of American Indians is intertwined with the intricate systems of kinship and family within tribes. The notion of family extends well beyond the nuclear family and includes the extended family. Overall, family is central in tribal communities.

Other common values identified among American Indian communities center on communal concerns (LaFromboise, Heyle, & Ozer, 1990). Within many tribal cultures emphasis is placed on the group rather than the individual, and demonstration of concern for group welfare is virtuous (Badwound & Tierney, 1988). Core American Indian values focus on responsibility to family and friends and cooperation (LaFromboise et al., 1990); the emphasis is placed on the ethic of cooperation and group commitment over the individual (Deyhle, 1995; Lamphere, 1977; Swisher, 1990).

The creation of American Indian culture centers on college campuses appears to have led to success in addressing the unique needs of American Indian students on predominantly White campuses, particularly with regard to acknowledging the value of community among American Indian cultures. Research has confirmed the need for such ethnic centers for ethnic minority students on predominantly White campuses (Astin, 1993; Day, 1999; Dell, 2000). D. L. Brown (2005) asserted, "having a place where Native American students feel like they belong and feel comfortable is extremely important to their success in higher education" (p. 93). To explore Brown's assertion, this chapter evaluates one such culture center at the University of Oklahoma, focusing on how its programs have addressed the factors identified as important to the academic success of American Indian students.

American Indian Students at the University of Oklahoma

The University of Oklahoma, a midsize public institution located in Norman, Oklahoma, has a predominantly White student population of approximately 25,000. Its American Indian student population, which numbers over

1,600 (6% of the total student population), is the largest ethnic minority population on campus. Oklahoma is home to 39 federally recognized tribes. The American Indian students on the campus represent tribes from throughout the state and nation and from reservation, rural, and urban communities.

In 1914, Senator Robert Owens supported efforts to establish an Indian studies program at the University of Oklahoma, which ultimately failed (Buffalohead, 1974; Carney, 1999). This initiative was repeated in 1937 with the same lack of success. However, as discussed in the next section, the following decades brought with them a spirit of change.

History and Development of an American Indian Culture Center

The Jim Thorpe Multicultural Center (JTMC) has served as a culture center for American Indian students at the University of Oklahoma for over 20 years. Named for the renowned Sac and Fox Olympic athlete Jim Thorpe, it was established as an American Indian center in the mid-1980s after originally serving as a dormitory for American Indian students. In the late 1980s, administration of the JTMC was transferred from the housing department to the Office of American Indian Student Services and it served no longer as a dormitory, but rather as a culture center for American Indian students.

Centrally located in a three-story house that originally served as a sorority house, the JTMC houses two conference rooms, a living room, a lounge, a dining room, a fully functional kitchen, and several offices. The living room is furnished with couches, chairs, and a television, and the upstairs lounge area with a sofa and recliner. The walls of the center are lined with pictures of its namesake, former students, and American Indian artwork. A trophy case at the back of the living room is filled with trophies that serve as evidence of the victories and accomplishments of past American Indian student groups. Memorabilia of current and former students displayed throughout the center pays homage to the American Indian population, both past and present, served by this center.

When it emerged as a culture center, the JTMC quickly became a hub for American Indian student life. The center housed offices for several American Indian student organizations and served as a central meeting place for American Indian students. Students often utilized the center as a resting place and study lounge between classes. It served as a place to hold meals,

Indian taco sales, receptions, and cultural activities. Most importantly, the JTMC became a place of familiarity and comfort for American Indian students; it became a place to reinforce the communal values of the American Indian students.

In the late 1990s, the center became a multicultural center, temporarily housing several ethnic minority student organizations. This came about partly because of the temporary displacement of several ethnic student organizations during the construction of a new student leadership center that would eventually house the offices of student organizations. Although it continued to primarily serve American Indian students, other ethnic student organizations began to utilize the center more frequently. This period marked the beginning of a slight shift in the function of the center, and a shift in the wider university toward a greater focus on multiculturalism. Responsibility for the oversight of the JTMC eventually moved from the Office of American Indian Student Services to the Center for Student Life, which houses American Indian Student Services. The center continues to be primarily utilized by American Indian students yet also maintains shared space with other student organizations.

As a hub for American Indian students at the University of Oklahoma, the center has been a central part of American Indian student life on campus for almost two decades. The JTMC has worked to reinforce the notion of community among the American Indian student population and continues to serve as a home away from home, a meeting place for students, a safe haven, a place of healing, and a culture center.

Student Programming at the Jim Thorpe Multicultural Center

The University of Oklahoma offers numerous services and programs to assist American Indian students on its campus. These programs are designed to address the barriers that many American Indian students face and to enhance their success. As the hub of the American Indian community, the JTMC is home to many of these programs and services.

New Student Orientation

Each year the Office of American Indian Student Services offers a new student orientation specifically for American Indian students. Designed to complement rather than replace the campus-wide new student orientation, the

American Indian student orientation serves as a means for new American Indian students to become acquainted with the university's American Indian community. The American Indian student orientation is held each year at the JTMC to introduce students to the resources available to them, including American Indian faculty, staff, students, alumni, programs, services, and student organizations. This orientation program helps new American Indian students identify and explore the numerous American Indian student organizations as it acquaints them with resources, services, and systems of support available to them on the campus and in the community.

Retention Programming

The American Indian students at the University of Oklahoma implemented a student-led retention program for their peers in 2001. This peer-mentoring retention program paired first-year students and sophomores with juniors, seniors, and graduate students and provided them with services geared toward their academic success and personal development. A student office for this program was traditionally housed in the JTMC (the program was later housed in the Office of American Indian Student Services), and many of the program events and meetings take place at the center.

Cultural Events

A number of cultural events are held at the JTMC each year, including hand games, cultural feasts, ceremonial events, and Native hymn singings. In addition, the center often serves as a gathering place for male American Indian students to come together for impromptu drumming sessions. The center serves as an ideal location for events that foster cultural reinforcement and renewal. As such, the center serves as a cultural sanctuary where American Indian students can go to express who they are as American Indian people and strengthen their ties to the American Indian community.

Student Activities

There are several American Indian student organizations on the University of Oklahoma campus. Many of these student organizations utilize the JTMC for meetings and activities throughout the year. By hosting weekly home-cooked meals prepared by the members of a local American Indian church, the JTMC provides the time and space for the development of fellowship among students and American Indian community members, who are an important source of support. The JTMC creates opportunities for the social interactions necessary for students to integrate into both the American Indian community and the university.

Sanctuary

Throughout its existence, the JTMC has served as a sanctuary for American Indian students on the University of Oklahoma campus. Its centrality to American Indian student life is evident on many levels. It provides a space in which students find comfort and a sense of belonging on a campus where they often experience feelings of isolation. During times of stress and tragedy, particularly when students encounter racism, the center serves as a safe haven where students can gather to seek healing and restoration. It offers a space where American Indian students can see themselves reflected in the larger campus community as they celebrate and strengthen their identity as American Indian people.

Recommendations

On the basis of our observations, we offer some recommendations to ensure the continued success of American Indian culture centers and American Indian students. First, American Indian culture centers must receive adequate institutional support. Institutions must acknowledge the important role that such centers play in the success of American Indian students. It is essential for institutions to provide the necessary funding to support and maintain these centers. Institutional support must include sufficient staffing of American Indian culture centers. Adequate staffing is vital to a center's ability to provide proper assistance and programming to American Indian students.

Institutions should be aware of the risks of a multicultural center that serves as a "one-stop shop" for all ethnic minority groups. In providing one support center for all ethnic minorities, they run the risk of diluting the services and the potential impact of a culture center. The needs of the various ethnic groups on college campuses are unique and must be addressed as such. When all ethnic groups are lumped together, the implication is often that their needs are the same and that there is a one-size-fits-all solution, which can interfere with the center's ability to adequately serve these populations (Patton, 2006).

Institutions should assess the needs of the American Indian student population on their individual campuses and develop programs and culture centers that address those needs. This must be done regardless of the size of the American Indian population on any individual campus. American Indian populations are unique, and so are their needs, and small or large, their needs are relevant.

If possible, institutions should try to create culture centers reflective of the tribal region in which they are located. American Indian tribal culture is extremely diverse; what is culturally relevant to one tribe may not be to another. Attempts should be made to work with area tribes and communities to develop centers that reflect the tribal culture(s) of the region. American Indian culture centers should provide a space to which not only the American Indian student community, but also the wider American Indian community is invited. Involvement from the outside American Indian community can provide vital support for American Indian students, especially those students far away from home.

Where Do We Go From Here?

Providing a space where American Indians students can feel safe, express and reinforce their cultural identity, and receive support is vital to their academic success. Such spaces reinforce their place within the wider campus community and provide a sense of belonging. These islands of sanctuary on predominantly White campuses play an important role in helping students gather the strength and support necessary for them to achieve success in higher education.

*Since this chapter was written the JTMC has been relocated to a newly renovated building on the southern part of the OU campus, and the original JTMC building is in the process of being demolished.

References

American Indian Higher Education Consortium. (2000). *Creating role models for change: A survey of tribal college graduates.* Washington, DC: Author.
Astin, A. W. (1993). *What matters in college: Four critical years revisited.* San Francisco: Jossey-Bass.

Badwound, E., & Tierney, W. (1988). Leadership and American Indian values: The tribal college dilemma. *Journal of American Indian Education, 28*(1), 9–15.

Belgarde, W. L. (1996). History of American Indian community colleges. In C. Turner, M. Garcia, A. Nora, & L. I. Rendón (Eds.), *Racial and ethnic diversity in higher education* (pp. 18–27). Boston: Pearson.

Benjamin, D. P., Chambers, S., & Reiterman, G. (1993). A focus on American Indian college persistence. *Journal of American Indian Education, 32*(1), 24–30.

Brown, D. L. (2005). American Indian student services. In M. J. Tippeconnic Fox, S. C. Lowe, & G. S. McClellan (Eds.), *Serving Native American students* (pp. 87–94). San Francisco: Jossey-Bass.

Brown, L., & Robinson Kurpius, S. E. (1997). Psychosocial factors influencing academic persistence of American Indian college students. *Journal of College Development, 38*, 3–12.

Buffalohead, W. R. (1974). Indian voices: The first convocation of American Indian scholars. In Aspen Institute for Humanistic Studies & American Indian Historical Society (Ed.), *Native American Studies programs: Review and evaluation* (pp. 161–190). San Francisco: Indian Historian Press.

Carney, C. M. (1999). *Native American higher education in the United States.* New Brunswick, NJ: Transaction.

Day, D. R. (1999). Perceptions of American Indian students of their experiences and factors related to retention in selected institutions of higher education. *Dissertation Abstracts International, 60*, 06A.

Dell, C. A. (2000). The first semester experiences of American Indian transfer students. *Dissertation Abstracts International, 61*, 02A.

Deloria, V. (1978). The Indian student amid American inconsistencies. In T. Thompson (Ed.), *The schooling of Native America* (pp. 9–26). Washington, DC: American Association of Colleges for Teacher Education.

Deyhle, D. (1992). Constructing failure and maintaining cultural identity: Navajo and Ute school leavers. *Journal of American Indian Education, 31*, 24–47.

Deyhle, D. (1995). Navajo youth and Anglo racism: Cultural integrity and resistance. *Harvard Educational Review, 65*, 403–444.

Dictionary.com. (n.d.). *Sanctuary.* Retrieved February 13, 2008, from http://diction ary.reference.com/browse/sanctuary

Falk, D. R., & Aitken, L. P. (1984). Promoting retention among American Indian college students. *Journal of American Indian Education, 23*(2), 24–31.

Garcia, R. L., & Goldenstein Ahler, J. (1992). Indian education: Assumptions, ideologies, strategies. In J. Reyhner (Ed.), *Teaching American Indian students* (pp. 13–32). Norman: University of Oklahoma Press.

Garrett, M. T. (1995). Between two worlds: Cultural discontinuity in the dropout of Native American youth. *The School Counselor, 42*(2), 186–195.

Horse, P. G. (2001). Reflections on American Indian identity. In C. L. Wijeyeshinghe & B. W. Jackson III (Eds.), *New perspectives on racial identity development: A theoretical and practical anthology* (pp. 91–107). New York: New York University Press.

Huffman, T. E. (1993). A typology of Native American college students. In T. E. Schirer & S. M. Branstner (Eds.), *Native American values: Survival and renewal* (pp. 67–80). Sault Ste. Marie, MI: Lake Superior State University Press.

Huffman, T. E. (1995). The tranculturation of Native American college students. In J. Macionis & N. V. Benokraitis (Eds.), *Seeing ourselves: Classical, contemporary, and cross-cultural readings in sociology* (pp. 200–208). Englewood Cliffs, NJ: Prentice-Hall.

Huffman, T. E. (1999). *Cultural masks: Ethnic identity and American Indian higher education.* Morgantown, WV: Stone Creek Press.

Huffman, T. E. (2001). Resistance theory and the transculturation hypothesis as explanations of college attrition and persistence among culturally traditional American Indian students. *Journal of American Indian Education, 40*(3), 1–39.

Huffman, T. E., Sill, M., & Brokenleg, M. (1986). College achievement among Sioux and White South Dakota students. *Journal of American Indian Education, 25*(2), 32–38.

Jackson, A. P., Smith, S. A., & Hill, C. L. (2003). Academic persistence among Native American college students. *Journal of College Student Development, 44,* 548–565.

LaFromboise, T. D., Heyle, A. M., & Ozer, E. J. (1990). Changing and diverse roles of women in American Indian cultures. *Sex Roles, 22*(7–8), 455–476.

Lamphere, L. (1977). *To run after them: Cultural and social bases of cooperation in a Navajo community.* Tucson: University of Arizona Press.

Lin, R. L. (1985). The promise and the problems of the Native American student. *Journal of American Indian Education, 25*(1), 6–16.

Lin, R. L., LaCounte, D., & Eder, J. (1988). A study of Native American students in a predominantly White college. *Journal of American Indian Education, 27*(3), 8–15.

Murguia, E., Padilla, R. V., & Pavel, D. M. (1991). Ethnicity and the concept of social integration in Tinto's model. *Journal of College Student Development, 32,* 433–439.

Noriega, J. (1992). American Indian education in the United States: Indoctrination for subordination to colonialism. In M. A. James (Ed.), *The state of Native America: Genocide, colonization, and resistance* (pp. 371–402). Boston: South End Press.

Pascarella, E. T., & Terenzini, P. T. (2005). *How college affects students.* San Francisco: Jossey-Bass.

Patton, L. D. (2006). The voice of reason: A qualitative examination of Black student perceptions of the Black culture center. *Journal of College Student Development, 47*(6), 628–646.

Pottinger, R. (1989). Disjunction to higher education: American Indian students in the Southwest. *Anthropology and Education Quarterly, 20,* 326–344.

Reddy, M. A. (1993). *Statistical record of Native North Americans.* Washington, DC: Gale Research.

Reyhner, J., & Eder, J. (2004). *American Indian education: A history.* Norman: University of Oklahoma Press.

Scott, W. J. (1986). Attachment to Indian culture and the "difficult situation." *Youth and Society, 17,* 381–395.

Snyder, T. D., Tan, A. G., & Hoffman, C. M. (2004). *Digest of education statistics 2003.* (NCES 2005–025). U.S. Department of Education, National Center for Education Statistics. Washington, DC: Government Printing Office.

Swisher, K. (1990). Cooperative learning and the education of American Indian/Alaskan Native students: A review of the literature and suggestions for implementation. *Journal of American Indian Education, 29,* 36–43.

Swisher, K., & Deyhle, D. (1989, August). The styles of learning are different, but the teaching is just the same: Suggestions for teachers of American Indian youth. *Journal of American Indian Education* (Special Edition), 1–14.

Thelin, J. R. (2003). Historical overview of American education. In S. R. Komives & D. B. Woodard (Eds.), *Student services: A handbook for the profession* (4th ed., pp. 3–22). San Francisco: Jossey-Bass.

U.S. Department of Education. (1998). *American Indians and Alaska Natives in postsecondary education.* Washington, DC: U.S. Government Printing Office.

U.S. Department of Education. (2006). *Digest of education statistics: 2006.* Washington, DC: U.S. Government Printing Office.

Wells, R. N. (1997). *The Native American experience in higher education: Turning around the cycle of failure II.* (ERIC Document Reproduction Service No. ED414108)

Willeto, A. A. (1999). Navajo culture and family influences on academic success: Traditionalism is not a significant predictor of achievement among young Navajos. *Journal of American Indian Education, 38*(2), 1–24.

Woodcock, D. B., & Alawiye, O. (2001). The antecedents of failure and emerging hope: American Indians and public higher education. *Education Policy Analysis Archives, 121,* 810–820.

Wright, B. (1996). The "untamable savage spirit": American Indians in colonial colleges. In C. Turner, M. Garcia, A. Nora, & L. I. Rendón (Eds.), *Racial and ethnic diversity in higher education* (pp. 122–134). Boston: Pearson.

NATIVE AMERICAN CULTURAL CENTERS

American Indian Center
University of North Dakota-Grand Forks, ND
Established 1972

Latino Native American Cultural Center
University of Iowa—Iowa City, IA
Established 1971

Native American Longhouse
Oregon State University—Corvallis, OR
Established 1971

Native American Cultural Center
Stanford University—Palo Alto, CA
Established 1974

Native American Cultural Center
Colorado State University—Fort Collins, CO
Established 1979

The Native American Cultural Center
University of South Dakota—Vermillion, SD
Established 1988

Dr. Josephine White Eagle Cultural Center
University of Massachusetts, Amherst—Amherst, MA
Established 1989

Native American Cultural Center (NACC)
Yale University—New Haven, CT
Established 1993

Native American Student Services Center
University of Northern Colorado—Greeley, CO
Established 1995

Wassaja Student Center
University of Arizona-Tucson, AZ
Established 1989

Zowie Banteah Cultural Center
Mt. Holyoke College—South Hadley, MA
Established 1995

Native American House (NAH)
University of Illinois—Urbana, IL
Established 2002

Native American Student and Community Center
Portland State University—Portland, OR
Established 2003

The First Nations Educational and Cultural Center
Indiana University—Bloomington, IN
Established 2007

Native American Educational & Cultural Center (NAECC)
Purdue University—West Lafayette, IN
Established 2007

4

ON SOLID GROUND

An Examination of the Successful Strategies and Positive Student Outcomes of Two Black Culture Centers

Lori D. Patton

I n 2002, *Black Issues in Higher Education* published an issue that focused on Black culture centers (BCCs) on college campuses. The cover article, "Black Culture Centers: Standing on Shaky Ground," raised important questions regarding the continued presence and relevance of BCCs in higher education. These questions included the following:

> Whom should cultural centers serve? And how? What should they be called? Add in culture and costs, and the next question to arise is, should there be a cultural center for every sizeable ethnic group on campus? (Hefner, 2002, p. 22)

According to Hefner, BCCs are standing on shaky ground as a result of the influx of an increasingly diverse student population, a dearth of financial resources, and their emphasis on social programs instead of academic programs. Although the questions raised by Hefner are important and can serve as a starting point for serious dialogue regarding the future of BCCs, this chapter focuses on demonstrating the ways in which BCCs are standing on solid ground.

The dominant discourse about BCCs suggests that these facilities are no longer relevant, have abandoned their original missions, and fail to meet the needs of diverse student populations (Hefner, 2002; Patton, 2006a). In this chapter, I argue that there is much that BCCs do that justifies their continued existence on college campuses. Using the findings from a qualitative study of the relevance and roles of BCCs, I contend that they do far more than they receive credit for, and that their successes demonstrate their relevance at predominantly White institutions (PWIs).

Historical Perspectives

The body of literature that examines BCCs is not extensive, and much of it is historical and/or anecdotal in nature. Most authors attribute the emergence of BCCs in the 1960s and 1970s to the student demands made during the Black Student Movement. The underlying impetus was the unwillingness of PWIs to engage with Black students as their presence on campus increased. Administrators and faculty at most institutions expected Black students to assimilate to the dominant environment. Thus PWIs were in every way less than welcoming to the incoming populations of Black students. According to Wolf-Wendel, Twombly, Tuttle, Ward, and Gaston-Gayles (2004):

> Black students were barely tolerated on many campuses and felt the sting of racism in class where they were simultaneously invisible and a spectacle. . . . Even on more progressive campuses, life was not structured to recognize and accommodate [their] needs and desires. (p. v)

Because PWIs were inhospitable and isolating environments, Black students galvanized to challenge the status quo of their institutions (Williamson, 1999). They planned sit-ins and protests and submitted to campus administrators a range of demands centering on the incorporation of Black Studies courses into the curriculum, focused recruitment of Black students, the hiring of additional Black faculty and staff members, and the creation of a house or center for Black students (Patton & Hannon, 2008). I contend the rise of BCCs is best understood in light of students' demands of university administrators (Patton, 2005). Black students did not simply insist on the creation of culture centers. Rather, their desire for the centers grew out of an increasingly prominent feeling of isolation and marginalization at PWIs. In 2005, I noted:

> Black students' demands for BCCs were inextricably intertwined with the yearning to see Black culture manifested throughout the entire system of

higher education. In essence they wanted to see their culture recognized in academics (curriculum and faculty), social life (student activities, residential life) and administrative affairs (financial aid, admissions). (p. 157)

Administrators at PWIs were often resistant to the demands of Black students, particularly their requests for the creation of Black Studies courses and BCCs; both efforts were perceived as separatist in nature and antithetical to the missions of colleges and universities. Black students responded to the lack of action and responsiveness by taking over administrative buildings, telling their stories to the press, and withdrawing from their institutions. Administrators at PWIs eventually succumbed to student demands following significant media attention that often cast their institutions in a negative light. The Black Student Movement and campus protests made the entire nation aware of the racial climate in the United States and inspired other social movements on campus. Thus, the emergence of culture centers was largely a result of Black students' efforts to make their campus environments conducive to their own survival, learning, and development (Patton, 2005; Williamson, 1999)

Benefits of BCCs

In addition to the historical literature that outlines the development of BCCs, another body of literature highlights the purpose of BCCs and the roles they have played at PWIs over time. While much of the literature is not empirically based, it offers concrete examples of the benefits of BCCs and demonstrates the need for practitioners and scholars to engage in examinations of BCCs.

Most often, BCCs are described as a home away from home for Black students at PWIs. According to Young and Hannon (2002), BCCs are "a safe haven, a place to retreat from the perceived hostility of an unwelcoming campus community." Princes (2005) indicated that BCCs were established to help Black students deal with the loneliness and isolation that many experienced at PWIs. In examining the philosophical foundations of BCCs, Stovall (2005) indicated that the central goals of these centers are to:

direct student frustrations into, not away from, academic activities; to guide students to challenge, rather than retreat from, unfairness in the classroom and in the campus community in general; to assist students in building a Black support system that constructs positive self and group identities; to provide avenues that will allow students to feel empowered vis-à-vis involvement in campus life, success in the classroom and intellectual growth; to provide the opportunity for African American, White, and all other students, faculty, staff administrators, as well as the surrounding campus community, to interact with and learn about African American culture and experience. (p. 106)

In a qualitative study, Black students indicated that BCCs were most beneficial in helping them adjust to campus life, provided them with experiences that led to participation in other campus activities, and gave them a sense of identity and historical relevance (Patton, 2006b). Despite the information available about the value of BCCs, several misconceptions about BCCs ultimately pose a challenge to their existence, including the notion that BCCs promote self-segregation and separatism, serve Black students only, and provide social rather than academic programs (Patton, 2006a). These misconceptions exist due to a lack of knowledge and information about the historical emergence of BCCs and the educational programming and events that take place at the centers.

Standing on Solid Ground

An examination of the challenges that BCCs face is warranted, yet it is also important to assess ways in which BCCs are succeeding. Rather than view BCCs as standing on shaky ground, it is imperative to highlight the solid ground upon which many BCCs stand in order to challenge deficit thinking about their existence. In this chapter, I offer two examples from a study that I recently conducted of BCCs; the centers included the Center for Black Studies at Northern Illinois University in DeKalb, Illinois, and the Malcolm X Institute at Wabash College in Wabash, Indiana. These centers are neither the most popular nor the best-known BCCs in the country. However, they are stellar examples of what makes BCCs a unique and relevant part of campus life. I was interested in identifying BCCs that emerged from student protests and demands and have managed to remain intact since their inception and investigating what these BCCs did "right" on their campuses.

The Black Studies Minor at the Center for Black Studies

The Center for Black Studies (CBS) at Northern Illinois University (NIU), a comprehensive public research university, houses the institution's minor in

Black Studies. The courses offered through the CBS are interdisciplinary in nature, focus on the Black experience in America, and address pertinent issues that affect the entire African diaspora as well as other cultures and ethnicities. The Black Studies classes are popular among students for several reasons, including the fact that they are standard three-credit-hour courses that any student can take to fulfill general education or minor studies requirements.

Students at NIU referred to the Black Studies courses as "eye opening." Monique, one of the students with whom I spoke, noted that "they've definitely been an eye-opener. Some of the things that I was a little ignorant to, I think, coming into college, they've made me realize some things about myself and my culture." The classes challenge students to think critically about the treatment of Blacks and other disenfranchised groups in society. Jalyn completed several of the courses and shared, "It always stimulates my mind a lot when I take these classes."

Black Studies courses encourage students to examine issues and consider possible solutions to dilemmas prevalent in Black communities. As students described their experiences, they noted how relieved they were to connect with course content and instructors; this was not always the case in other classes. Many of the students stated that they enrolled in Black Studies courses because they viewed the classes as opportunities to learn about themselves. The impact of the courses is so strong that students often recommend the classes to other students. Howard noted:

> I took a class, personally, because I thought it would be something like, oh, it's probably going to be an easy A to take the class . . . and then once I got to class, I took Racism in American Culture and then that class opened my eyes to a whole lot more. You know, I was shocked and I ended up loving the class and I got an easy A out of it because you actually want to do the reading. In [some of] my other classes, we just blow off the reading. I was actually reading more books because they were a lot more interesting. I mean, the class, they made it really interesting. It was an eye-opener. . . . I feel like the class, I think, just had me thinking differently. . . . It just, it opened my eyes to a lot of stuff. And I mean things I probably wouldn't have thought of before. I mean, it's important. That's, like, stuff that I can actually take with me outside of college. That's stuff I definitely retained.

The Black Studies classes at NIU are essential because they are the venues through which many Black students learn about the CBS. David admitted that had it not been for a Black Studies class, he would not have had any type of involvement with the center. He noted, "Honestly, without that class, I probably would never have stepped in this place the whole semester."

A large number of Black Studies courses are taught in the CBS classroom. Once students are exposed to the center through class attendance, they have opportunities to meet the staff and learn about the center's resources, programming, and student organizations. Some CBS staff members teach Black Studies courses, which connects students with the people responsible for the center and others on campus who partner with the CBS. The classes are also a major draw for students of other ethnicities. There is a strong possibility that student involvement at the CBS would be negatively affected if the Black Studies minor were moved to a different location. Student exposure to the CBS could dwindle without the presence of Black Studies courses. At the time Michelle was interviewed for this study, she had already taken six Black Studies classes. She explained what those classes meant to her:

> I tell people that if I didn't have those courses, I couldn't make it through the week just taking my major courses, because I have no connection to them. But it's the Center for Black Studies, and I tell every student, "You need to at least take one course there and you need to get hooked up with that building, get to know those teachers, get to know the people there, because that's what's going to keep you."

The physical environment of the CBS emphasizes the importance of the Black Studies minor. The classroom used for Black Studies courses sits in the center of the building, which clearly indicates a focus on educating students about Black culture and life and stresses the important role of education in the Black community. The CBS clearly has a very strong academic influence on campus in addition to offering support to Black students.

Fostering Brotherhood at the Malcolm X Institute

The process through which students are initiated into the Malcolm X Institute (MXI) at Wabash College, a private liberal arts college for men, is unique. Prospective members must participate in an associate member program, which involves volunteering in the MXI's mentoring program, planning events, and learning about Black history and culture. An important part of the associate member program is the development of a clear understanding of the history and purpose of the MXI. The culminating experience of the associate member program involves the planning and implementation of the Kwanzaa program and completion of tests that address history and other information students learn during the membership process. The program is designed to enhance students' understanding of Black culture and provide them with privileges that other students do not receive, such as 24-hour access to the MXI.

Perhaps the most interesting thing about the associate member program is the fact that White fraternity members constantly and erroneously liken MXI membership to a fraternity. As a result, accusations of "dirty rushing"—or attempts to make a fraternity look bad in order to persuade a prospective member to join one fraternity rather than another—are common. MXI members are sometimes accused of telling Black students and others to join the MXI instead of joining a White fraternity. However, MXI members who participated in this study made it abundantly clear that the MXI is not a fraternity even though it sponsors fraternal-like activities, such as recruiting, conducting service projects, sustaining traditions, and expressing brotherhood. In fact, several MXI members also belong to Black fraternities on other campuses.

No other BCC that participated in this study offered a membership option requiring students to go through a special process. However, MXI participants were quick to point out that students who do not go through the associate member process are not excluded from MXI programs. The program was created to foster a greater sense of belonging, camaraderie, and brotherhood, in light of the fact that the college had not taken any steps toward inviting Black fraternities to campus. Several of the students commented on the similarity between the associate member program and pledging a fraternity. Steven claimed:

> I'm quick to point out that it's not—that we do have Black fraternity members on campus but, you know, I can't argue [with] the fact that it is a quasi-fraternity. I mean we have . . . a fraternal-like nature. I guess that

would be the best way of putting it. We are, you know, we're a close brotherhood; we call ourselves a brotherhood. We have associate pledges written
into our constitution. We do everything traditionally.

Students also explained what associate members do in order to receive full
membership as brothers in the MXI. Trebor explained that "the associates
program is . . . it's like a pledgeship, no hazing, you know. Basically you've
got to learn the history of the building and, you know, some Black history
and show your commitment." Michael added that "you take several tests,
on the history, on Black Studies things, you know, Kwanzaa . . . as well as
do presentations. You know . . . you have to plan the Kwanzaa programs."
The planning of the Kwanzaa celebration is considered a culminating experience in the associate member program, after which associates become MXI
members. Michael elaborated:

> They [associate members] do not have access to the building whenever they
> want, but that's a really big thing that separates them from a member. I
> mean, they participate in the exact same thing[s] as we do. At the end of
> their associate program at the end of the semester, we have to vote on
> them, make sure they met their requirements for things like KQ and K,
> that's the mentoring program. We look at their record, like have they been
> attending meetings, MXI functions, and we vote, the brothers vote, and
> then, like, we initiate them in and then they're brothers.

As one of the older members of the MXI, Steven witnessed changes and
transitions in the associate member program over the years. He spoke openly
about what he believed to be central differences between the MXI and a
fraternity:

> Like, they [fraternity members] cross the burning sand, the associate
> pledges cross the river, so to speak. So I don't think it's modeled after [a
> fraternity]. . . . We've had fraternity members be chairmen and leaders of
> our institute, but I don't think any of our traditions really model it. I know
> of none that I've done so far. . . . We have our traditions. I don't like to
> call them initiations, because it's not a fraternity, but we have our tradi-
> tions that we do on a yearly basis with new associates . . . and that kind of
> thing brings you together as a class.

Current members of the MXI made special efforts to recruit first-year students. When asked about the recruitment process and why MXI members

make special efforts to target the Black freshmen, Charles explained that "usually they need it. I mean, I feel like they need it." It is important to the upper-class Black men on campus to get new students acclimated to Wabash and provide them with immediate connections on campus. Caeser also offered insight into the benefits of being involved:

> So, you know, it just really motivated me to hang out with them and, you know, I really felt like I was making a difference for something, for something on campus, even though whether it was successful or not, I felt like I was doing something to, you know, make that difference.

Being involved with the MXI was particularly important and beneficial to Caeser given the obstacles he faced during his high school years and his lack of knowledge about Black experiences:

> One of the big things [about] the associate program is just that we, they, stress the education of Black history and Black culture. They never try to change, like, who you are; they just want to teach you about Black culture and Black history and, you know, Black music, the Black experience like Kwanzaa, great Black leaders—things like that—because, I mean, a lot of Black people don't know about their own history. I sure didn't before I came here. And, you know, when you learn about those things, it makes you feel like you're more, I don't know, it just makes you feel more Black. It just makes you feel better, like you know all these great things about your people, and that's one of the things that motivated me to be a history major too, just learning about all these different minority cultures around the world, like our own heritage.

Membership in the MXI provided Caeser with support and brotherhood. He also mentioned the fraternal aspects of MXI:

> You know, it just feels like you've got someone you can just count on, you know, just to roll with sometimes. You know, when times get rough, everybody does come together. I mean, there are times when people don't get along, all the brothers don't get along, but when times get tight, everybody comes together . . . We're not a Greek fraternity, but it is fraternal. I mean, guys stick together.

Students stated that the majority of MXI members are non–African American students who are interested in learning about Black culture and want to be involved. This is commonly unrecognized by critics of the MXI. Although Black members of the MXI were welcoming of international students, White students, and other student populations, they expressed concerns about getting more Black students involved. Some of the greatest obstacles are the small number of Blacks enrolled at Wabash, the fact that many Black students are recruited to Wabash to play sports and their schedules do not allow time for participation in other extracurricular activities, and difficulty attracting students who simply are not interested in MXI membership.

Overall, most of the MXI members interviewed for this study claimed that their affiliation with the MXI is beneficial. One of the participants shared that when Black members of the MXI graduate from Wabash, they consider themselves MXI alumni in addition to Wabash alumni. The student also commented that when alumni visit campus, they come to the MXI first. Alumni make donations to the MXI and sponsor programs; their involvement demonstrates an allegiance to the survival of the MXI as a support for Black students at Wabash College.

The small-college atmosphere of Wabash allows the MXI to have a central role on campus in terms of cultural programming and Black male student involvement. This facility serves a number of purposes on campus, such as a gathering spot for students, a programming body, and the Wabash version of a Black student union. These efforts are spearheaded by students who serve in elected positions, such as MXI chairman, membership chair, and programming chair. Furthermore, the MXI is an academic facility as well. While no courses are offered through the MXI, several classes are held in the building. Similar to the CBS at NIU, courses held at the MXI result in increased student exposure to the facility.

An additional notable characteristic of the MXI is its staffing structure. Currently, there is only one professional on staff—the director. While small staffs are not uncommon for small colleges or BCCs, the role of the MXI director sets it apart from other BCCs. Many of the students interviewed for this study expounded on the leadership structure of the MXI. The director oversees the facility and budget, yet the MXI chairman and other students who comprise the elected leadership body actually run the center. The director's role was described by students as advisory in nature, whereas the student leadership makes a great deal of the decisions about programming and funding.

Staying Relevant

I chose to highlight NIU's CBS and Wabash's MXI because the centers play an important and unique role in their respective campus communities. The Black Studies minor at the CBS and the associate member program at the MXI are central components that bring exposure to their centers. Both offer educational programming to teach students about Black history and culture, and have been successful in involving students of various races, ethnicities, and cultures. At the CBS, the courses are a draw not only for Black students but also for students who need to complete general course requirements or have interest in pursuing the minor. Moreover, the interdisciplinary nature of the courses is attractive to a diverse array of students. At the MXI, the associate member program fosters brotherhood, leadership, involvement, and identity development. The programs not only provide academic benefits to students but also usher in opportunities for involvement and leadership experiences.

As the relevance of BCCs is called into question, it is essential to highlight programs at which they are successful. BCCs should identify what makes them unique and communicate their successes to their campuses and the broader higher education community. By clearly doing so, BCCs can work toward enhancement to ensure that they remain successful and relevant. Moreover, such efforts should become the key pieces that maintain the uniqueness of BCCs. Finally, BCC programs should be evaluated to ensure that they meet the goals of the center and support the institution's mission.

References

Hefner, D. (2002). Black cultural centers: Standing on shaky ground? *Black Issues in Higher Education, 18*(26), 22–29.

Patton, L. D. (2005). Power to the people! A literature review of the impact of Black student protest on the emergence of Black culture centers. In F. Hord (Ed.), *Black culture centers and political identities* (pp. 151–163). Chicago: Third World Press.

Patton, L. D. (2006a). Black culture centers: Still central to student learning. *About Campus, 11*(2), 2–8.

Patton, L. D. (2006b). The voice of reason: A qualitative examination of Black student perceptions of Black culture centers. *Journal of College Student Development, 47*, 628–646.

Patton, L. D., & Hannon, M. D. (2008). Collaboration for cultural programming: Engaging culture centers, multicultural affairs, and student activities offices as partners. In S. Harper (Ed.), *Creating inclusive campus environments for cross-cultural learning and student engagement* (pp. 139–154). Washington, DC: NASPA.

Princes, C. D. (2005). The precarious question of Black cultural centers versus multicultural centers. In F. Hord (Ed.), *Black culture centers: Politics of survival and identity* (pp. 135–146). Chicago: Third World Press.

Stovall, A. J. (2005). Why Black culture centers? The philosophical bases for Black culture centers. In F. Hord (Ed.), *Black culture centers: Politics of survival and identity* (pp. 102–112). Chicago: Third World Press.

Williamson, J. A. (1999). In defense of themselves: The Black struggle for success and recognition at predominantly White colleges and universities. *Journal of Negro Education, 68,* 92–105.

Wolf-Wendel, L. E., Twombly, S. B., Tuttle, K. N., Ward, K., & Gaston-Gayles, J. L. (2004). *Reflecting back, looking forward: Civil rights and student affairs.* Washington, DC: NASPA.

Young, L. W., & Hannon, M. D. (February 14, 2002). The staying power of Black cultural centers [Editorial]. *Black Issues in Higher Education, 18,* Last Word.

AFRICAN AMERICAN
CULTURAL CENTERS

Paul Robeson Cultural Center
Rutgers University—New Brunswick, NJ
Established 1967

ABLE (Allied Blacks for Liberty and Equality) Center for Black Culture
Knox College—Galesburg, Illinois
Established 1968

Afro-American Cultural Centers
University of Iowa—Iowa City, IA
Established 1968

Black/African American Culture Center
Colorado State University—Fort Collins, CO
Established 1968

H. Fred Simons African American Cultural Center
University of Connecticut—Storrs, CT
Established 1968

John D. O'Bryant African-American Institute
Northeastern University—Boston, MA
Established 1968

Neal-Marshall Black Culture Center
Indiana University—Bloomington, IN
Established 1968

Africana Center
Tufts University—Medford, MA
Established 1969

Afro-American Cultural Center
Yale University—New Haven, CT
Established 1969

Black Community Services Center
Stanford University—Palo Alto, CA
Established 1969

Black Cultural Center
Iowa State University—Ames, IA
Established 1969

The Conney M. Kimbo Black Cultural Center
Grinnell College—Grinnell, IA
Established 1969

John L. Warfield Center for African & African American Studies
University of Texas—Austin, TX
Established 1969

Afro-American Cultural Center
Eastern Illinois University—Charleston, IL
Established 1970

Black Cultural Center
Purdue University—West Lafayette, IN
Established 1970

Black Cultural Center
Swarthmore College—Swarthmore, PA
Established 1970

Bruce D. Nesbitt African American Cultural Center
University of Illinois at Urbana-Champaign—Urbana, IL
Established 1970

David A. Portlock Black Cultural Center
Lafayette College—Easton, PA
Established 1970

Malcolm X Institute of Black Studies
Wabash College—Crawfordsville, IN
Established 1970

Black Cultural Center, Black House
Rensselaer Polytechnic Institute—Troy, NY
Established 1971

Boling Black Cultural Resources Center
Wright State University—Dayton, OH
Established 1971

The Institute of Black Culture (IBC)
University of Florida—Gainesville, FL
Established 1971

Nyumburu Cultural Center
University of Maryland—College Park, MD
Established 1971

Gaines-Oldham Black Culture Center
University of Missouri—Columbia, MO
Established 1972

Malcolm X Cultural Center
University of Massachusetts—Amherst, MA
Established 1972

Betty Shabazz House
Mt. Holyoke College—South Hadley, MA
Established 1973

Black Cultural Center
University of Tennessee—Knoxville, TN
Established 1975

Center for Black Culture
University of Delaware—Newark, DE
Established 1975

Lonnie B. Harris Black Cultural Center
Oregon State University—Corvallis, OR
Established 1975

The Center for Black Cultural and Student Affairs
University of Southern California—Los Angeles, CA
Established 1977

Luther Porter Jackson Black Cultural Center
University of Virginia—Charlottesville, VA
Established 1977

Marcus Garvey Cultural Center
University of Northern Colorado—Greeley, CO
Established 1982

Black Cultural Center
Berea College—Berea, KY
Established 1983

The Mary Lou Williams Center for Black Culture
Duke University—Durham, NC
Established 1983

The Bishop Joseph Johnson Black Cultural Center
Vanderbilt University—Nashville, TN
Established 1984

Avery Research Center for African American History and Culture
College of Charleston—Charleston, SC
Established 1985

Center for Black Culture
West Virginia University—Morgantown, WV
Established 1987

African American History and Culture House (AAHCH)
University of Missouri—Kansas City, MO
Established 1988

The Sonja Haynes Stone Center for Black Culture and History
University of NC-Chapel Hill—Chapel Hill, NC
Established 1988

African American Cultural Resource Center
University of Arizona—Tucson, AZ
Established 1989

African American Resource Center
University of California Santa Cruz—Santa Cruz, CA
Established 1989

Hale Black Cultural Center
The Ohio State University—Columbus, OH
Established 1989

African American Cultural & Research Center
University of Cincinnati—Cincinnati, OH
Established 1991

Black Cultural Center
Virginia Polytechnic Institute and State University—Blacksburg, VA
Established 1991

Wilbur N. Daniel African American Cultural Center
Austin Peay State University—Clarksville, TN
Established 1991

African American Cultural Center
Louisiana State University—Baton Rouge, LA
Established 1993

Center for Black Studies
Northern Illinois University—DeKalb, IL
Established 1993

African American Cultural Center
University of Georgia—Athens, GA
Established 1994

Upperman African American Cultural Center
University of North Carolina, Charlotte—Charlotte, NC
Established 1995

Makuu Black Cultural Center
University of Pennsylvania—Philadelphia, PA
Established 2000

PART TWO

THEORETICAL PERSPECTIVES AND CULTURE CENTERS

5

COUNTERSPACES IN A HOSTILE PLACE

A Critical Race Theory Analysis of Campus Culture Centers

Tara J. Yosso and Corina Benavides Lopez

A lot of Latinos who come to the university are first generation and so when they come to a university like this, where there's not that many Latinos, they get culture shock and they want to go home. . . . We do a lot of events within the halls that relate back to the culture just so that the students can feel a little bit more welcome in the halls and a little bit more comfortable. 'Cause it is very hard coming into a university that's not—where you don't see a lot of yourself.[1]

I n the preceding passage, Sofia, a Latina undergraduate at a rural Research I university in the Midwest, spoke to the marginalization that Students of Color experience at that historically White institution. She shared this in order to explain the creation of a student-initiated organization dedicated to offering cultural activities in the residence halls. Listening to this young woman's reflections, we are reminded of bell hooks's (1990) observation that "We know better the margin as site of deprivation. . . . We know less the margin as site of resistance" (p. 151). Utilizing critical race theory (CRT), this chapter examines culture centers as counterspaces forged in the margins of historically White colleges and functioning as transformative sites of resistance for Students of Color.

We begin this discussion by describing CRT as an analytical framework used to examine the persistence of racism in higher education. According to most university brochures, college represents a time of unbridled optimism, exciting challenges, and opportunities. Few students anticipate that their college experience might be marked by gendered racism in the questioning of their physical presence, academic merits, and cultural knowledge on and around campus (Smith, Yosso, & Solórzano, 2007; Solórzano, Ceja, & Yosso, 2000). Certainly recruitment brochures would not advertise the fact that many universities foster a campus climate wherein Whites enjoy a sense of entitlement while racial minorities face charges that they are unqualified and out of place.

We argue that traditional discourse about diversity in higher education helps maintain negative campus racial climates across the U.S. higher education system. Well-intentioned theories, policies, and practices of diversity tend to uncritically view the experiences of White middle-class students as the standard. CRT recenters the discussion on the histories and lived experiences of People of Color.

Next, we present some undergraduate students' reflections on their participation in culture centers on historically White campuses. This discussion reveals that the transition to the college campus for many Students of Color begins with their confronting subtle, yet stunning racial microaggressions that aim to remind them of "their place" at the margins of the university. Amid such messages of rejection, culture centers can provide a physical, epistemological, social, and academic counterspace for Students of Color to build a sense of community and nurture "critical resistant navigational skills" (Solórzano & Villalpando, 1998). We assert that culture centers disrupt the White privilege and entitlement pervasive on historically White university campuses by empowering students to choose the margin "as site of resistance—as location of radical openness and possibility" (hooks, 1990, p. 153).

Critical Race Theory

> Racism is especially rampant in places and people that produce knowledge
> . . . By bringing in our own approaches and methodologies, we transform
> that theorizing space. (Anzaldúa, 1990, pp. xix, xxv)

The late Chicana activist-scholar Gloria Anzaldúa asserted that People of Color must work to transform academia's discursive spaces by drawing on their "own approaches and methodologies." As we focus the research lens on People of Color, we validate often-overlooked forms of knowledge grounded in a legacy of resilience and resistance to racism and other forms of subordination. This act of recentering the debate about racial inequality in schools on the histories and lived experiences of People of Color has been a collaborative process of creating a new framework of CRT in education (e.g., Dixson & Rousseau, 2005; Ladson-Billings & Tate, 1995; Lopez & Parker, 2003; Lynn & Adams, 2002; Lynn, Yosso, Solórzano, & Parker, 2002; Parker, Deyhle, Villenas, & Crossland, 1998; Yosso, 2006).

Rooted in progressive community and scholarly traditions, CRT originated as an academic movement among legal scholars questioning the slow progress of civil rights legislation in the 1980s. In extending CRT to the fields of education and sociology, our work identifies CRT's genealogical antecedents in critical activist and scholarly traditions such as ethnic studies, women's studies, and critical pedagogy. Drawing on the strengths of these traditions and the historical hindsight of previous theoretical blind spots, CRT exhibits five tenets:

1. The *inter*centricity of race and racism with other forms of subordination: CRT starts from the premise that race and racism are central, endemic, permanent, and a fundamental part of defining and explaining how U.S. society functions (Bell, 1992; Russell, 1993). CRT acknowledges the inextricable layers of racial subordination based on race as well as on gender, class, immigration status, surname, phenotype, accent, and sexuality (e.g., Crenshaw, 1989, 1991; Valdes, 1998).

2. The challenge to dominant ideology: CRT challenges White privilege and refutes the claims of objectivity, meritocracy, color blindness, race neutrality, and equal opportunity that institutions of higher education make to camouflage the self-interest, power, and privilege of dominant groups (e.g., Calmore, 1992; Solórzano, 1997).

3. The commitment to social justice: CRT's social and racial justice research agenda exposes the "interest-convergence" of civil rights gains in education (Bell, 1987) and works toward the elimination of racism, sexism, and poverty, as well as the empowerment of People

of Color and other subordinated groups (e.g., Freire, 1970, 1973; Solórzano & Delgado Bernal, 2001).

4. The centrality of experiential knowledge: CRT recognizes the experiential knowledge of People of Color as legitimate, appropriate forms of data, and critical to understanding, analyzing, and teaching about racial subordination (e.g., Delgado Bernal, 2002).

5. The transdisciplinary perspective: CRT extends beyond disciplinary boundaries to analyze race and racism within both historical and contemporary contexts (e.g., Calmore, 1997; Delgado, 1984, 1992; Gutiérrez-Jones, 2001; Harris, 1993; Olivas, 1990).

Though individually these tenets are not new, as a framework CRT challenges us to be explicit about how theory informs our research methods and pedagogy, and to take action guided by the lived experiences of those injured by racism (Solórzano, 1997, 1998). Anzaldúa (1990) noted, "In our mestizaje theories we create new categories for those of us left out or pushed out of existing ones" (pp. xxv–xxvi). Indeed, a CRT analysis of historically White colleges and universities honors Anzaldúa's call to "transform" institutions of higher education by framing the dialogue around the knowledge and histories of marginalized communities.

Racial Microaggressions

Over 100 years after W. E. B. DuBois (1903/1989) warned that "the problem of the color-line" (p. 29) would continue to challenge U.S. society, racism and sexism persist in both covert and overt forms in higher educational settings (Smith, Altbach, & Lomotey, 2002). Using multi-method research tools to analyze campus racial climate experiences, scholars document a pervasive sense of White male privilege and a troubling level of "accepted" racial bigotry (e.g., Allen & Solórzano, 2001). In social and academic spaces on these college campuses, African American and Latina/o students daily experience subtle, yet stunning interpersonal and institutional racial assaults, which Chester Pierce has termed racial microaggressions (see Davis, 1989; Pierce, 1970, 1974, 1995; Yosso, Smith, Ceja, & Solórzano, 2009). From interpersonal remarks, such as "When I talk about those Blacks, I wasn't talking about you," and "I don't think of you as a Mexican" to racial jokes and institutional neglect, these "acts of disregard" cause immense stress (Solórzano, 1998, p. 125). In their various forms, racial microaggressions send messages implying that People of Color are unintelligent, foreign, criminally prone, and deserving of socially marginal status (see also Constantine, 2007; Constantine & Sue, 2007; Sue et al., 2007). Students of Color spend considerable time and energy deciphering the layers of these racial affronts, uncovering assumptions about gender, class, immigrant status, and other forms of subordination. If they confront their assailants, they may also expend additional energy and time defending themselves against accusations of being "too sensitive." Over time, the mundane but extreme stress caused by racial microaggressions (Carroll, 1998) can lead to mental, emotional, and physical strain—what William Smith (2004) has termed "racial battle fatigue" (see also Smith, Yosso, & Solórzano, 2006). Moreover, Students of Color experience the accumulation of racial microaggressions as a rejection of their presence at the university.

Race and Gender Marginality

Racial microaggressions are one form of everyday, systemic racism, which serve to keep Students of Color "in their place" at the margins of historically White universities. For example, Kenneth González (2002) documents the social, physical, and epistemological "cultural starvation" of Chicano undergraduates at an urban liberal arts public west coast college. His research demonstrates that in social spaces, students find themselves a numerical racial/ethnic minority with very little, if any, political power. This isolation leaves them with a clear sense that communicating in any language other than English (e.g., Spanish) is inappropriate. Students' physical world also elicits cultural alienation, featuring campus sculptures, buildings, flyers, and office postings that do not reflect Chicana/o histories or experiences. The cars and clothes of the predominately White student body further evidence the physical reproduction of White middle-class culture. Moreover, González (2002) noted that the epistemological world of the Chicanos in his study featured very little access to Faculty of Color and a paucity of ethnic studies curriculum. The institutional maintenance of this "apartheid of knowledge" effectively "marginalizes, discredits, and devalues the scholarship, epistemologies, and other cultural resources" Students and Faculty of Color bring to the academy (Delgado Bernal & Villalpando, 2002, p. 169). Such marginalization may impact the adjustment, academic performance, sense of comfort, sense of value, and ultimately the persistence of Students of Color (Smith, 2009).

The "cultural starvation" of students in Gonzalez's study resonates with Sofia's remarks at the beginning of this chapter. As she describes the cultural isolation endured by Latinas/os in the residential halls on her rural Research I Midwestern campus, she details survival strategies students developed to culturally nourish and replenish themselves.

> You're not going to see your food there. You are not going to watch Spanish [language] television. . . . You are not going to hear Spanish on the radio station. Nothing that you're used to is here . . . especially in the halls. So what we did is . . . we created an organization for the halls that helped with all those things. (University of Illinois at Urbana-Champaign, n.d.-2)[2]

Sofia collaboratively worked to create a cultural sense of home in the residence halls with Spanish-language books, culturally authentic meals, and extracurricular cultural activities. Similarly, the students in González's study took it upon themselves to establish a cultural sense of home in their dorm room by covering their walls with Chicana/o cultural symbols (e.g., posters and pictures), playing Chicana/o music loudly (despite complaints from neighbors), and speaking to each other in Spanish. In addition, they reached out by telephone or drove home to visit with family members and friends from their hometowns. To counter the cultural starvation they experienced, these students also sought out Chicana/o studies courses, Chicana/o faculty, and Chicana/o student organizations

White students do not bear the extra load of confronting race and gender marginality in college. Like their counterparts, Students of Color balance a full load of courses, sometimes work two jobs to afford their academic and living expenses, and participate in campus and community activities. Acknowledging that these students also endure gendered racism and marginalization becomes difficult when universities are busy boasting about race-neutral policies and a color-blind yet diverse institution of higher education.

Naming and Challenging a Diversity of Convenience

We broadly define campus racial climate as the overall racial environment of the university that could potentially foster outstanding academic outcomes and graduation rates for all students but too often contributes to poor academic performance and high dropout rates for Students of Color (e.g., Hurtado, Milem, Clayton-Pedersen, & Allen, 1998; Solórzano, Allen, & Carroll, 2002). A positive campus racial climate features: (a) the inclusion of Students, Faculty, and Administrators of Color; (b) a curriculum reflecting the historical and contemporary experiences of People of Color; (c) programs to support the recruitment, retention, and graduation of Students of Color; and (d) a mission that reinforces the institution's commitment to diversity and pluralism (e.g., Guinier, Fine, & Balin, 1997; Hurtado, 1992, 1994).

We distinguish between diversity of convenience, the form most often endorsed by universities, and genuine diversity or pluralism, which seems increasingly difficult to realize in an era of "color-blind," "race-neutral" politics. Evidenced in reactionary and superficial policies to increase the size of underrepresented groups, diversity of convenience can actually contribute to a hostile campus racial climate. Beyond portraying a racially diverse group of students in recruitment brochures, historically White universities do not necessarily commit to providing equal access and opportunities for Students of Color, let alone promise an inviting, positive campus racial climate. Genuine racial diversity or pluralism refers to underrepresented racial and ethnic groups being physically present *and* treated as equals on the college campus. All administrators, faculty, and students affirm one another's dignity by demonstrating readiness to benefit from each other's experience and willingness to acknowledge one another's contributions to the common welfare of the college. Evidence of genuine diversity would include programs to compensate communities the university has historically underserved and initiatives to remedy social inequalities the institution has perpetuated.[3] Such efforts may disrupt the institutional status quo and destabilize the university's historical racial power base.

Instead, colleges tend to endorse diversity to the extent that it serves White students. Derrick Bell (1980, 1987, 2004) has identified this practice of allowing People of Color to benefit from society's institutions only at the convenience of White society as "interest convergence" (see also Dudziak, 1988, 2000). Bell's critique helps explain the contradiction when universities celebrate diversity with ethnic food and *fiestas* while failing to provide equal access and opportunity to Students of Color. If, as research suggests, enrolling Students of Color helps White students become more racially tolerant, livens up class dialogue through more diverse points of view, and prepares

White students to gain employment in a multicultural, global economy, then what is the role of Students of Color?

Seemingly, in return for admission, universities expect Students of Color to be a source of educational enrichment for Whites. This pattern of prioritizing the needs of White students occurs "often with a complete lack of self-consciousness" because "White supremacy creates in Whites the expectation that issues of concern to them will be central in every discourse" (Grillo & Wildman, 1995, pp. 566–567). CRT guides our purposive shift of this discussion, and allows us to see that culture centers often take on the responsibility of preparing racially marginalized students to become the next generation of service providers, leaders, and role models for Communities of Color. In fact, many college culture centers come to fruition as a result of student protest and community demands for equal treatment in social institutions. The next section briefly demonstrates the ways campus culture centers utilize the margin as a space to foster students' survival and resistance strategies. This occurs with the knowledge that Students of Color navigate a negative campus racial climate very differently than White students.

Stages of Passage for Students of Color on Historically White Campuses

> Rather than demand that students of color attending mainstream institutions of higher education undergo initiation rites that inevitably lead to their cultural suicide, a more protean cultural model of academic life should prevail. Such a model should contend that students of color on predominately White campuses be able to affirm, rather than reject, who they are. (Tierney, 1999, p. 89)

In his critique of Vincent Tinto's (1993) stages of passage model, William Tierney calls for a more complex understanding of how African American students maintain their "cultural integrity" on historically White university campuses. Tinto's model contends that undergraduate students engage in three stages of passage early on in college: separation, transition, and incorporation. During the separation stage, students disassociate from their pre-college community (i.e., family, friends). The transition stage takes place during and after separation, when students let go of their old norms and behaviors and acquire new college norms and behaviors. Finally, according to Tinto, incorporation refers to students' integration process into various college communities. Tierney (1999) believes these stages "assume low-income, urban students of color must drop or reconfigure their cultures and identities of origin if they are to succeed in college" (p. 88). We share this concern and ask: If this model centers on the experiences of White middle-class students, how can it account for the experiences of Students of Color? If this model is insufficient, then what are the stages of passage for under-graduate Students of Color?

To address these questions, we listened to the reflections of some Chicana/o and Latina/o students who attended a public comprehensive liberal arts urban college in California and participated in the campuses' five culture centers. We first share a brief history of the origins of the culture centers at Inland State[3] to contextualize the significance of their role as counterspaces.

Reclaiming Diversity at Inland State

At its founding in the late 1930s, Inland State served an all-White male student population.[4] The university began enrolling White women in the early 1960s, and Students of Color later in the decade. Statewide demographic shifts, community activism, and legal mandates forced institutions of higher education to begin to take "affirmative" steps toward racial and gender diversity. Eventually, Inland State's mission statement articulated a commitment to respecting differences and diversity, and a goal of preparing students to be leaders in a changing multicultural world.

In the mid-1990s, a series of state initiatives aiming to restrict social services, educational access, and opportunity for Communities of Color, youth, and immigrants made their way to the ballot box (e.g., California's proposi-tions 187, 209, 227). As voters expressed increasing conservative and reaction-ary views against racial diversity, students demanded that their universities demonstrate progressive and critically reflective actions to affirm diversity. For example, student protestors in Central and Southern California demanded the departmentalization of Chicana/o studies and the establish-ment of diversity (ethnic and women's studies) course requirements.

At Inland State, a group of multiracial students walked out of their classes, marched across campus, and took over the president's office. With the support of community members and key faculty and staff, these students demanded that the university acknowledge racial/ethnic diversity through the creation of spaces that students could call their own. Students expressed frustration with what they called the hypocrisy of the university, which celebrated diversity in its mission statement while marginalizing and rendering invisible racially/ethnically diverse students.

As a result of this well-planned protest and deliberate process of articulating students' demands, Inland State established three centers in a historical building in the middle of campus focused on Chicana/o and Latina/o, Asian American and Pacific Islander, and African American/Black communities. Students' continued insistence that the university recognize and honor their voices and experiences soon led to the creation of two more centers representing Lesbian, Gay, Bisexual, Transgender, and Native American communities.

Now, more than a decade later, the five culture centers function as social, epistemological, and physical counterspaces fostering social justice efforts in and around the university. The institutionalized and interpersonal forms of racism that intersect with multiple layers of subordination still persist, albeit more subtly. However, when students confront this multidimensional racism in the classroom and campus community, the culture centers provide a counterspace to facilitate their survival and resistance.

Though the student protestors demanded that the institution demonstrate a genuine commitment to racial and gender diversity, the culture centers now bear primary responsibility for nurturing a positive, pluralist campus climate in terms of race and gender. Because People of Color remain underrepresented in the ranks of faculty and administration, the culture centers also serve the unanticipated function of providing a counterspace for Faculty of Color, who are otherwise isolated in predominately White departments. Faculty of Color may bring their lunch to eat in the culture centers, and some integrate their course curricula with the center's programming. In the absence of racial diversity in the leadership of the university, the responsibility for each center's coordinator and the director of the five centers to serve as role models increases. For example, while the university has become a designated "Hispanic Serving Institution," this demographic signifier has not necessarily resulted in structural or policy changes to better serve Chicana/o, Latina/o students. There remains a sociopolitical urgency for the culture centers (and the Students and Staff of Color within these spaces) to do the daily diversity work for the institution.

The following student reflections shed light on how Students of Color utilize the culture centers at Inland State as a navigational resource. Their remarks indicate that the stages of passage for Students of Color on historically White college campuses transform the margins into a place of resistance and possibility.

Culture Shock

> Black folks coming from poor, underclass communities, who enter universities of privileged cultural settings unwilling to surrender every vestige of who we were before we were there . . . must create spaces within that culture of domination if we are to survive whole, our souls intact. Our very presence is a disruption. (hooks, 1990, p. 148)

As hooks observes, Students of Color at historically White universities disrupt the "natural" state of campus life. The incessant racial microaggressions these undergraduates confront upon their arrival communicates their presence is suspect and that they should expect to be treated like intruders. So, while Tinto's (1993) model presumes that students are readily welcomed and equitably rewarded for assimilating into mainstream college life, the reality for most Students of Color does not support this assumption. The separation stage suggests successful undergraduates break from their home community physically, emotionally, and socially to initiate their transition into the university. Severing these ties would exacerbate the marginalization students confront. Indeed, to survive and resist the racism they encounter, they create and participate in counterspaces that exhibit the cultural resources of their families[5] and home communities (e.g., Carter, 2003; Delgado-Gaitan, 2001; González et al., 1995; González & Moll, 2002; Yosso, 2005).[5] For example, Jose, a Latino undergraduate student at Inland State, took a staff job at the Chicana/o and Latina/o culture center in part because

> It was really a home away from home . . . that I could come to when I was struggling with class, when I was unsure about my major and my career plans and much more. It was a place to learn and expand my knowledge of my culture and other cultures as well. . . . Coming from Eastside High School, where almost the entire school was Latino, this center helped me deal with the culture shock I experienced at the university.

In addition to engaging in a multicultural experience outside the classroom, Jose received academic and career advice. In this home away from home, he realized he would not have to struggle alone. The centers give students space to vent, commiserate, and encourage each other about how to manage the messages of rejection they experience. These social and academic counter-spaces validate the very cultural knowledges and histories of People of Color, which are regularly dismissed or marginalized in other university spaces (Solórzano et al., 2000; Whitmire, 2004).

Francisco, a Queer Chicano student who volunteered with the culture centers and held a leadership position in university governance, explains, "For me, the centers became a home in a new environment that allowed me to exist, feel accepted at, and connected. . . . The culture centers offered validation that is so important for minority and first-generation students in college." His remarks confirm the significance of the culture centers in nurturing academic confidence for Students of Color and affirming the value of their existence on campus. Motivated to support marginalized students as they negotiate the rejection that they experience at a historically White university, Francisco recently completed his master's degree in student affairs.

Community Building

> For me this space of radical openness is a margin—a profound edge. Locating oneself there is difficult yet necessary. It is not a "safe" place. One is always at risk. One needs a community of resistance. (hooks, 1990, p. 149)

Building a "community of resistance" on the margin may require courage, vigilance, and diligence. Students of Color seek out safe campus spaces and communities where they can process and respond to the rejection that they experience attending a historically White college. This is very different from Tinto's transition stage, during which students acquire new socio-academic skills and values and join new networks in their new college environment through a process of leaving behind their previous attitudes and behaviors. The counterspaces Students of Color build represent the cultural wealth of their home communities (see Yosso, 2005).

At Inland State, the culture centers help students construct spaces of resistance on the margin by building on the array of cultural knowledge, networks, skills, and abilities cultivated in Communities of Color. A Latina alumna, Rita, described the significance of this community-building process for historically underrepresented first-generation students:

Having been the first one in my family and extended family to attend and graduate from college, the center soon was the family I had on campus. I cannot recall having a professor or teacher throughout my years [in school], looking like me or coming from a similar background. The coordinator of the center provided me with a role model, someone who I could aspire to be like.

Rita worked as a student staff member and volunteer at the culture centers and later served as a student representative in university governance. Inspired by her Chicana role model and the leadership experience she gained through the center, Rita went on to complete a master's degree in student affairs. Similar to Francisco, Rita demonstrates a commitment to giving back to her community, on and off campus, as a role model for marginalized students making their way through college.

Critical Navigation Between Multiple Worlds

We come to this space through suffering and pain, through struggle. . . . We are transformed, individually, collectively, as we make radical creative space which affirms and sustains our subjectivity, which gives us a new location from which to articulate our sense of the world. (hooks, 1990, p. 153)

In the process of building and participating in "radical creative spaces" on historically White campuses, Students of Color critically navigate multiple worlds. This process of building communities reflective of the cultural knowledge acquired from their families woven together with insights and skills garnered from the university transforms students "individually, collectively" (hooks, 1990, p. 153). As a result, students engaging in this process gain a socially conscious worldview and "critical resistant navigational skills" (Solórzano & Villalpando, 1998) unaccounted for by Tinto's incorporation stage. Indeed, at this point in Tinto's stages of passage model, when students become integrated parts of the college, the university represents the center of a student's world. This is not necessarily the case for Students of Color, who have been fostering communities that bridge their worlds of home and school.

Students of Color carry the community cultural wealth and aspirations of their families with them to the university. They incorporate the cultural

values of their families and communities into the university, while also utilizing college resources to fulfill their family and community needs. Culture
centers support students' critical navigation between these worlds. For example, students and staff preserve the historical memory of the fight to create
the culture centers by sharing the struggle with each new generation of
undergraduates. This process of recovering and recounting collective history
reminds students of their responsibility to honor those who came before
them and to carry on their legacy.

Staff and faculty allies work alongside students to increase educational
access and equity within and beyond campus. Indeed, culture centers help
students realize how their struggle to graduate is connected to a larger struggle for social justice beyond the academy. At the same time, the staff and
faculty affiliated with culture centers support Students of Color in their
efforts to graduate, often in spite of institutional neglect.

When Students of Color and campus culture centers engage in services
promoting outreach, recruitment, and retention for their historically White
universities, they are often confronted by accusations of self-segregation.
Octavio Villalpando (2003) argued that such claims misrepresent the very
real and necessary acts of self-preservation for People of Color in higher education. Indeed, CRT provides a useful framework for exposing the hypocrisy
of blaming the victims of discrimination for taking action to survive a hostile
campus climate. Eva, a Latina preparing to graduate from Inland State,
explains her own process of moving beyond the shock of rejection to engage
in community building to develop skills of critical navigation between multiple worlds:

> When I first arrived, I thought the cultural centers were a form of separa-
> tion. I thought that they separated the campus by ethnicities. . . . Now I
> see cultural centers as a celebration of different cultures and as a way of
> slowing assimilation, which takes our identity away from us. . . . For me
> they helped bring back the culture I had completely lost in the K–12 sys-
> tem. . . . It's also a place that welcomes those who do have that culture
> shock. . . . I see it as a place that creates opportunities for other students
> to learn about what they may be defensive against, afraid of, or just curious
> about. . . . The cultural centers have turned my little ignorant world upside
> down. . . . I would not be who I am today without the cultural centers.

Eva's involvement with her campus culture centers allowed her to experience the value of counterspaces for surviving a system of culturally "subtractive schooling" (Valenzuela, 1999).

Discussion

> Resistance can take the form of momentous acts of organized, planned, and disciplined protests, or it may consist of small, everyday actions of seeming insignificance that can nevertheless validate the actor's sense of dignity and worth. (Caldwell, 1995, p. 276)

In this chapter, we argued that theory and policy in higher education tend to uncritically center on the experiences and voices of White male students. Historically White colleges may endorse policies and practices of diversity while at the same time enabling White interests to "take back the pivotal focus" (Grillo & Wildman, 1995, p. 567). In these contexts Students of Color often endure a negative and even hostile campus climate. Utilizing a CRT framework, we documented how some Students of Color survive and resist in these settings by creating and participating in counterspaces. As a case in point, we described how five culture centers founded as a result of "momentous acts of organized, planned, and disciplined protests" at Inland State engage in "everyday actions" that "validate [students'] sense of dignity and worth" (Caldwell, 1995, p. 276).

Centering our analysis on the lived experiences of Students of Color, we also critiqued the assumptions underlying Tinto's stages of passage model, namely that students successfully transition into college life by separating from their home communities. In listening to the reflections of Inland State students and alumni, we found at least three stages of passage unaccounted for in Tinto's (1993) model. We further examined how the five campus culture centers facilitate students' passage through these stages of rejection, community building, and critical navigation between multiple worlds (see also Yosso, 2006; Yosso et al., 2009). We argued that culture centers on historically White university campuses such as Inland State embody the tenets of a CRT framework:

   1. Centrality of race/racism with other forms of subordination: Culture
      centers place the experiences and histories of Students of Color at

the forefront of their missions, vision statements, and programming. Through university-wide retreats and multiracial events, these counterspaces emphasize the intersectionality of students' racial identity to engage in discussion about marginality based on gender, class, immigration status, sexuality, and language.

2. Challenge to dominant ideology: Culture center programming affirms a revisionist history of People of Color and focuses on academic advancement (as opposed to remediation) in outreach and retention efforts. This deliberate work to move beyond food and fiestas also challenges color-blind diversity approaches, wherein some students' scholarly merits, physical presence, cultural values, immigration status, and primary language are unfairly questioned, while other students enjoy a false sense of entitlement.

3. Commitment to social justice: Culture centers often take the lead in campus diversity struggles (e.g., defending affirmative action in all its forms, challenging on-campus hate crimes). Such actions may not endear the centers to university administrators but do reaffirm the need for their physical and epistemological presence on historically White conservative campuses. Culture center resources (e.g., guidance, information) also prepare Students of Color to be advocates of pluralism in graduate school and beyond.[6]

4. Centrality of experiential knowledge: The daily functioning of culture centers revolves around the cultural skills, networks, abilities, and knowledge that students, faculty, and staff utilize to survive and resist racism and other forms of subordination. Building on this community cultural wealth (Yosso, 2005) and their own cultural intuition (Delgado Bernal, 1998), peer counselors, professional counselors, and staff co-construct programming, services, and day-to-day culture center activities that exemplify and exhibit their experiential knowledge.

5. Transdisciplinary perspective and historicity: To foster student achievement, culture centers draw on various disciplines, from the humanities and social sciences to math, science, and engineering. This often occurs reciprocally through direct collaborations with ethnic and women's studies departments or individual faculty members interested in center-supported programs and materials that expand on class themes. These structured opportunities to apply theoretical

knowledge outside the classroom and to engage in projects where students see themselves as participants in history link the academy with the community.

Rooted in a mission of social justice and an action agenda to promote critical navigational skills for their multiracial communities, campus culture centers nurture resilience and resistance and ultimately promote retention and academic achievement well beyond graduation. As a framework, CRT challenges us to recognize and honor the work of creating and maintaining physical, epistemological, social, and academic counterspaces for racially marginalized students. Culture centers dedicate themselves to this work, which, for the most part, historically White institutions fail to do. It is our hope that in documenting the significance of these counterspaces, we contribute to ongoing struggles of survival and resistance in the margins of higher education.

Notes

1. Sofia is the pseudonym of a Latina student whose anonymous remarks are electronically archived in a series of interviews collected in a cross-campus initiative at the University of Illinois at Urbana-Champaign (n.d.-2) called Ethnography of the University. Undergraduate students conduct and analyze many of the interviews in this ongoing research, which began in 2002–3, with a focus on six areas, including race and the university. The description of the initiative explains:

> Whether spoken of in the context of "diversity" or "multiculturalism," race is at the heart of the American university—its history, its contemporary challenges, and its futures. This project examines ways in which the U.S. university and the American college experience are indelibly racialized. In particular, this project examines longstanding U.S. debates and decisions on affirmative action. (University of Illinois at Urbana-Champaign, n.d.-1, p. 4)

2. Portions of this chapter draw on previously published research about campus racial climate and racial microaggressions for African American and Latina/o undergraduates (see Solórzano, Ceja, & Yosso, 2000 and Yosso, Smith, Ceja, & Solórzano, 2009).

3. The work of universities then would bring about the improvement of social services (e.g., medical, judicial, educational) for communities of color. Universities would also be engaged in developing a strong pool of leaders and role models within Communities of Color (see Yosso, Parker, Solórzano, & Lynn, 2004).

4. We used an open-ended e-mail prompt to ask a sample of students and alumni who participated over a five-year period in Inland State's culture centers to reflect on their experiences. We focus here on the answers given by Chicana/o and Latina/o respondents, and use their chosen self-identifying terms (e.g., Queer Chicano). We use the fictitious name Inland State and pseudonyms to maintain confidentiality and protect the anonymity of those who shared their reflections.

5. We use the term "families" in a broad sense of kinship, acknowledging that more traditional connotations carry race, class, and heterosexual assumptions. Family may include immediate family, friends, extended kin (aunts, uncles, grandparents), and chosen family, both living and long passed on.

6. In the process of participating in these counterspaces, Students of Color develop leadership skills and a renewed commitment to social justice. They find the support and resources necessary to realize their goal of giving back to their communities with their degrees. At Inland State, for example, the culture center coordinators and director serve as role models and equip students with the tools and insights they need to become role models in their communities.

References

Allen, W., & Solórzano, D. G. (2001). Affirmative action, educational equity, and campus racial climate: A case study of the University of Michigan Law School. *Berkeley La Raza Law Journal, 12*(2), 237–363.

Anzaldúa, G. E. (1990). Haciendo caras: Una entrada. In G. E. Anzaldúa (Ed.), *Making face, making soul/haciendo caras: Creative and critical perspectives by feminists of color* (pp. xv–xxviii). San Francisco: Aunt Lute Books.

Bakke v. Regents of the University of California, 438 U.S. 265 (1978).

Bell, D. A. (1980). *Brown v. Board of Education* and the interest-convergence dilemma. *Harvard Law Review, 93*(3), 518–533.

Bell, D. A. (1987). *And we are not saved: The elusive quest for racial justice.* New York: Basic Books.

Bell, D. A. (1992). *Faces at the bottom of the well: The permanence of racism.* New York: Basic Books.

Bell, D. A. (2004). *Silent covenants:* Brown v. Board of Education *and the unfulfilled hopes for racial reform.* New York: Oxford University Press.

Caldwell, P. M. (1995). A hair piece: Perspectives on the intersection of race and gender. In R. Delgado (Ed.), *Critical race theory: The cutting edge* (pp. 267–277). Philadelphia: Temple University Press.

Calmore, J. O. (1992). Critical race theory, Archie Shepp, and the fire music: Securing an authentic intellectual life in a multicultural world. *Southern California Law Review, 65*, 2129–2231.

Calmore, J. O. (1997). Exploring Michael Omi's "messy" real world of race: An essay for "naked people longing to swim free." *Law and Inequality, 15*(1), 25–82.

Carroll, G. (1998). *Environmental stress and African Americans: The other side of the moon.* Westport, CT: Praeger.

Carter, P. (2003). "Black" cultural capital, status positioning, and schooling conflicts for low-income African American youth. *Social Problems, 50*(1), 136–155.

Constantine, M. G. (2007). Racial microaggressions against African American clients in cross-racial counseling relationships. *Journal of Counseling Psychology, 54*(1), 1–16.

Constantine, M. G., & Sue, D. W. (2007). Perceptions of racial microaggressions among Black supervisees in cross-racial dyads. *Journal of Counseling Psychology, 54*(2), 142–153.

Crenshaw, K. (1989). Demarginalizing the intersection of race and sex: A Black feminist critique of antidiscrimination doctrine, feminist theory, and anti-racist politics. *University of Chicago Legal Forum, 1989,* 139–167.

Crenshaw, K. (1991). Mapping the margins: Intersectionality, identity politics, and the violence against Women of Color. *Stanford Law Review, 43*(6), 1241–1299.

Davis, P. (1989). Law as microaggression. *Yale Law Journal, 98*(8), 1559–1577.

Delgado, R. (1984). The imperial scholar: Reflections on a review of civil rights literature. *University of Pennsylvania Law Review, 132,* 561–578.

Delgado, R. (1992). The imperial scholar revisited: How to marginalize outsider writing, ten years later. *University of Pennsylvania Law Review, 140,* 1349–1372.

Delgado Bernal, D. (1998). Using Chicana feminist epistemology in educational research. *Harvard Educational Review, 68*(4), 555–582.

Delgado Bernal, D. (2002). Critical race theory, LatCrit theory, and critical raced-gendered epistemologies: Recognizing Students of Color as holders and creators of knowledge. *Qualitative Inquiry, 8*(1), 105–126.

Delgado Bernal, D., & Villalpando, O. (2002). An apartheid of knowledge in academia: The struggle over the "legitimate" knowledge of Faculty of Color. *Equity and Excellence in Education, 35*(2), 169–180.

Delgado-Gaitan, C. (2001). *The power of community: Mobilizing for family and schooling.* Lanham, MD: Rowman and Littlefield.

Dixson, A. D., & Rousseau, C. K. (Eds.). (2005). Special issue on critical race theory in education. *Race Ethnicity and Education, 8*(1), 1–127.

DuBois, W. E. B. (1989). *The souls of Black folks.* New York: Bantam. (Originally published 1903)

Dudziak, M. L. (1988). Desegregation as a cold war imperative. *Stanford Law Review, 41*(1), 61–120.

Dudziak, M. L. (2000). *Cold war civil rights: Race and the image of American democracy.* Princeton, NJ: Princeton University Press.

Freire, P. (1970). *Education for critical consciousness*. New York: Continuum.

Freire, P. (1973). *Pedagogy of the oppressed*. New York: Seabury Press.

Gonzalez, K. (2002). Campus culture and the experiences of Chicano students in a predominantly White university. *Urban Education, 37*, 193–218.

Gonzalez, N., & Moll, L. C. (2002). Cruzando El Puente: Building bridges to funds of knowledge. *Educational Policy, 16*(4), 623–641.

Gonzalez, N., Moll, L. C., Tenery, M. F., Rivera, A., Rendon, P., Gonzales, R., & Amanti, C. (1995). Funds of knowledge for teaching in Latino households. *Urban Education, 29*(4), 443–470.

Grillo, T., & Wildman, S. (1995). Obscuring the importance of race: The implications of making comparisons between racism and sexism (or other -isms). In R. Delgado (Ed.), *Critical race theory: The cutting edge* (pp. 564–572). Philadelphia: Temple University Press.

Guinier, L., Fine, M., & Balin, J. (1997). *Becoming gentlemen: Women, law school, and institutional change*. Boston: Beacon Press.

Gutiérrez-Jones, C. (2001). *Critical race narratives: A study of race, rhetoric, and injury*. New York: New York University Press.

Harris, C. I. (1993). Whiteness as property. *Harvard Law Review, 106*, 1707–1791.

hooks, b. (1990). *Yearnings: Race, gender, and cultural politics*. Boston: South End Press.

Hurtado, S. (1992). The campus racial climate: Contexts of conflict. *Journal of Higher Education, 63*(5), 539–569.

Hurtado, S. (1994). The institutional climate for talented Latino students. *Research in Higher Education, 35*(1), 21–41.

Hurtado, S., Milem, J., Clayton-Pedersen, A., & Allen, W. (1998). Enhancing campus climates for racial/ethnic diversity: Educational policy and practice. *Review of Higher Education, 21*(3), 279–302.

Ladson-Billings, G., & Tate, W. (1995). Toward a critical race theory of education. *Teachers College Record, 97*, 47–68.

Lopez, G., & Parker, L. (Eds.). (2003). *Interrogating racism in qualitative research methodology*. New York: Peter Lang.

Lynn, M., & Adams, M. (Eds.). (2002). Critical race theory in education: Recent developments in the field [Special issue]. *Equity and Excellence in Education, 35*(2).

Lynn, M., Yosso, T. J., Solórzano, D. G., & Parker, L. (Eds.). (2002). Critical race and qualitative research [Special issue]. *Qualitative Inquiry, 8*(1).

Olivas, M. (1990). The chronicles, my grandfather's stories, and immigration law: The slave traders chronicle as racial history. *Saint Louis University Law Journal, 34*, 425–441.

Parker, L., Deyhle, D., Villenas, S., & Crossland, K. (Eds.). (1998). Critical race theory and education [Special issue]. *International Journal of Qualitative Studies in Education, 11*(1).

Pierce, C. M. (1970). Offensive mechanisms. In F. B. Barbour (Ed.), *The Black seventies* (pp. 265–282). Boston: Porter Sargent.

Pierce, C. M. (1974). Psychiatric problems of the Black minority. In S. Arieti (Ed.), *American handbook of psychiatry* (pp. 512–523). New York: Basic Books.

Pierce, C. M. (1995). Stress analogs of racism and sexism: Terrorism, torture, and disaster. In C. V. Willie, P. P. Rieker, B. M. Kramer, & B. S. Brown (Eds.), *Mental health, racism, and sexism* (pp. 277–293). Pittsburgh: University of Pittsburgh Press.

Russell, J. (1993). On being a gorilla in your midst, or, the life of one Black woman in the legal academy. *Harvard Civil Rights–Civil Liberties Law Review, 28,* 259–262.

Smith, W. A. (2004). Black faculty coping with racial battle fatigue: The campus racial climate in a post-civil rights era. In D. Cleveland (Ed.), *A long way to go: Conversations about race by African American faculty and graduate students at predominantly White institutions* (pp. 171–190). New York: Peter Lang.

Smith, W. A. (2009). Campuswide climate: Implications for African American students. In L. C. Tillman (Ed.), *The SAGE handbook of African American education* (pp. 297–309). Thousand Oaks, CA: Sage.

Smith, W. A., Altbach, P. G., & Lomotey, K. (Eds.). (2002). *The racial crisis in American higher education: Continuing challenges for the twenty-first century* (Rev. ed.). Albany: State University of New York Press.

Smith, W. A., Yosso, T. J., & Solórzano, D. G. (2006). Challenging racial battle fatigue on historically White campuses: A critical race examination of race-related stress. In C. A. Stanley (Ed.), *Faculty of color: Teaching in predominantly White colleges and universities* (pp. 299–327). Bolton: Anker Publishing.

Smith, W. A., Yosso, T. J., & Solórzano, D. G. (2007). Racial primes and Black misandry on historically White campuses: Toward critical race accountability in educational administration. *Education Administration Quarterly, 43*(5), 559–585.

Solórzano, D. G. (1997). Images and words that wound: Critical race theory, racial stereotyping, and teacher education. *Teacher Education Quarterly, 24,* 5–19.

Solórzano, D. G. (1998). Critical race theory, racial and gender microaggressions, and the experiences of Chicana and Chicano scholars. *International Journal of Qualitative Studies in Education, 11,* 121–136.

Solórzano, D. G., Allen, W., & Carroll, G. (2002, Spring). A case study of racial microaggressions and campus racial climate at the University of California, Berkeley. *UCLA Chicano/Latino Law Review, 23,* 15–111.

Solórzano, D. G., Ceja, M., & Yosso, T. J. (2000). Critical race theory, racial microaggressions, and campus racial climate: The experiences of African American college students. *Journal of Negro Education, 69*(1–2), 60–73.

Solórzano, D. G., & Delgado Bernal, D. (2001). Critical race theory, transformational resistance, and social justice: Chicana and Chicano students in an urban context. *Urban Education, 36,* 308–342.

Solórzano, D. G., & Villalpando, O. (1998). Critical race theory, marginality, and the experience of minority students in higher education. In C. Torres & T. Mitchell (Eds.), *Sociology of education: Emerging perspectives* (pp. 211–224). Albany: State University of New York Press.

Sue, D. W., Capodilupo, C. M., Torino, G. C., Bucceri, J. M., Holder, A. M. B., Nadal, K. L., & Esquilin, M. (2007). Racial microaggressions in everyday life: Implications for clinical practice. *American Psychologist, 62*(4), 271–286.

Tierney, W. G. (1999). Models of minority college-going and retention: Cultural integrity versus cultural suicide. *Journal of Negro Education, 68*(1), 80–91.

Tinto, V. (1993). *Leaving college: Rethinking the causes and cures for student attrition* (2nd ed.). Chicago: University of Chicago Press.

University of Illinois at Urbana-Champaign. (n.d.-1). *Ethnography of the university.* Retrieved from http://www.eotu.uiuc.edu/what/whitepaper.pdf

University of Illinois at Urbana-Champaign. (n.d.-2). *Examining diversity at the University of Illinois.* Retrieved from http://www.eotu.uiuc.edu/live/examining/examiningdiversity/examiningdiversity.htm

Valdes, F. (1998). Under construction: LatCrit consciousness, community and theory. *La Raza Law Journal, 10*(1), 1–56.

Valenzuela, A. (1999). *Subtractive schoolings: U.S.-Mexican youth and the politics of caring.* Albany: State University of New York Press.

Villalpando, O. (2003). Self-segregation of self-preservation? A critical race theory and Latina/o critical theory analysis of findings from a longitudinal study of Chicana/o college students. *International Journal of Qualitative Studies in Education, 16*(5), 619–646.

Whitmire, E. (2004). The campus racial climate and undergraduates' perceptions of the academic library. *Libraries and the Academy, 4*(3), 363–378.

Yosso, T. J. (2005). Whose culture has capital? A critical race theory discussion of community cultural wealth. *Race, Ethnicity, and Education, 8*(1), 71–93.

Yosso, T. J. (2006). *Critical race counterstories along the Chicana/Chicano educational pipeline.* New York: Routledge.

Yosso, T. J., Parker, L., Solórzano, D. G., & Lynn, M. (2004). From Jim Crow to affirmative action and back again: A critical race discussion of racialized rationales and access to higher education. *Review of Research in Education, 28,* 1–25.

Yosso, T. J., Smith, W. A., Ceja, M., & Solórzano, D. G. (2009). Critical race theory, racial microaggressions, and campus racial climate for Latina/o undergraduates. *Harvard Educational Review, 79*(4), 659–690.

6

CRITICAL BORDERS

Student Development Theoretical
Perspectives Applied to Culture Centers

Mary F. Howard-Hamilton, Kandace G. Hinton,
and Robin L. Hughes

Middle Urban University (MUU) is a large public institution located in Circle City, which has a population of 500,000 residents, of whom 35% are African American, 40% are White, 7% are Asian American, and 3% identify themselves as "other." The Latina/o population, estimated to hover around 15%, has tripled each year since 2000. In contrast, the university enrolls 35,000 students, and students of African descent make up only 5% of the total population. The breakdown of faculty, staff, and students by race and faculty rank is shown in Table 6.1.

A recent survey conducted by a national educational policy analyst found recruitment and retention of students and employees of color at all levels to be inadequate. In addition, there has been a mass exodus of graduating seniors of color to attend graduate schools in surrounding states. A recent survey showed that students leave the city and state to attend more diverse institutions. According to the survey, one of the students' major complaints is that there are few faculty, administrators, and students of color with whom to interact. One student stated, "We are uncertain about whether they have our best interests at heart—the university, I mean."

TABLE 6.1

Students, Faculty, and Staff by Race/Ethnicity at Middle Urban University

	White	African American	Latina/o	Native American	Asian American	Other
Students	81%	7%	3%	1%	3%	5%
Non-tenured faculty	90%	1%	3%	<1%	3%	3%
Tenured faculty	90%	3%	2%	<1%	2%	3%
Upper-level administrators	98%	1%	<1%	<1%	<1%	<1%
Administrative staff	92%	3%	3%	<1%	<1%	<1%
Custodial and hourly staff (full time)	10%	65%	20%	<1%	<1%	3%

Middle Urban Leadership: About Culture Centers

MUU's provost, Dr. Able (a 62-year-old White male who has been employed at the institution since 1970), has continually stated to the academic community that there is no need for a culture center on campus. The MUU campus newspaper published an article quoting the provost as saying:

> We live and thrive in a nation, state, and city that are equitable. I have never experienced any racism on this campus or in this city. It simply does not exist. This so-called center would only promote the balkanization of students, faculty, and scholarly life, as it probably has on campuses all across the country. Any president or administrative staff member who supports such a center [at another institution] will never be hired on this campus. Quite simply, I will never support such a facility.

Under Dr. Able's leadership, the institution does not support affirmative action in hiring and believes that culture centers produce "reverse" racism. The sentiments of the vice president of student affairs are similar to those articulated by the provost. She vociferously asserted that:

> There are just no data that support the contention that a Black cultural center is needed on campus and can increase retention. If data exist, then let me see it, and even if it does exist, what will keep other students from asking for a White culture center? I have to be fair and not engage in reverse discrimination! We have overcome issues of race. Simply put, race does not matter here at Middle Urban.

Current: A Series of Fortunate Events

In 2007, MUU Black, Latina/o, Native American, and Asian American students presented evidence that several ethnic/racial minority organizations were being denied services by offices throughout the campus. Specifically, rooms for meetings and parties were no longer available, food service and security costs escalated, and the student government challenged their membership processes, claiming that they were not inclusive. The student coalition held a rally and march on campus, which culminated in a press conference, at which a student leader stated:

> We want to be leaders to promote social justice and equity. How can these things occur when our own provost is so blind to injustices—so supportive of

institutional injustices, [and] structural and systemic racism? We demand a
cultural center because we pay tuition, we want to be connected to this univer-
sity, we want to begin our own traditions, we want a place to call home, and
when we graduate we want to be proud to call MUU our alma mater!

Assessing the Environment

The Middle Urban University case involves a series of issues that commonly occur on college campuses across the country. The vast majority of American institutions are not immune to retention and attrition problems among students of color and insensitive administrators and faculty who overtly use their White privilege to subjugate others, as well as the dismissal and denial of the need for a safe space for ethnic/racial minority groups to call home on a college campus. Title VI of the Civil Rights Act of 1964 provided the motivation for postsecondary institutions to open their doors to underrepresented groups (Kaplin & Lee, 1997). The law declares that no person should be denied participation in or benefits of any program or activity receiving federal assistance on the basis of his or her color or national origin. Specifically, discriminatory acts are illegal and institutions should actively seek to "increase rather than limit the opportunities available to minority students and faculty" (Kaplin & Lee, 1997, p. 559). There are several theoretical lenses that can be used to help students, faculty, and administrators better understand the difficult discussion of diversity. After the theories are carefully dissected for appropriate interpretation, they can provide a framework for practice. Furthermore, these theories can inform institutional leaders of the importance and need for culture centers on campus. When students are asked what attracts them to a particular campus environment, they say that it is the appearance and physical setting of the institution (Gaines, 1991; Strange & Banning, 2001). "Education is an endeavor that is most sensitive to ambiance; students respond all their lives to memories of the place that nourished their intellectual growth" (Gaines, 1991, p. 11). So how does Middle Urban University want to be remembered? As a place that denied students' passionate requests? Or as a place whose appearance did not reflect or respect the students' racial/ethnic identities?

The phrase "identity politics" (Rhoads, 1998, p. 623) has been used to negatively describe student unrest that is connected to discrimination based on race, gender, or sexual orientation. However, we argue that there should be a counter-interpretation of the term. "Identity politics" can describe the participatory democratic process in which students of color "seek to build a truly multicultural society through the colleges and universities they inhabit" (Rhoads, 1998, p. 623). The case of Middle Urban University is a clear example of identity politics (one that involves the participation of various groups of color), with African American students protesting along with other students of color. They made their voices heard by creating organizational disruption in order to forcibly heighten the administrators' and the community's awareness of the problems on campus and ultimately engaged in institutional reform (Rhoads, 1998). The administrators of MUU spoke of the possibility of reverse racism and the balkanization of students should a culture center be established on campus. Rhoads (1998) referred to this as "tribal isolationism" (p. 644). The administrators in this case claimed that students of color, the tribes, would isolate themselves based upon separatist philosophies. How can the students' actions be perceived as passionate pleas for institutional improvement? Are the administrators viewing the protest from a privileged and ethnocentric frame of reference? Understanding the various developmental shifts among faculty, administrators, and students requires knowledge of racial identity and environmental theories in order to appreciate how cultural groups adapt to and coexist with the dominant group.

Environmental Theories

Kurt Lewin crafted the equation $B = f(P \times E)$, which means behavior is a function of a person's interactions with the existing environment. Application of Lewin's interactionist paradigm to the case of Middle Urban University and the student coalition's fight for a culture center makes it clear that their behavior is a function of two things: personal anger at and frustration with the administration because they are not listening and interaction with an environment that is extremely negative, stressful, resistant, and inhibiting (Strange & Banning, 2001). Critical human geographers would emphasize the importance of recognizing universities and classrooms as crucial locales of "socially activist engagement" (Hay, 2001, p. 141). The students who are protesting should be given a platform to discuss their perceptions of the campus environment and why they find the culture to be toxic.

That platform should be the classroom, because there is no other safe space or place for them to engage in dialogue. Hay (2001) noted that faculty should engage in radical pedagogy, using the classroom "as a site of practical political engagement" (p. 141). If faculty raised their levels of consciousness and connected classroom interactions with social political issues, they would teach students how to engage in powerful conversations about oppression, domination, and inequities within the university environment as well as the broader communities. Hay (2001) proffered that

> Students and teachers move daily from university to home, to work, to clubs and councils, carrying with them skills and knowledge developed and refined in all of those milieu [*sic*]. We need to ensure therefore that we do not make our offices, tutorial rooms, and lecture halls places in which practices of injustice are played out and perpetuated. They must instead be models of intellectual and social emancipation. (p. 142)

It is through this act of giving voice to students by changing classroom strictures and structures that faculty can reform educational and institutional practices, thus changing the world (Hay, 2001).

Higher education sociologists (antonio & Muñiz, 2007; Gumport, 2007) believe that there has been a radical shift in the social and cultural geography of the university environment since the beginning of the century, a view that parallels the philosophy of critical human geographers. Antonio and Muñiz (2007) identified several challenges for higher education: (1) creating equitable access, (2) fostering learning and development for a diverse student body, (3) managing campus conflict brought about by diverse voices, (4) hiring and retaining faculty of color, and (5) "reconciling conflict surrounding the dominance in the general education curriculum of a white male, European, and European American canon over works by non-Western and racial minority scholars" (p. 267). The study of campus climate has prompted higher education sociologists to study self-segregation and the socialization process of racial/ethnic minority groups—specifically, how diversity and racial tension have brought about a need for different models of campus community and the important roles all students and faculty play in making the environment inclusive.

These challenges can be seen in the case of Middle Urban University. Self-segregation among students of color occurs because they need a space where they are visible rather than always being invisible on predominantly White campuses (Patton, 2006). They need a place that allows them to convene and have their voices heard in addition to celebrating their unique histories and backgrounds. Patton argues against the premise that culture centers are a bastion of self-segregation, reminding scholars that everyone can use the centers and that they serve as an educational and social resource.

Environmental design theorists (Moos, 1986; Oldenburg, 1989; Strange & Banning, 2001) have shared their beliefs regarding the importance of a place that students can call their own that is not part of the traditional public space. These students need a place they perceive as safe and open to personalization as well as ownership. Oldenburg (1989) calls these spaces a "third place." This area is not a residence hall, functional office area, or classroom building. Instead, "Much like a familiar hangout, a third place tends to bind people together in a defined space where typical roles and responsibilities are lifted temporarily while new relationships and connections are explored in a unique and comfortable culture" (Strange & Banning, 2001, p. 146). There is a need for faculty, administrators, and students to become comfortable with the discourse about diversity and be willing to physically be in the same domain as persons who are not part of the dominant culture. Several racial identity theories provide cognitive and psychosocial frameworks useful for dissecting the levels of disengagement to engagement among Whites, who may not be aware of the privileges that not only exist on college campuses but also are part of their own individual ideology.

Racial Identity Theories

The faculty, staff, and students at Middle Urban University should recognize the vast personal and institutional privileges that are overtly and covertly granted to them based upon their race and dominant status at the institution. When administrators verbally dismiss the importance of a culture center and others consciously or unconsciously support their decision, the dominant group's power and privilege are perpetuated throughout the campus climate (Hobgood, 2000; Katz, 2003; McIntosh, 1988). Dismantling Whiteness (Hobgood, 2000) can be exceptionally challenging; however, understanding the behaviors associated with White racial identity may help to challenge and support racist behaviors.

White Racial Identity

Hardiman's White identity development model (2001) was created as a prescription for Whites to help transform society and experience the evolution of a liberated racial identity. The five-stage model is composed of worldviews that range from a naive perspective about people of color to acceptance of the need to see oneself as privileged. One ultimately transforms by taking responsibility for dismantling one's privileged positions in society and finally understanding systemic oppression. The Helms model of White racial identity development (Hardiman, 2001; Helms & Cook, 1999; Torres, Howard-Hamilton, & Cooper, 2003) is comprised of six statuses and offers an analysis of how White people unconsciously become racist. This model views racism as something that is learned from authority figures who see themselves not as White but as individuals without a race. As an individual's raceless identity is covertly reinforced and supported, eventually he or she observes how others overtly embrace their ethnicity, which causes cognitive dissonance for the individual. The dissonance manifests itself in the form of racist actions and behaviors, as well as angst among Whites, because there are very few role models that embrace a multicultural worldview. If a White person is able to understand the systemic power of racism along with the behavioral implications of oppression, he or she may become a supporter of a society that empowers all people and might help dismantle these constructs.

The models of White identity development presented here were selected because of their impact in the counseling, student affairs, and psychology literature. The models are grounded in empirical studies and have been used in numerous theses, dissertations, and articles. The models have been used in the counseling canon for over 25 years and there is an instrument, the White Racial Identity Development Scale, that measures an individual's status according to Helms's model (Helms & Cook, 1999). The adversaries of the students of color in the Middle Urban University case are willing neither to relinquish their privilege nor to empower the students of color on campus. In terms of their racial identity stage, they have no social consciousness of race and are not willing to examine who they are and how systemic racism provides them with a comfortable environment in and outside the classroom. It is through the demonstrations and demands of the students of color that Whites on campus may begin to observe how the university discriminates, giving Whites a significant advantage over marginalized groups. Whites also need to be challenged by non-racist Whites who are at higher stages so they can model how to be allies to underrepresented groups. In addition, non-racist Whites can verbalize how racism negatively affects everyone on campus by writing policies and designing programs to raise White racial consciousness and by hiring diverse faculty and staff. Overall, engaging in a dialogue with Whites about race, racism, oppression, and privilege allows others to gauge their level of consciousness, thus structuring a conversation that will promote growth and understanding following Helms and Cook's (1999) as well as Hardiman's (2001) models. Culture centers have historically been places where ethnic minority groups have found solace and comfort in the opportunity to engage in open and honest dialogue with each other and with members of the dominant culture.

Ethnic/Racial Minority Identity Development

There are numerous models of identity development that are geared toward a special racial/ethnic population. Helms and Cook (1999) provided a summary of selected models enumerating the stages of identity development and descriptions of individuals from different racial/ethnic groups. This section, however, focuses on Atkinson, Morten, and Sue's minority identity development model (1998), which can be applied to cross sections of racial/ethnic groups. The five stages of the minority identity development model are delineated as follows (Parker, Archer, & Scott, 1992; Torres, Howard-Hamilton, & Cooper, 2003):

1. Conformity: Racial/ethnic minorities have an intellectual and cultural connection with Whites. They absorb the values, beliefs, and history of the dominant culture yet understand very little about their own racial/ethnic heritage.
2. Dissonance: This is a questioning phase that occurs because the racial/ethnic minority individual has gotten a wake-up call to racism and negative feelings are attached to this dramatic realization.
3. Resistance and immersion: There is a complete rejection of conformity behaviors and a renewal and self-awakening to the history and values of the individual's racial/ethnic group.
4. Introspection: Individuals ask themselves, "Why am I rejecting the dominant culture?" and "Is there a way I can reconcile the feelings of anger and resentment toward the dominant culture?" Members of

racial/ethnic minorities ask these and other questions as they attempt to balance and resolve their feelings toward White Americans.

5. Synergetic articulation and awareness: An intellectual breakthrough occurs when the racial/ethnic minority individual resolves his or her issues with the dominant culture and begins to value people from all cultures.

The students of color in the Middle Urban University case have moved through the first four stages of the minority identity development model. There was universal acceptance and support of the dominant culture, which involved subscribing to the rules and regulations as well as taking courses that did not include a diversity of perspectives, when they began matriculating at MUU. Once the students began to grow intellectually and break free from a dualistic banking education mind-set (a prescribed or routinized method of thinking and teaching), an epiphany occurred. The students began to question why their voices were not heard on campus and their experiences did not resonate in the textbooks they were reading. They found that they needed a safe place where they could speak about the issues and problems they were encountering on campus—thus the request for a third place or culture center.

Students in the fourth stage of racial identity development are encouraging the administrators at MUU to become more receptive to sharing the campus with non-dominant groups. Unfortunately, there are students who are angry about the way Whites have abused their privileges. Concomitantly there are Whites who idealize their race and hold negative and distorted perceptions of racial/ethnic minority groups. Overall, there is an impasse in the communication process, so it is incumbent upon Whites who are at the autonomy state, along with African Americans who are identity aware, to move the two groups closer together in their thinking and beliefs. In these conversations, it is most important that the provost, chancellor, and president of MUU clearly support the non-dominant group and explain why it is important to support diversity initiatives on campus.

Tatum (1997) has stated that the stress that Black students endure on a daily basis in predominantly White environments moves them to find refuge in a safe space by sitting together in the cafeteria. She further stated that in order for Black students to transition through the stages of racial identity development, they need to be able to "practice their language in

Black student unions and cultural centers and at college dining halls on predominantly White campuses all over the United States" (Tatum, 1997, p. 77). If safe spaces like culture centers are not available, it may become impossible for students of color to learn how to move beyond their anger at the dominant culture and find their voices in order to become empowered to enact change not only on the college campus but in their professional environments after graduation. Tatum cautioned White colleges about the extreme psychological duress that Black students endure when they are exposed to uncaring and insensitive environments and stressed the important role that cultural space can have in ameliorating their estrangement from the campus. She proffered that "having a place to be rejuvenated and to feel anchored in one's cultural community increases the possibility that one will have the energy to achieve academically as well as participate in the cross-group dialogue and interaction many colleges want to encourage" (Tatum, 1997, p. 80).

Programming Recommendations

Administrators who work in culture centers should use theories to design programs, direct their conversations with students, and create mission/vision statements or strategic plans. Effective programs that promote the multicultural growth and development of faculty, staff, and students on campus should be designed and implemented. Some ways to increase racial/ethnic sensitivity are facilitating workshops and encouraging faculty to teach their courses in the culture center on campus. This gives all students an opportunity to understand the function and mission of the center.

Programs can include the Game of Oppression, distributed by the National Association of Student Personnel Administrators (http://www .NASPA.org) and described as "an interactive tool for diversity education." The activity can be facilitated by a team of racially diverse facilitators to encourage authentic dialogue about issues of oppression and dominance in the lives of the participants. The game can be used to engage students in a discussion about prejudice and discrimination that challenges them to think beyond their current White racial identity status or ethnic/racial minority identity stage. Panel discussions with faculty, staff, and students about current diversity topics can also challenge the way students think about race. Movie nights and book club discussions that center on the effects of racism on college students keep students of color engaged because they offer an opportunity for students to share their methods of survival and their counterstories in a supportive environment. An activity that was quite successful at Indiana University Bloomington was a sorority exchange between African American women in Black Greek organizations and women living in traditional sorority houses. The women spent an evening in the culture center and had discussions about race, gender, and oppression and engaged in some of these activities to gain insight into the issues women face on college campuses.

The culture center can also be a place of political engagement. A racial/ethnic task force can be created, and its members can serve as leaders and spokespersons regarding discrimination on campus, or it can serve as a support group for students who need to have their voices heard. The group can assist in creating anti-discrimination policies and can support multicultural programming on campus. The individuals on the task force should be White faculty and staff who are at the higher stages of racial identity development as well as faculty and staff of color.

Conclusion

Overall, we have been amazed that the historical trends in higher education have led us full circle from the Black power movement in the 1970s and 1980s to the current climate, in which we see students making the same demands today on college campuses. We are struggling with the reversal of many policies that provided equity and access to scholarships, programs, and academic disciplines for students of color on college campuses. However, campuses can do the right thing by finding champions on campus who are ready to develop policies and articulate them clearly and succinctly. They must be the leaders who can model the intellectual and psychosocial transformation that must occur in order for a strategic plan for the development of a culturally sensitive and dynamic campus to be implemented.

There is a need for leaders to make assured decisions about the changes that need to occur on campus. Leaders must listen carefully to students of color who are damaged by the racial barriers overtly and covertly situated on campus (Feagin, Vera, & Imani, 1996). In addition, the administrators must take the students' demands seriously and "recognize them fully as legitimate members of the campus community, and . . . engage them in a meaningful dialogue directed at integrating campus culture and social structures" (Feagin et al., 1996, p. 167). It is shameful that conversations about the need for a safe place and space on college campuses must take center stage and students must shout, scream, and use precious emotional energy in order for these issues to be addressed. Culture centers are powerful tools for enhancing the growth and development of all students on campus. They provide an environment for stimulating discussions about race, gender, religion, sexual orientation, and other topics that are relevant on college campuses today. Tatum (1997) argued, "If White students or faculty do not understand why Black or Latino or Asian cultural centers are necessary, then they need to be helped to understand" (p. 80). The use of theory to inform the proper practice and implementation of programs can guide administrators' actions, thus assuring all constituents that they do practice what they preach.

References

antonio, A. L., & Muniz, M. M. (2007). The sociology of diversity. In P. J. Gumport (Ed.), *Sociology of higher education: Contributions and their contexts* (pp. 266–294). Baltimore: Johns Hopkins University Press.

Atkinson, D. R., Morten, G., & Sue, D. W. (1998). *Counseling American minorities: A cross cultural perspective* (5th ed.). San Francisco: McGraw-Hill.

Feagin, J. R., Vera, H., & Imani, N. (1996). *The agony of education: Black students at White colleges and universities.* New York: Routledge.

Gaines, T. A. (1991). *The campus as a work of art.* Westport, CT: Praeger.

Gumport, P. J. (Ed.). (2007). *Sociology of higher education: Contribution and their contexts.* Baltimore: Johns Hopkins University Press.

Hardiman, R. (2001). Reflections on White identity development. In C. L. Wijeyesinghe & B. W. Jackson III (Eds.), *New perspectives on racial identity development: A theoretical and practical anthology* (pp. 108–128). New York: New York University Press.

Hay, I. (2001). Critical geography and activism in higher education. *Journal of Geography in Higher Education, 25*(2), 141–146.

Helms, J. E., & Cook, D. A. (1999). *Using race and culture in counseling and psychotherapy: Theory and process.* Needham Heights, MA: Allyn & Bacon.

Hobgood, M. E. (2000). *Dismantling privilege: An ethics of accountability.* Cleveland, OH: Pilgrim Press.

Kaplin, W. A., & Lee, B. A. (1997). *A legal guide for student affairs professionals.* San Francisco: Jossey-Bass.

Katz, J. H. (2003). *White awareness: Handbook for anti-racism training* (2nd ed.). Norman: University of Oklahoma Press.

McIntosh, P. (1988). *White privilege and male privilege: A personal account of coming to see correspondence through work in women's studies* (Working Paper No. 189). Wellesley, MA: Center for Research on Women.

Moos, R. H. (1986). *The human context: Environmental determinants of behavior.* Malabar, FL: Krieger.

Oldenburg, R. (1989). *The great good place.* New York: Paragon House.

Parker, W. M., Archer, J., & Scott, J. (1992). *Multicultural relations on campus: A personal growth approach.* Muncie, IN: Accelerated Development.

Patton, L. D. (2006). Black culture centers: Still central to student learning. *About Campus, 11*(2), 2–8.

Rhoads, R. A. (1998). Student protest and multicultural reform: Making sense of campus unrest in the 1990s. *Journal of Higher Education, 69*(6), 621–646.

Strange, C. C., & Banning, J. H. (2001). *Educating by design: Creating campus environments that work.* San Francisco: Jossey-Bass.

Tatum, B. D. (1997). *"Why are all the Black kids sitting together in the cafeteria?": And other conversations about race.* New York: Basic Books.

Torres, V., Howard-Hamilton, M. F., & Cooper, D. L. (2003). *Identity development of diverse populations: Implications for teaching and administration in higher education.* San Francisco: Jossey-Bass.

7

RESITUATING CULTURE CENTERS WITHIN A SOCIAL JUSTICE FRAMEWORK

Is There Room for Examining Whiteness?

Michael Benitez Jr.

Throughout the 1970s and 1980s this nation's colleges and universities were faced with extremely testing times following *Brown v. Board of Education*, the civil rights movement, and the Black student movement in the preceding two decades (Hord, 2005; Lewis, 1998; Patton & Hannon, 2008; Princes, 1994; Williams, 1987). Such historical moments, coupled with sociopolitical pressures, drove the passage of legislation closely examining inequitable practices and legally addressing student access and equality in education (see Crenshaw, Gotanda, Peller, & Thomas, 1995; Wolf-Wendel, Twombly, Nemeth-Tuttle, Ward, & Gaston-Gayles, 2004). As a result, the enrollment of underrepresented racial/ethnic populations, particularly African Americans, at predominantly White institutions (PWIs) steadily increased, and campuses across the United States were prompted to strategize and formulate approaches to address the demographic change that began to drastically transform the academic landscape in higher education (Patton, 2006b; Powell, 1998; Princes, 1994).

This shift in student representation, coupled with Black student activism and demands, required campus leaders to implement a broad range of initiatives addressing the sociocultural and academic needs of a growing population of ethnic and racially minoritized[1] students across college campuses

(Chang, 2005). This process led to the establishment of multiple initiatives (i.e., Black culture centers, ethnic and cultural studies, and minority student services) to serve a wide range of student populations (Foster & Long, 1970; Vellela, 1999). Today, universities continue to struggle to meet the needs of ethnic and racially minoritized students on their campuses. Whereas initial efforts were geared toward Black students, given their central role in the Black student movement and their insistence on being admitted to PWIs, the racial and cultural dynamics of higher education have steadily changed over time. Today's struggle is rooted in a different context that extends beyond the Black-White binary that once dominated cultural discourse to one of multicultural consideration. Attention has shifted to populations such as Asian American and Pacific Islanders, Latinas/os, Native Americans, and women and lesbian, gay, bisexual, and transgender students.

Shifting away from a Black-White binary and moving toward a more critical and inclusive multicultural paradigm requires us to consider the implications of such institutional transitions. Questions that are important to address in the process of social and contextual alteration include; what is lost and gained in the process of moving beyond the Black-White paradigm? Who does or does not benefit from moving beyond the traditional conceptualization of meeting the needs of minoritized groups on university and college campuses? Such institutional cultural and spatial shifts also bring to the surface some important questions posited by Princes as part of a paper she presented at the 1994 Annual Conference of the Pennsylvania Black Conference on Higher Education pertaining to the role of multicultural and Black cultural centers on college campuses. More specifically, she asked "does it make sense to replace a center that has traditionally and perhaps adequately addressed the issue of racial harmony when there is much evidence that suggests the need for more understanding among whites?" Or "does it make better sense to develop an inclusive organization," such as a multicultural center that can assure similar commitment and support to Black cultural centers? (Princes, 1994, pp. 45–46). She argued that as college campuses diversified their enrollment, different groups would inquire about resources specifically aimed to meet their social and cultural needs. Conversely, such a shift also brings to light the complexity of cultivating and sustaining inclusive campus atmospheres. As such, college campuses should not only focus on meeting the needs of minoritized ethnic and racial groups but also direct attention and resources toward examining how race-specific and multicultural spaces can assist White students in coping with the diversification of college campuses and academia and how such diversity challenges White identity (Sallee, Logan, Sims, & Harrington, 2009).

It is also critical to examine how spaces such as culture centers can benefit White students by helping them "produce a new anti-racist identity" (Bedard, 2000, p. 41). This sort of examination must account for sociohistorical constructions of power and privilege among Whites, move beyond educating Whites about other cultures, and focus more on how White students can learn about themselves and their positionality given their exposure to and interactions with students from different racial/ethnic cultures (Ortiz & Rhoads, 2000). In this chapter, I briefly examine and situate Princes's "precarious question" (1994) in the context of current campus cultural shifts and diversification and examine how race-specific culture centers (RSCCs) and multicultural centers (MCCs) can serve White student bodies on campus. In the process, I utilize a comprehensive framework based on social justice and antiracism discourse to situate my argument. Finally, I offer suggestions for the future employment of MCCs and RSCCs as politicized and symbolic spaces for deconstructing Whiteness and cultivating collective consciousness across ethnic/racial groups.

Increasingly Diverse Student Populations: RSCCs and MCCs in a Multiracial/Multiethnic Context

During the final two decades of the 20th century, the Asian American and Latina/o college student populations tripled, Native American enrollment increased by 80%, and African American student enrollment increased by 56% (American Council on Education, 2003). A recent report released by the American Council on Education found that the total minority enrollment in American colleges and universities increased 50%, from 3.4 million students to 5 million students between 1995 and 2005, with students of color making up 29% of the population across college campuses in the United States (Mikyung, 2008). Overall, there was a 46% increase among African Americans, a 66% increase among Latinas/os, a 31% increase among Native Americans, and a 37% increase among Asian Americans (Mikyung, 2008). Such a change in student composition requires campus leaders to continually revisit the fluidity of student enrollment and the newly created campus climate dynamics cultivated through these phenomena. It is essential that institutional leaders acknowledge the multiplicity of voices and experiences present throughout the socio-academic fabric of the campus and encourage inter- and cross-cultural engagement among students in meaningful and purposeful ways (Chang, 2005; Chesler, Lewis, & Crowfoot, 2005; Patton & Hannon, 2008). As Chang (2005) noted in "Reconsidering the Diversity Rationale," campuses "must create additional opportunities and expectations for students to interact across racial and other social differences" (p. 11). This includes students of minoritized racial/ethnic backgrounds, who have historically been underrepresented in higher education and whose experiences are often relegated to the margins of campus life, as well as White students, who have historically experienced privilege, entitlement, and inequitable practices that favor them in higher education (Bonilla-Silva, 2003; Gewirtz, 1998; Young, 1990).

One of the ways in which college campuses have attempted to promote racial and ethnic diversity and meet students' needs has been through the establishment of culture centers (Asante, 2005; Patton, 2006b; Princes, 1994). Culture centers have historically afforded a safe space for critical thinking and dialogue, represented political spaces of resistance in hostile academic environments, and served as a home away from home for students of color (Hord, 2005; Patton, 2006a, 2006b). MCCs and RSCCs provide a local context for initiating a range of political, social, and cultural events to support and affirm students' experiences in pursuing their academic goals while preserving their cultural ties and roots (Jones, Castellanos, & Cole, 2002). The findings of a case study conducted by Jones et al. (2002) examining ethnic minority student experiences at a PWI indicated that all minoritized racial and ethnic groups "were pleased with the services provided by the cross cultural center" (p. 30) and perceived the campus culture center as welcoming and nurturing. They added that the cross-cultural center served as a beneficial space that promoted the retention of ethnic and racially minoritized students (Jones et al., 2002). Some students described the center as a relaxed, stress-free atmosphere where they felt comfortable addressing personal and social issues; others identified the center as a "haven, a home away from home, a place I can be myself, and a part of my roots" (p. 30).

Asian students identified the center as a "different experience from the rest of the university, more positive and pleasant." It was referred to as "a place to think of one's identity and pick up cultural pieces." Latino students identified the center as "a home away from home" where Native Americans associated the center as a "place to interact with other tribe members," "a place that provides strength for my community to work together," and "a location with a sense of camaraderie which helps to solidify identity." (Jones et al., 2002, p. 30)

Such responses speak to these students' experiences and validate the need for culture centers. For many, these spaces of critical engagement on homogenous White campuses affirm identity, build community, and cultivate leadership (Tatum, 2004); serve as nonthreatening spaces for cultural expression, empowerment, and pride (Patton, 2006a); and serve as anti-oppressive political spaces of consciousness for students of color in pursuit of historical acknowledgement and self-identity (hooks, 1990). These spaces have been shown to address the needs of students of color, but should they also serve White students? If so, in what capacity? Furthermore, how should RSCCs and MCCs operate in a way that not only preserves their mission of serving students of color but also allows for outreach to White students while promoting and fostering inclusive cross-cultural engagement? Moreover, the precarious question of RSCCs versus MCCs remains to be addressed, not only in the context of increasingly diverse student populations across college campus, but also in the context of racial and ethnic tensions involving politics and identity (Sefa Dei & Calliste, 2000). A clear call has been made for these centers to integrate and expand their missions (Hefner, 2002; Patton, 2006a).

Situating Whiteness and Antiracism Discourse in RSCCs and MCCs

Just as critical and valuable as the creation and cultivation of a space for the social, intellectual, and spiritual development of students of color is the need to address the social development of White students, many of whom have had little to no cross-cultural engagement and are unaware of White privilege and the dominant White discourses that permeate campus culture (Freire, 2000; Gewirtz, 1998, 2006; hooks, 2003; Ortiz & Rhoads, 2000). Gewirtz (1998) argued that "a politics of recognition or an ethics of otherness involves not only a commitment to respond to others and otherness but also a commitment to avoiding practicing the power of surveillance, control, and discipline upon others" (p. 476). Most of the current literature does not delve into the value, or lack thereof, of considering the impact of MCCs and RSCCs on the experiences of White undergraduates across college campuses. Historically, foundations for multicultural initiatives in education were originally intended to oppose dominant trends of Whiteness in the academy. However, today's students bring new ways of conceptualizing diversity issues with them to college campuses. These new ideas, attitudes, and viewpoints differ in many ways from those of previous generations (DiMaria, 2007). To be clear, I am not implying that racism and other issues that affect students of color are no longer prevalent; rather, administrators must become responsive to shifting demographics when considering current RSCC and MCC discourses (Gay, 2000; Sefa Dei & Calliste, 2000). Given my experience as the director of both a BCC and an MCC, I admit that it is unrealistic to believe that there is a program or space that appeals to all students. As such, spaces aimed at fostering and encouraging cultural and political engagement should be developed based on the best interest of the students within specific contexts shaped by structural and institutional policy, conditioning, and spatial depoliticization (Mohanty, 2003). Too often, spaces such as RSCCs and MCCs rely on homogeneous theoretical impositions that assume students' needs can be met in the same way or that models found to be effective for one ethnic/racial group within a given context are applicable to other groups in their respective contexts, with no consideration for shifting spatial dynamics. Perhaps it is not necessary to erect a center for every group, but rather current spaces (centers), as well as newly created spaces (centers and programs), can be used to strategically, politically, and equitably address diverse needs.

Given the sociohistorical conditions that have led to the dissonance and disconnect between culture centers and White students, a more progressive response to the discourse is conceptualizing culture centers as possible spaces for the social deconstruction of "Whiteness" and racial superiority. This might best be understood within an antiracist social justice education framework. These spaces cannot exist in the absence of purpose, and therefore it is critical that faculty and staff working closely with RSCCs and MCCs cultivate an environment that is inclusive of not only those who are labeled and viewed as multicultural but also those who have been, since the development of multicultural discourse, constructed as independent of multicultural discourse (Ortiz & Rhoads, 2000; Sallee et al., 2009; Sefa Dei & Calliste, 2000). Recentering RSCCs and MCCS in a social justice framework indicates an important shift in focus toward questions such as; whom does diversity serve? How and why are processes of normalcy constructed? How are such spaces navigated so that conversations on diversity reveal the dangers of power and privilege to both the oppressor and the oppressed?

A focus on both the needs and development of ethnic and racially minoritized students, as well as the development of White privileged students, politicizes the multiculturalization process as one that intentionally creates a space or spaces on campus for what Mohanty (2003) refers to as co-implication, "the idea that all of us share certain histories as well as certain responsibilities: ideologies of race define both White and Black people" (p. 203), as well as members of all ethnic and racial groups who cannot be categorized in terms of the Black-White binary. More specifically, I call upon campuses to look not only at how they are addressing issues affecting minoritized groups but at how to engage students in a multicultural campus, be it through cultural programming, diversified curricula, race-specific centers, or multicultural centers (Sallee et al., 2009) that challenge the dominant culture via critical multiculturalism as opposed to celebrations of commoditized multiculturalism (referred to by Mohanty, 2003). This process is paramount in the recentering of RSCCs and MCCs in a social justice antiracist framework, for it implies that marginalized and privileged ethnic/racial cultural groups need to engage in a space where White students are challenged to think about their own identity by interacting with students of other races and ethnicities (Ortiz & Rhoads, 2000; Sallee et al., 2009) in a space cultivated on the basis of the experiences of the subjugated, not the privileged. There are numerous theoretical frameworks that focus on White identity development, but Hardiman's model of White identity development and Helms's model of White racial identity development (Hardiman, 2001) are most often referred to in the higher education literature. In the case of RSCCs and BCCs however, I refer to Ortiz and Rhoads (2000), who offer a five-step model of deconstructing Whiteness that I believe is political, intentional, and multicontextual. Further, the model is situated in a social justice and multicultural framework, conceptualized in and informed by antiracism education, and aimed at helping White students navigate a series of steps

that involve "understanding culture, learning about other cultures, recognizing and deconstructing white culture, recognizing the legitimacy of other
cultures, and developing a multicultural outlook" (Ortiz & Rhoads, as cited
in Sallee et al., 2009, p. 211). On the basis of my experience with social justice
in higher education, I believe this model more accurately captures the need
to view such spaces as "political and cultural sites" (Tastsoglou, 2000, p. 101)
that can be altered, readjusted, and socially contextualized (Kincheloe, Slattery, & Steinberg, 2000). Not only to challenge and serve racial/ethnic
minoritized and privileged students within that space, but also as a means to
contemplate the fluidity of identity development as a process that is pedagog-
ically circular and reciprocal as opposed to linear (Bedard, 2000). Given that
my goal is not to descriptively elaborate on the aforementioned theoretical
frameworks, I refer those who wish to gain a deeper awareness of how to
create a multicultural space inclusive of White students on campus to Ortiz
and Rhoads (2000) and Sallee et al. (2009) for a more in-depth discussion
on the deconstructing Whiteness model.

Recentering RSCCs and MCCs in Social Justice Framework: White Bodies Included

Bell (1997) describes social justice education as a democratic, inclusive, and
participatory process focused on affirming human agency and cultivating
equitable spaces where people can collaborate to create change and representation of diverse voices and experiences. hooks (2003) articulated the following in *Teaching Community*: "Black people/people of color who truly believe
that white people cannot change can only embrace the logic of victimhood"
(p. 53). Her words suggest the need for diversity educators to find value in
inclusive attempts to reach racial equity by considering how Whites can also
contribute to the process of attaining racial equity. Bell (1997) conceptualized social justice pedagogy as an approach that "enables us to think clearly
about our intentions and the means we use to actualize them" (p. 4), and a
framework that permits us to challenge and contest how we approach issues
grounded in social justice and diversity education. Doing so, according to
Bell (1997), will lead us to continually revisit our approaches to conceptualizing social justice while creating new ones as we encounter changing social
conditions, the absence of support and resources, and individual and structural resistance. As such, social justice education aims to construct a societal

vision based on full and equal participation of all groups in any given community that is collectively shaped by practices of injustice and oppression.

It is critical to consider the abstract nature of social justice and how easily both the process and goal can be depoliticized if they are not considered contextually and comprehensively. Both Gewirtz (2006) and Young (1990) contended that social justice must be considered as an abstract and ambiguous multidimensional paradigm that must be understood within its local contexts and politics of identity. More specifically, Gewirtz (1998) has spoken to the recognizable nature of social justice education and argued the need for openness to unassimilated otherness. In particular, I refer to the need for campus constituents to be open to inter- and cross-cultural engagement based on the experiences of students of minoritized and racialized ethnicities as opposed to the Eurocentric epistemological and ontological ideologies often employed to meet the needs of students of minoritized ethnic and racial backgrounds. Doing so situates justice as "freedom from oppressive relations" (Gewirtz, 1998, p. 476) and allows for more utilitarian anti-oppressive and antiracist processes that inform a commitment to inclusive social and politicized activities.

During a recent visit to Iowa, Carlos Cortes, author of *The Making and Re-Making of a Multiculturalist,* referred to social justice as a moving target (personal communication, November 10, 2008). The concept of a moving target captures the essence of social justice advocacy, contextualization, and praxis. Many times I have realized that social justice is an obscure, depoliticized, and intangible presence in education that can easily be misguided if not conceptualized holistically and equitably (Gorski, 2006; Hu-DeHart, 2000). Similarly, I have observed issues around race and ethnicity addressed by apolitical movements within social justice frameworks in higher education, where the role of RSCCs and MCCs has been restricted and limited to ahistorical watered down celebrations of cultural awareness that fail to address issues of power relations, dominant discourse, and hegemonic resistance (Mohanty, 2003). Tatum (2007) has pointed out that "white students and students of color often have a desire to connect with one another across racial lines" (p. 101). Similarly, Sallee et al. (2009) referred to several studies by scholars who address the positive developmental (social, cognitive, cultural) impact of exposing White students to different races/ethnicities and the benefits that accrue to both privileged and marginalized racial/ethnic groups on campus. This goal can be addressed compellingly through critical safe spaces such as RSCCs and MCCs if discussion is grounded on a politicized social justice base. However, let me be clear that my goal is not to utilize such spaces to meet the needs, or lack thereof, of White students enrolled in academia, as most institutions of higher education across the United States have been historically assembled on, and informed by the premise of Whiteness. Part of my aim is to advocate the necessity for and further integration of such spaces (culture centers—be they RSCCs or MCCs) founded and created in response to political movements grounded on marginalized identities. In addition, my aim is to bring to light how such spaces can also be conceptualized and used to deconstruct and reconstruct Whiteness in the academy.

For White students, who have not been a central consideration in the establishment of culture centers, I suggest the need to carve a space in the margins (culture centers) where they can also engage in a provocative process of coming to know Whiteness on the experiences of oppressed minoritized populations and interrogating dominant discourses that typically deny their own ethnic and racial histories, which in turn contributes to the cycle of oppression (Bedard, 2000). Tim Wise (2008) spoke to this phenomenon in an article titled "On White Pride and Other Delusions." Wise described the sentiments of White folks frustrated by the absence of White culture centers and White history thematic celebrations, and by academic institutions' overemphasis on non-dominant discourses related to oppressed groups. In his book *Pedagogy of the Oppressed*, Paulo Freire (2000) asserted, "If students are not able to transform their lived experience into knowledge and to use the already acquired knowledge as a process to unveil new knowledge, they will never be able to participate rigorously in a dialogue as a process of learning and knowing" (p. 19). This requires a broad-based lens rooted in the framework of social justice education and inclusive of theories for liberatory and anti-oppressive praxis (hooks, 1994).

Through this process of inclusion and expansion of RSCC and MCC objectives, White students identify connections or similarities between racism and intersecting social justice issues. This includes gender, class, sexuality, and other issues that White students are likely to view as more salient points of entry than race and ethnicity. In seeking innovative methods to build bridges between White students and culture centers (Asante, 2005), White students who normally would not consider culture centers legitimate spaces of social justice inquiry and engagement begin to (1) acknowledge racism and ethnic inequality as legitimate social justice issues of focus and contestation; (2) view RSCCs and MCCs as contemporary spaces of struggle and resistance for all, regardless of the racial/ethnic group for which they were originally intended to serve; (3) become more likely to engage with non-White peers in a nonthreatening space; and (4) learn to think critically about race, which enables them to make Whiteness visible and take note of and embrace others' perspectives (Moore, 2006). This shift in contextual thinking and positioning is not meant to target minoritized students of color or White students specifically, but rather to lead to a better understanding of the historic significance of these cultural contexts as local spaces of dissent in higher education that advance the social justice agenda from racial/ethnic non-dominant critical perspectives, be they Latina/o, African American, Asian Pacific American, or First Nation or other multicultural experiences and narratives (Darder & Torres, 2004).

Essential considerations of inquiry from this position, however, raise the following questions: Should White students even be considered in the establishment and operationalization of these spaces? If so, can MCCs serve White students in a manner different from RSCCs? These questions should not focus on whether or not one or the other can serve White students differently or more effectively. Nor should they focus on the extent to which White students should be considered in terms of the role of MCCs and RSCCs at PWIs. Rather, the focus should be placed on what strategies campuses can implement to maintain the mission and work of culture centers without losing the historical foundation, significance, and symbolism of these spaces. Strategies include, but are not limited to, using these culture centers as spaces for building community during orientation; hosting classes, diversity workshops, and critical inter- and cross-cultural programs; making social justice advocacy central to the centers' missions; and making hiring inclusive (Harper & Quaye, 2009). However, these spaces cannot exist in the absence of purpose and politics. Griffiths (2003) provides the following fluid interpretations of how social justice might be grasped as a framework for education: "Social justice depends on both recognition and redistribution, the issues need to be understood in terms both of little stories and of grand narratives; that is, both localized issues and large-scale theorizing about them" (p. 55). Thus, it is essential that social justice serve not as an equalizer of struggles but rather as an intersecting ground for equity and self-reflexivity

(Mohanty, 2003; Tastsoglou, 2000). Making social justice central to these culture centers is not meant to water down or minimize the individual as well as collective struggles of minoritized racial/ethnic groups. Nor does it serve to comfort White students. Instead, it is a call for administrators and faculty to see the value of these spaces in engaging White students in conversations about Whiteness, racism, and other issues related to power, dominance, and social justice education from a critical non-Eurocentric antiracist lens aimed at cultivating politicized discourse and shattering homogenous ideology.

Future Directions for Campuses Grappling With the Precarious Question and Whiteness

Undoubtedly, there is some literature that criticizes both RSCCs and MCCs on college campuses and student development (Chesler, Lewis, & Crowfoot, 2005; Moore, 2006; Princes, 1994; Watkins, 1994). Often these critiques address the extent to which such centers segregate students as opposed to uniting them, therefore preventing the development of a critical collective consciousness. Others have argued that RSCCs and MCCs serve as depoliticized social spaces that promote celebratory representations and cultural tourism rather than promoting diversity and social justice (Gorski, 2006; Hu-DeHart, 2000; Patton, 2006a; Rothenberg, 2007; Watkins, 1994). On one hand, MCCs (by their title alone) seem to represent unity, acceptance, mutual respect, and equality. This salient goal of unity and false collective consciousness, however, runs the risk of amputating the centers from the political, historical, and social contexts and movements that paved the way for their foundation (Watkins, 1994). On the other hand, RSCCs (by their racial designation alone) could be perceived as catering to only one group and alienating White students rather than focusing on critical interrogation of the dominant culture, serving as a safe space for multiethnic students, and promoting equity (Hord, 2005). Rothenberg (2007) correctly argued that "we need to return to a version of multiculturalism that combines celebration with attention to issues of dominance and subordination, hierarchy, power, and privilege" (p. 49).

Important to the advancement and achievement of campuses wrestling with this question is the role of educators in addressing multiculturalism in academia and from multiple critical lenses. This requires strategic and careful processes by which those who identify with the movement can still meaning-fully view and approach both RSCCs and MCCs as political spaces of histor-ical context, depth, and scope and with a vision for inclusiveness and equity. Chesler et al. (2005) captured this portrait best when they referred to student-oriented programs as critical challenges that involve "maintaining a balance between emphasizing separate social identities and building a trans-group consciousness or community" (p. 253). Part of this process is the need to consider those who are labeled the multiethnic and multiracial, as well as other minoritized groups whose experiences and identities have been rele-gated to the margins of the multicultural canon, and stigmatized or pigeon-holed as independent of this process; such as women; lesbian, gay, bisexual, transgender people; people with different abilities; people whose first lan-guage is not English; people of nondominant faiths; and folks who are at an economic disadvantage. In the end, both RSCCs and MCCs might prove useful to White students as long as they are rooted in and operate out of an antiracist social justice framework—one inclusive of multiple and shifting theoretical frameworks aimed at creating inclusive spaces of resistance, reflection, and transformation with the understanding that we can neither diminish these centers' cultural relevance nor minimize their symbolic and political roots.

Note

1. I utilize the term minoritized as opposed to minority in this paper to refer to the process [action vs. noun] of student minoritization. My choice of text in this case assumes that there is a history of structural and institutional actions that have over time limited access to, and led to a lack of presence among students of color in higher education labeled as racially and ethnically different from the norm. Doing so also challenges the physical and spatial fixture often associated with how minority is often employed in most literature focused on similar issues to a more critical understanding of how minority came to be constructed socially over the course of history and how students continue to be minoritized in contemporary spaces of higher education.

References

American Council on Education. (2003). *20th anniversary: Minorities in higher edu-cation annual status report*. Washington, DC: Author.

Asante, M. K. (2005). Challenging orthodoxies: The case for the Black cultural center. In F. L. Hord (Ed.), *Black cultural centers* (pp. 37–40). Chicago: Third World Press.

Bedard, G. (2000). Deconstructing Whiteness: Pedagogical implications for anti-racism education. In G. J. Sefa Dei & A. Calliste (Eds.), *Power, knowledge and anti-racism education: A critical reader* (pp. 41–56). Halifax, Nova Scotia, Canada: Fernwood.

Bell, L. A. (1997). Theoretical foundations for social justice education. In M. Adams, L. A. Bell & P. Griffin (Eds.), *Teachings for diversity and social justice: A sourcebook* (pp. 3–15). New York: Routledge.

Bonilla-Silva, E. (2003). *Racism without racists: Color-blind racism and the persistence of racial inequality in the United States.* Lanham, MD: Rowman & Littlefield.

Chang, M. (2005). Reconsidering the diversity rationale. *Liberal Education, 9*(1), 6–13.

Chesler, M., Lewis, A., & Crowfoot, J. (2005). *Challenging racism in higher education: Promoting justice.* Lanham, MD: Row& Littlefield.

Crenshaw, K., Gotanda, N., Peller, G., & Thomas, K. (1995). *Critical race theory: The key writings that formed the movement.* New York: New Press.

Darder, A., & Torres, R. D. (2004). *After race: Racism after multiculturalism.* New York: New York University Press.

DiMaria, F. (2007, September 21). Exploring millennial students' views on diversity. *Hispanic Outlook,* pp. 22–24.

Foster, J., & Long, D. (1970). *Protest! Student activism in America.* New York: William Morrow.

Freire, P. (2000). *Pedagogy of the oppressed.* New York: Continuum.

Gay, G. (2000). *Culturally responsive teaching: Theory, research, and practice.* New York: Teachers College Press.

Gewirtz, S. (1998). Conceptualizing social justice in education: Mapping the territory. *Education Policy, 13*(4), 469–484.

Gewirtz, S. (2006). Towards a contextualized analysis of social justice in education. *Educational Philosophy and Theory, 38*(1), 69–81.

Gorski, P. (2006). Complicity with conversation: The de-politicizing of multicultural and intercultural education. *Intercultural Education, 17*(2), 163–177.

Griffiths, M. (2003). *Actions for social justice in education: Fairly different.* Philadelphia: Open University Press.

Hardiman, R. (2001). Reflections on White identity theory. In C. L. Wijeyesinghe & B. W. Jackson III (Eds.), *New perspectives on racial identity development: A theoretical and practical anthology* (pp. 108–128). New York: New York University Press.

Harper, S., & Quaye, S. J. (2009). *Student engagement in higher education: Theoretical perspectives and practical approaches for diverse populations.* New York: Routledge.

Hefner, D. (2002). Black cultural centers: Standing on shaky ground? *Black Issues in Higher Education, 18*(26), 22–29.

hooks, b. (1994). *Teaching to transgress: Education as the practice of freedom.* New York: Routledge.

hooks, b. (2003). *Teaching community: A pedagogy of hope.* New York: Routledge.

Hord, F. L. (Ed.). (2005). *Black cultural centers.* Chicago: Third World Press.

Hu-DeHart, E. (2000). The diversity project: Institutionalizing multiculturalism or managing differences? *Academe, 86*(5), 39–42.

Jones, L., Castellanos, J., & Cole, D. (2002). Examining the ethnic minority student experience at predominantly White institutions: A case study. *Journal of Hispanic Higher Education, 1*(1), 19–39.

Kincheloe, J. L., Slattery, P., & Steinberg, S. R. (2000). *Contextualizing teaching: Introduction to education and educational foundations.* New York: Addison, Wesley, Longman.

Lewis, J. (1998). *Walking with the wind: A memoir of the movement.* New York: Simon and Schuster.

Mikyung, R. (2008). *Minorities in higher education, 2008: Twenty-third status report.* Washington, DC: American Council on Higher Education.

Mohanty, C. T. (2003). *Feminism without borders: Decolonizing theory, practicing solidarity.* Durham, NC: Duke University Press.

Moore, R. M. (2006). *African Americans and Whites: Changing relationships on college campuses.* Lanham, MD: University Press of America.

Ortiz, A. M., & Rhoads, R. A. (2000). Deconstructing Whiteness as part of a multicultural educational framework: From theory to practice. *Journal of College Student Development, 41*(1), 81–93.

Patton, L. D. (2006a). Black culture centers: Still central to student learning. *About Campus, 11*(2), 2–8.

Patton, L. D. (2006b). The voice of reason: A qualitative examination of Black student perceptions of Black culture centers. *Journal of College Student Development, 47*, 628–646.

Patton, L. D., & Hannon, M. (2008). Collaboration for cultural programming: Engaging culture centers, multicultural affairs, and student activities offices as partners. In S. Harper (Ed.), *Creating inclusive campus environments for cross-cultural learning and student engagement* (pp. 139–154). Washington DC: NASPA.

Powell, M. H. (1998). Campus climate and students of color. In L. A. Valverde & L. A. Castenell Jr. (Eds.), *The multicultural campus: Strategies for transforming higher education* (pp. 95–118). Walnut Creek, CA: Sage.

Princes, C. D. (1994). *The precarious question of Black cultural centers versus multicultural centers.* (Report No. HE028386). Paper presented at the Annual Conference of the Pennsylvania Black Conference on Higher Education, Harrisburg, PA. (ERIC Document Reproduction Service No. ED383273)

Rothenberg, P. (2007). Half-empty or half-full? "Diversity" in higher education today. *Liberal Education, 93*(1), 44–49.

Sallee, M. W., Logan, M. E., Sims, S., & Harrington, P. (2009). Engaging White students on a multicultural campus: Developmental needs and institutional challenges. In S. Harper & S. J. Quaye (Eds.), *Student engagement in higher education: Theoretical perspectives and practical approaches for diverse populations* (pp. 199–221). New York: Routledge.

Sefa Dei, G. J., & Calliste, A. (Eds.). (2000). *Power, knowledge and anti-racism education: A critical reader.* Halifax, Nova Scotia, Canada: Fernwood.

Tastsoglou, E. (2000). Mapping the unknowable: The challenges and rewards of cultural, political, and pedagogical border crossing. In G. J. Sefa Dei & A. Calliste (Eds.), *Power, knowledge, and anti-racism education: A critical reader* (pp. 98–121). Halifax, Nova Scotia, Canada: Fernwood.

Tatum, B. D. (2004, April 2). Building a road to a diverse society. *The Chronicle of Higher Education,* pp. B6–B7.

Tatum, B. D. (2007). *Can we talk about race? And other conversations in an era of school resegregation.* Boston: Beacon Press.

Vellela, T. (1999). *New voices: Student political activism in the '80s and '90s.* Boston: South End Press.

Watkins, W. H. (1994). Multicultural education: Towards a historical and political inquiry. *Education Theory, 44*(1), 99–116.

Williams, J. (1987). *Eyes on the prize: America's civil rights years, 1954–1965.* New York: Penguin.

Wise, T. (2008). *Speaking treason fluently: Anti-racist reflections from an angry White male.* Berkeley, CA: Soft Skull Press.

Wolf-Wendel, L. E., Twombly, S. B., Nemeth-Tuttle, K., Ward, K., & Gaston-Gayles, J. L. (2004). *Reflecting back, looking forward: Civil rights and student affairs.* Washington, DC: NASPA.

Young, I. M. (1990). *Justice and the politics of difference.* Princeton, NJ: Princeton University Press.

PART THREE

ADMINISTRATIVE AND PRACTICE-ORIENTED ISSUES FOR CULTURE CENTERS

8

VIEWING CULTURAL PRACTICE THROUGH A LENS OF INNOVATION AND INTENTIONALITY

Strategies for Student Personnel Administrators in Culture Centers

Toby S. Jenkins

O n any given day on any given campus, you are likely to find two professionals at two different points in their careers facing the same challenge—effectively managing cultural learning on a contemporary college campus. One professional faces this challenge with years of experience and a portfolio of successes. Having weathered the changing climate of colleges through several decades, the professional sees no reason not to follow the traditional format of brown bag presentations, film series, lectures, panels, and tributes. The problem—students aren't responding, seats are empty, and frustration is high. Moreover, students are being blamed for being apathetic and lacking an interest in culture.

Fresh out of a graduate program, the other professional is armed with excitement, enthusiasm, and theories. The office is decorated, the degree is on the wall, and the professional has begun to develop relationships with students. But now that the transition from student to new practitioner has been made, much more is expected—the new professional must thoughtfully guide students' growth, know more than just the stages of development and be able to creatively brainstorm initiatives and programs that address the critical stages of student development, and establish more than a basic understanding of racial difference among college students; that is, he or she must educate and expose them to cultures with which many people are not even familiar. The problem lies in the fact that actual cultural practice is not covered in graduate school, change and results are expected but sufficient guidance is not provided, and the new professional has no idea where to begin.

Professionals throughout campuses—those involved in student activities, student engagement, multicultural affairs, civic engagement, and culture centers—face these challenges. The millennial data provided by Strauss and Howe (2000) remind us that every year the cultural outlook changes and influences how college students engage and what they expect of the college experience. However, much too often, individual professional practices are not as dynamic and as quick to evolve. Some professionals seem to be moving at horse-and-buggy speed in their willingness to change and meet contemporary student interest. Though moving at a faster pace, the approach to graduate education and campus-based professional development of staff still seems to be occurring at more of the pace of a cruise ship than racing ahead with a future focus. How many of us have entered careers without any formal and ongoing professional development programs? How many look forward to the annual conference as the only means of learning about new approaches to practice? And how many have graduated still unsure of even how to do "practice"? This lack of practical training can have significant effects on the service that we provide to students.

When the professional concentration on culture, multiculturalism, and diversity is added to this challenge, it becomes even more problematic, as these are highly sensitive and contentious issues that must be handled not only with caution but through professional knowledge. Universities verbally espouse a commitment to these issues but do very little to ensure staff can effectively manage, replicate, and create culture on a contemporary college campus. These professionals require expertise in cultural studies, student development, and program implementation. And the field must begin to establish viable cultural practice models that guide professional practice, including program development, office management, and student advising.

The tri-sector practitioners model (TSPM) was developed to provide such a framework to both new and veteran professionals facing the challenges and mandates of providing more culturally engaging spaces and opportunities outside the classroom. The model, a collaborative effort between myself and a colleague at another institution, brought together our several years of experience in higher education. Having experienced significant success in creating cultural education programs and garnering greater institutional investment in cultural initiatives both inside and outside university culture centers, we sought to articulate the professional philosophy and strategy that underscored much of our work in a model that could be shared with and adopted by colleagues to inform their practice. This model places value on the knowledge that is produced as a result of practice. It recognizes that key professional learning takes place in the field as well as through the pages of research articles.

The model has utility in various student affairs environments and is particularly viable as a holistic approach to cultural practice in university culture centers. The TSPM identifies three core services, programs, and initiatives that should be offered by university culture centers to ensure that there is not a deficit or imbalance in programming and services. Within each sector are also three essential components of practice that provide specific examples for professionals to follow. In previous articles, we have only shared the programming component of the model (Jenkins & Walton, 2005, 2006, 2008). For this chapter, I expand the model to include community building and administrative services. As a model, the TSPM serves as a starting point for any professional faced with transforming an office or implementing change for better cultural practice. In this regard, this model is developed specifically for cultural practitioners. Cultural practitioners are those charged with bringing cultural theory, heritage, and ideology to practice on campus (Jenkins & Walton, 2008). Cultural practice is the art of designing and building authentic and meaningful cultural experiences. The TSPM is a framework that can be used to develop a comprehensive portfolio of cultural programs and services.

The Tri-Sector Practitioners Model in Detail

This chapter dissects the model in detail and provides a description of, literature support for, and practical examples of each area of the model. It also highlights the three primary components that ensure that cultural practice, in both programming and administrative management, is intentional and interwoven into the office culture. These three broad areas are community building and outreach, administrative practices, and cultural programming (see Figure 8.1).

Sector I: Community Building and Outreach

The focus of community-building initiatives is to grow the culture center's relationship with and outreach to various constituents, including students, alumni, parents, campus departments, and city, state, and national professional colleagues. There are three key strategies for community building: effective marketing, strategic campus and community involvement, and outreach to multiple communities.

Comprehensive Marketing Campaigns

If you don't tell them, they definitely won't come. Transforming a culture center means nothing if no one is even aware of the center. A general marketing rule is that marketing should comprise 10%–15% of the overall budget

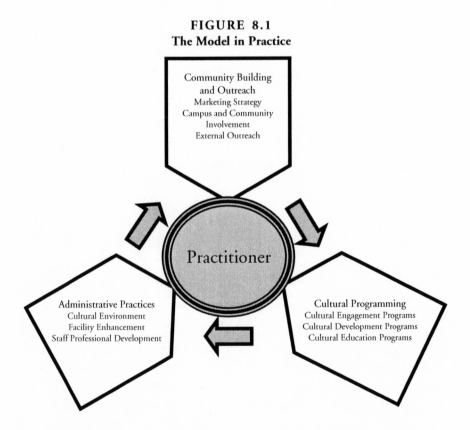

FIGURE 8.1
The Model in Practice

(Kotler & Armstrong, 1996). In addition, for any specific program, 10%–15% of the overall budget should be dedicated to marketing for the center itself. A viable marketing campaign involves much more than creating posters, fliers, and brochures. A multidimensional strategy for sharing your message with the community is key. Money should be allocated for brochures, newspaper ads, mass-produced posters, website enhancement, mass mailings to students and parents. For example, one of our major cultural programs has a total budget of about $25,000, not including marketing. Fifteen percent of this can be rounded up to $4,000. This means that in order to see an audience attendance that warrants a $25,000 program, we must invest at least $4,000 in marketing the event. We do this by developing a comprehensive marketing strategy outlined in Table 8.1.

For this campaign, thousands of pieces of publicity are distributed, several ads are bought to reach a wide audience, and many forms of free PR and promotional tactics are used to advertise one event. The result—over 3,000 students attend this campus event each year. To truly see major results in student participation, an equally strong effort should be invested in public relations and marketing to students. Taking the time during one semester to research all available publicity venues on your campus can result in many more semesters of high attendance and interest in the culture center. Marketing renewal should be annual and the marketing campaign should be updated each year to include new mediums. And of course this section cannot come to a close without addressing the issue of institutional support. Our cultural center, like many, operates on an extremely small budget. The budget for this one program is about 3 times the budget provided us by the institution. How do we do it? We raised all the funds for 2 years from various campus partners. After executing a successful event for 2 years, we were provided with the majority of the program budget by our division. Rather than being limited by a lack of support or focusing our energy on complaining about the lack of institutional support, we did the necessary work to prove that we could offer a major cultural experience worth the institution's investment.

Strategic Campus and Community Involvement

Culture center staff should be actively involved on campus and present in spaces outside the center. We must meet students where they are in order to eventually get them into our centers and our programs. This means having staff regularly attend student meetings, student-sponsored programs, and

TABLE 8.1
World Cultural Festival Marketing Budget

Item	Unit Cost	Number	Total
Advertising			
Student newspaper advertisement (1/2 page)	$668.00	3	$2,004
Banners (per sq. foot) posted externally on campus and within the student union	$400.00	2	$800
Publicity			
Handbills sent to all residential students (four handbills per sheet)	$0.04	1,913	$66.96
Flyers (black and white)	$0.04	500	$20.00
Flyers (color) posted in classroom buildings	$0.60	500	$360.00
Posters (12″ × 18″) posted in residence halls	$0.85	550	$467.50
Color easel posters (placed in seven residence halls and in the cultural center)	$55.00	8	$440.00
Facebook invitation	Free		
Listserv invitation	Free		
Letter to faculty and staff (sent to a mailing database of 300 faculty and staff members)	Free		
Campus TV public service announcement	Free		
Press release to student newspaper and local paper (pitch feature story)	Free		
Inclusion in student newsletters	Free		
Promotions			
Promotional items (t-shirts)	$5.00	50.00	$250.00
Visits to student organization meetings, mentoring groups, and classes	Free		
Total			**$4,408.46**

residence hall programs. Staff should also make regular appearances in class-rooms and at orientation sessions, welcome programs, and workshops sponsored by other departments. Because many campuses are large, complex structures, it can often be overwhelming to consider developing relationships with several units across campus. Approaching relationship building in a very strategic way by identifying the top five to ten campus departments to which the culture center should be connected and then dividing staff so that each individual serves as a liaison to two or three of these departments can make this a more manageable goal. Each year, culture center staff can add more departments or reexamine relationships to determine if changes to the list should be made. And remember, liaisons can also be graduate assistants and graduate interns, particularly if your office has a small staff. The key to developing liaisons is being strategic. It is important that you determine priorities regarding what relationships need to be built, which are already strong, and which existing ones require constant nurturing. Even with a large staff, our human resources can't be all things to all people. As a strategic leader, it is important for you to align relationships in a visionary way to enhance others' exposure to and awareness and support of your center.

Of course academic teaching remains one of the most important ways to gain regular exposure to students and to make them aware of the culture center. Teaching classes can offer opportunities for both personal relationship building and strategic academic support through the incorporation of culture center programs into the classroom experience. This provides students with very rich and diverse course experiences and greater awareness of their diverse campus resources. Each year, I teach a cultural leadership course in the African and African American studies department at my institution. Culture center programs are integrated into the course content and all students who have taken the course have continued to be involved with the culture center after completing the course.

Because culture centers are born out of the model of community culture centers in urban centers such as the District of Columbia, Detroit, Philadelphia, and Chicago, they are often viewed as both a campus and community resource (Jenkins & Walton, 2008). In order to create effective community programs, culture center staff, particularly directors, must be keyed into the national and international agendas of the cultural communities that they serve. This requires culture center staff to participate in conferences, symposia, and town hall meetings, outside higher education, such as the Congressional Black Caucus or the NAACP; attend national policy and political events; and establish relationships with national foundations. Because education is usually included on the national agenda of most underrepresented communities, it is vital that we interact with and hear from the community regarding their needs so that we can better serve them.

Outreach to Multiple Communities

During my tenure as Director of the Paul Robeson Center at Penn State University, one of our many community-building initiatives has been an annual summer newsletter to the parents of students of color. The *PRCC Parent Newsletter* was created to keep parents of color connected to the Penn State campus community and the cultural center. This mailing highlights PRCC programs and services and opportunities for student involvement and offers suggestions for parental support of college students of color. University alumni represent another important constituent community. Alumni outreach is essential for a variety of reasons. Alumni often serve as *griots*, the community historians, of the cultural center. They can remind us of those things that should not be changed and are an essential part of the culture center's history. They are also often the greatest supporters of necessary change and growth and can provide human and financial support for these efforts—their investment in the cultural center is often strong and personal. But most important, opportunities to interact with alumni provide current students with models and mentors who can motivate, inspire, and understand their experiences.

Sector II: Administrative Practices

It is necessary for student affairs professionals and their operations to foster both a physical and cultural environment that effectively meets student needs and ensures that all resources—both human and physical—are culturally sensitive. The environment that we create plays a major role in meeting students' needs. By ensuring that centers are physically structured to be of real use to students and encouraging staff in the center to establish a cultural environment of warmth and welcome, we recognize that culture is not only about celebration, ritual, and tradition but also about space, rootedness, and belonging. These administrative practices involve three areas of concentration: cultural environment creation, staff professional development, and institutional commitment.

Creating a Cultural Environment and Enhancing Facilities

Culture centers should consistently be reminded of their obligation to serve as a cultural safe space where students of color can see themselves reflected, embraced, and valued. Culture centers across the country range in size and scope from very small, one-office, one-person operations to very large organizations housed in multimillion-dollar buildings with several staff members. This makes establishing standards for practice somewhat difficult, as budget differences tend to mirror facility differences. In this chapter, we focus on models of practice. Therefore, with regards to space, we focus on the most ideal facility offerings for culture centers rather than the typical facility format. When we are planning for change or developing innovative strategies within a limited space, it is important to start from a model of excellence and challenge ourselves to determine how we can capture the essence of what is offered at model facilities regardless of our space constraints. For example, at our center, we have no viable space for intimate cultural programs. There is no space in the culture center that can accommodate an audience of 150. Rather than being limited by the constraints of our center, we have reconceptualized spaces like our library and used it for innovative programming and we have taken the essence of the culture center into residence halls and redecorated and transformed study lounges in the halls into warm and intimate cultural spaces for programs. Our presence is so great at these satellite events that students comment that they feel they are in the culture center itself.

Some of the most viable facilities around the country can be found at institutions like the University of North Carolina at Chapel Hill, Purdue University, Indiana University, and the University of Maryland. These culture centers are in fully functioning buildings that allow the scope of the centers to grow and transform beyond what students or the university might have envisioned 30 years ago when the centers were established. To clearly understand why adequate facilities are needed, we must first look closely at what the word "culture" means. Too often, in student affairs, "cultural services" are seen as any small space for students of color, a few programs, or a staff member dedicated to multicultural affairs—whatever that means. Hofstede (1997) provided a detailed definition of culture that illustrates the scope and complexity of this concept:

> Culture refers to the cumulative deposit of knowledge, experience, beliefs, values, attitudes, meanings, hierarchies, religion, notions of time, roles,

spatial relations, concepts of the universe, and material objects and possessions acquired by a group of people in the course of generations through individual and group striving. Culture is the systems of knowledge shared by a relatively large group of people. . . . Culture in its broadest sense is cultivated behavior; that is the totality of a person's learned, accumulated experience which is socially transmitted, or more briefly, behavior through social learning. . . . A culture is a way of life of a group of people—the behaviors, beliefs, values, and symbols that they accept, generally without thinking about them, and that are passed along by communication and imitation from one generation to the next. (p. 2)

The importance of culture centers' diverse practical outputs will be discussed later, but here it is important to understand that multiple programs, initiatives, and services are needed for a culture center to fully approach culture and to address the multiple belief systems, behavior patterns, social traditions and rituals, customs, histories, and habits of various ethnicities. To adequately provide such services, the best facilities offer lounge space for social gatherings, cultural libraries that both archive important cultural collections and allow patrons to study, offices for cultural student organizations, adequate storage space for cultural artifacts and props that are needed for events, dance studios in which cultural dance troupes can practice, classrooms/auditorium space allowing for innovative partnerships across academic and student affairs as well as weekend cultural classes for youths, multiple programming spaces to allow for both large-scale and intimate programs, sufficient administrative office space to allow for the growth of staff and the establishment of grant-funded positions (Fulbrights, graduate assistantships, etc.), conference rooms that provide culturally engaging meeting spaces, and up-to-date technology throughout the building to allow for programmatic approaches that appeal to the learning styles of today's college students. But it is not enough to just build an adequate facility. It is important for time to be devoted to renewing and upholding the legacy of providing a culturally stimulating space—that is, one that reflects students' cultural experiences, feels like home, and makes all feel immediately welcome.

Paramount to upholding this mission is ensuring that the facility houses visual images, written messages, physical spaces, and human resources that are culturally welcoming. To put this value into practice, cultural art exhibitions should be showcased in both formal and informal spaces. The old notion that art belongs in galleries should be challenged by creative approaches that place art where students are—in computer labs, social lounges, student organization offices, and even restrooms. Why miss an opportunity to expose students to art? All spaces in a culture center should be culturally welcoming. It does not seem to make sense to make lobbies and performance spaces culturally engaging but allow libraries and computer labs in the culture center to remain institutional. Those of us who know the joy of an urban cultural café where the walls are painted warm colors, ethnic art graces the walls, jazz or neo soul plays softly in the background, and crowds of college-age consumers work diligently for hours can recognize the importance of transforming the computer labs and social lounges in culture centers into more contemporary spaces that merge social, cultural, and work experiences. Our spaces should be ones in which students do not have to choose between these aspects of their lives.

Examining various definitions of culture can help us to understand this need for renewal. Hill Collins (1986) provided one of the most relevant definitions of culture as:

> the symbols and values that create the ideological frame of reference through which people attempt to deal with circumstances in which they find themselves. Culture . . . is not composed of static, discrete traits moved from one locale to another. It is constantly changing and transformed, as new forms are created out of old ones. Thus, culture . . . does not arise out of nothing: it is created and modified by material conditions. (p. S22)

Contemporary ethnic cultures include new values, habits, and behaviors that have emerged from old ones. The old saying "If it ain't broke, don't fix it" may not work with this population, as the culture center environment may not be broken—it may be outdated. Students, who live in a society where cell phones, PDAs, and computers become outdated every year, may not even attempt to use outdated college environments. Therefore, it is critical that professionals find creative ways to renovate, redecorate, and mix historical art in a contemporary context in their facilities. Exposing students to historical forms of cultural expression remains important, but it must be done in ways and in environments that are appealing. Students of color resist the institutional feel of spaces even in university culture centers. Therefore, our spaces must be renewed and transformed into contemporary and culturally vibrant environments.

Professional Development for Staff

A dedicated effort to increase the cultural knowledge of staff is another critical administrative issue. Staff must have expertise in three major areas in order to work effectively as cultural practitioners: college student development, cultural/ethnic studies, and program administration. In our chapter in Harper's *Creating Inclusive Campus Environments for Cross-Cultural Learning and Student Engagement,* we defined cultural practitioners as:

> those professionals that are charged with implementing cultural programs after the institution identifies the need for increased cultural experiences. These professionals put culture into practice—they transform it from a value or professional ethic into a living, physical experience. . . . Cultural practitioners are more than advisors. They go beyond the traditional role of student organization support resource and do the work of creating and implementing institutionally sponsored cultural programs. (Jenkins & Walton, 2008, p. 89)

It is important that as cultural practitioners, staff take seriously their role to educate and replicate cultural practices on college campuses. It is important not only to provide these opportunities, but to also ensure that they are authentic, deeply engaging, and institutionally impactful. Too often the institution relies on the outdated practice of depending on students to provide all cultural programs on campus. This is often disguised as student self-governance or agency. However, a culturally vibrant institution is one that offers multiple programs and initiatives planned by both students and the institution. On a campus that truly values diversity, there are never too many cultural offerings.

An Institutional Commitment

Culture centers should lead the charge on providing institutional cultural programs. Undoubtedly, our students have much to offer and share regarding their cultures. They also have much to learn. Many ethnic/racial minority students are educated in the same deficient educational systems as their White peers and come to college knowing very little about their cultural histories (Jenkins, 2003). Therefore, college is an opportunity for students to learn about others as well as themselves, and this learning can take place both inside and outside the classroom. Out-of-class learning can only be deeply meaningful if staff members develop their professional expertise and knowledge of the ethnicities and cultures that they serve. Professional development should focus on growing staff knowledge of the cultures and ethnicities of our students, understanding how issues of culture and race impact college student development, developing expertise in program implementation, including theory into cultural practice, planning events, and assessing programs. Institutional programs should be ones that are highly developed and intentional. Institutional events should be ones in which time, money, and expertise come together to create a highly complex, professionally planned, and deeply engaging cultural event. Institutional programs should not mirror student programs in scale, scope, complexity, or appearance. They should offer students a model for excellence in programming.

To achieve this, professionals must have a lifelong commitment to continued study through courses, reading, conferences, and international travel/ immersion trips. As the world becomes even more globally connected, general expectations of cultural knowledge among university staff have grown. In addition, we now serve an even greater number of international students and American students with study abroad experience, which makes it increasingly important for cultural practitioners to have international immersion experiences and firsthand exposure to the cultures of various ethnic communities. This can improve staff's ability to facilitate cultural immersion trips for students on their campuses. Such experiences should not be solely tied to credit-bearing courses—leadership initiatives, heritage month programs, and cultural history trips can all include a component of education abroad. This requires strong support and encouragement for such professional growth from the university. Gone are the days when a hardworking cultural practitioner was on campus all day—we should expect international experiences from cultural administrators. We must build upon and strengthen professional ties with universities in the native countries and continents of our students of color, including Africa, the West Indies, and South America. Such partnerships can provide greater knowledge for our professionals and greater experiences for our students.

Finally, customer service training is a critical administrative component of effectively managing a culture center. All staff from full-time workers to work study students should engage in ongoing customer service training, as warm and welcoming interactions comprise the essence of culture centers. The synergy of all components of the center, from engaging spaces to the

student centeredness of the staff, should foster an environment that is culturally attractive to students.

Sector III: Cultural Programming

This section describes the three major types of programming that should be
offered in culture centers and the viability of the development of multiple
initiatives in each of these three areas. The result is a portfolio that is diverse
and appeals to students with a variety of interests, learning styles, and developmental needs. I also offer examples of how I adapted this model as a
framework to guide the programs offered by the Paul Robeson Cultural Center at Penn State University. These examples illustrate how to translate the
philosophical concepts of cultural education, cultural engagement, and cultural development into practice.

Cultural Education Programs

Scholarly and cultural education programs integrate interdisciplinary study
and learning into creative cocurricular programming venues. Approaching cultural diversity from an academic context, these programs provide the entire
campus community with opportunities to engage in scholarship and interactive cultural learning outside the classroom. In addition, cultural education
initiatives include partnerships on K–16 curriculum transformation efforts and
educational change with regard to cultural education on a global level. At
Penn State's culture center, we have hosted several education programs,
including traditional lecture panels and brown bag presentations. However, as
we approached renewing our programming to meet the needs of contemporary college students, we have taken a different approach to education.

The Cultural Arts in Social Action Initiative

The Cultural Arts in Social Action Initiative was designed in response to the
growing need to develop both critical art consumers and performers in a
society dominated by popular culture. Many of America's youths are over-
whelmed by the media, film, magazines, and music videos, which influence
beliefs regarding what is an authentic representation of a population's culture. The project is driven by Maulana Karenga's theory of social artistic
responsibility. According to Karenga (1997), socially responsible artistic
expression must meet three qualifications: (1) it must be functional, possess-
ing the ability to address social issues, particularly those affecting oppressed
and marginalized communities; (2) it must be collective, representing the

fullness of the cultural experience of a people; and (3) it must be committed to offering a motivation for the realization of a people's true potential and active work against social limitations.

In recent years, spoken word has grown in popularity and become a major publicly accessible form of artistic expression. Through the many spoken word lounges in major cities, the HBO Def Poetry Series, and the numerous open-mic events on college campuses across the country, spoken word has become both popular and commercialized. However, as an art form, it continues to hold weight as an authentic grassroots means of social expression. Through spoken word, public and community-based artists are able to fully and honestly give voice to relevant local and global issues in ways not offered by traditional media venues. In the media, non-White racial groups remain underrepresented in terms of employment and are represented stereotypically and associated with violent crime across the programming spectrum from entertainment to the nightly news. It is important for consumers to understand that popular culture represents a major source of information on various cultures to audiences around the world (Noriega, 2001). In television dramas, male characters outnumber female 3:1, and in soap operas women are outnumbered 7:3. Even in children's television, males dominate by 70%–85% (Ingham, 1995). This makes leveraging access to more balanced art forms and ideas a priority for organizations that are dedicated to meaningful cultural production. For our nation to continue working toward its goal of becoming a truly open and democratic society, it is vital for future social leaders and artists to be encouraged to understand how the content of art and entertainment influences attitudes, beliefs, and ideas.

Specifically, some groups have become particularly concerned with the degrading ways in which communities of color are portrayed in popular media such as music and music videos. In response, several movements in higher education have surfaced to directly challenge such misrepresentations and to elevate the collegiate consumer market's expectations of art. One example is the Take Back the Music Campaign, sponsored by *Essence Magazine* and Spelman College. This campaign was initiated in an attempt to encourage critical discussion of these issues and exploration of the effects of these images (Take Back the Music Campaign, 2007). The Cultural Arts in Social Action Initiative seeks to join this critical conversation through exploration of a model educational experience that integrates popular forms of arts and intensive study on social issues with the goal of developing artistic content that is more reflective of cultural communities and that brings attention to relevant social issues. The outcomes will enhance both the experience of the audience in their consumption of art and the artists as they expand the scale and scope of their craft. The initiative involves several components:

1. Seminar meetings and arts workshops: The seminar brings together a small group of student artists (undergraduate and graduate) who are interested in engaging in the development of their poetry and musical skill sets. As part of an interactive program experience, students unite poetry/spoken word and music in joint complex performances that focus on critical contemporary social issues. Through weekly workshop trainings, the Cultural Arts and Social Action seminar concentrates on two critical areas of artistic development: (1) exploration of social issues of interest, transference of issues into artistic expression, and integration of multiple art forms into performance pieces (artistic content) and (2) performance and stage presence, exploration of personal styles, and improvisational skill building (artistic delivery). This contemporary approach to cultural arts is a great way to teach students about historical eras of socially conscious artistic expression such as the Black arts movement and the Harlem Renaissance.

2. Local and regional performances: The emerging student artists who participate in the Cultural Arts and Social Activism experience represent the potential of today's young artist to embody the community connectedness and social dedication of great artists such as the late Paul Robeson, for whom the culture center at Penn State is named. These students form a community-based performance group called Collective Energy. Collective Energy served as the headliner at the regular Bed Spoken Word Lounge on the University Park campus and also traveled to give performances at local schools, after-school programs, and other Penn State campuses. The group creatively introduced their collegiate peers as well as Pennsylvania communities to relevant social issues through the use of the arts.

3. Cultural Arts in Action Spring Break Initiative: Collective Energy established an online arts scholarship project in partnership with a similar group of student artists at the University of the West Indies (UWI), the Word Sound Power performance group within the Center for Creative Arts and Arts in Education Department. The students exchanged scholarly articles, news stories, and artifacts focused

on critical social problems, issues of social ethics, and histories of oppression in the United States and Trinidad. Both groups then transformed this scholarship into artistic performances. The groups came together in a Cultural Arts in Action Spring Break experience at the University of the West Indies in Trinidad. The spring break exchange and cultural immersion took place at the Center for Creative and Festival Arts at UWI. This is a dynamic academic-based initiative that focuses on developing and delivering interactive arts programs on relevant social issues for the local community. The UWI performance arts groups have performed internationally and received numerous national awards for their community involvement in Trinidad. This field experience provided Penn State students with a broader understanding of developing socially responsible art and creating community arts programs. In addition, it extended the reach of the artistic presentations of Penn State students to global audiences. Upon their return, students presented on the process of transforming research into artistic practice and shared examples at brown bag research presentations at the culture center at Penn State.

Cultural Engagement Programs

Cultural engagement programs provide opportunities for students, faculty, staff, and the community to experience the practice, celebration, and demonstration of culture. These programs serve to enhance the campus climate and social environment by providing opportunities for what Jeffrey Milem and Kenji Hakuta (2000) have called cultural and diversity interaction.

The World Cultural Festival

At the Paul Robeson Cultural Center, one of our many cultural engagement programs is the World Cultural Festival. The purpose of this campus-wide festival is threefold:

- To increase exposure to and understanding of global cultures
- To construct a vibrant celebration of multiculturalism and global diversity in the State College area
- To offer students, administration, faculty and staff, and the local community an opportunity to meet, to socially engage, and to be educationally stimulated

The festival includes a global bazaar experience with several tent displays across the HUB Lawn featuring cultural displays, educational posters, and artwork representing the five corners of the world; a We Are Penn State tent that features Penn State paraphernalia and university information; and cultural entertainment throughout the event. Students can relax on the grass and enjoy cultural performances on the main stage as well as music provided by a DJ.

Finally, the event features a Taste of the Diaspora featuring food samples from all over the world. Faculty and staff are invited to serve and interact with students. Staff and faculty members ranging from vice presidents and vice provosts to staff assistants volunteer to serve our students! This festival first took place on a smaller scale in the fall of 2005 and it now attracts about 2,000 students.

This initiative is logistically planned by the culture center with the help of a campus-wide planning committee. It is important to note that the program is widely supported, with over 20 campus departments cosponsoring it, including student affairs units and academic colleges.

Cultural Student Development Initiatives

Culturally based student development initiatives seek to creatively integrate cultural education, cultural theories, and cultural practice into college student development programs. By infusing social, historical, and contemporary issues affecting communities of color into culturally and communally engaged leadership and civic development opportunities, these programs offer a practical application of the theoretical ideals of the social change model of leadership (Higher Education Research Institute, 1996), Robert Greenleaf's Theory of Servant Leadership (1996), and contemporary perspectives on millennials, the hip hop generation, and leadership.

The Cultural Leadership Institute

The Cultural Leadership Institute was one of our primary cultural development initiatives. Cultural leadership fellows are introduced to the leadership models and practices of past leaders of color and provided with opportunities to explore current challenges faced by college students of color and current leadership needs of various cultural communities and to participate in leadership experiences outside the university. The program includes weekly course meetings; a cultural journey that allows students to immerse themselves in community-based culture; leadership participation in campus-based confer-ences; and cultural engagement through campus cultural events. Twenty cul-tural leadership fellows participate in this experience each year. Students who have participated in the program have indicated that the program gave them an increased understanding of their personal and cultural values, a better knowledge base of the contributions and practices of leaders of color as well as the principle of servant leadership, and more positive attitudes about maintaining or establishing close relationships with oppressed communities.

Assuming the Challenge of Cultural Practice

Cultural practice in university culture centers is a complex endeavor. Univer-sity culture centers see culture as the multidimensional experience that it is rather than treating it as a goal that can be accomplished through a few cele-brations and a major annual lecture. Creating a productive center that offers a rich variety of programs, services, and initiatives requires visionary, strate-gic, and intentional administrative leadership. It is undoubtedly hard work. However, the resulting presence of a dynamic and innovative culture center on campus can affect the entire campus community across all professional levels (students, faculty, staff) and all cultures, races, and ethnicities. The learning experience and campus climate are made better for all. What I am suggesting in this chapter is elevating the culture center's status so that it is viewed as a major institutional resource. To achieve this, innovation and dili-gent effort are required in conceptualizing programs, reaching out across the campus, marketing to all students rather than a small segment of the popula-tion, and developing a staff work ethic of competency and excellence. Keep-ing one's professional finger on the pulse of change management, professional development, facility management, customer service practices, and cultural program development allows the cultural life of the campus to remain vibrant and grow creatively.

References

Greenleaf, R. K. (1996). Part two: Essays on power, management and organizations. In D. M. Frick & L. C. Spears (Eds.), *Robert K. Greenleaf on becoming a servant-leader*. San Francisco, CA: Jossey-Bass.

Higher Education Research Institute. (1996). *A social change model of leadership development: Guidebook version III.* Los Angeles: Graduate School of Education and Information Studies, University of California.

Hill Collins, P. (1986). Learning from the outsider within: The sociological significance of Black feminist thought. *Social Problems, 33*(6), S14–S32.

Hofstede, G. (1997). *Cultures and organizations: Software of the mind.* New York: McGraw-Hill.

Ingham, H. (1995). *The portrayal of women on television.* Retrieved from http://www.aber.ac.uk/media/Students/hzi9401.html

Jenkins, T. (2003, May-June) The color of service. *About Campus, 8*(2), 30–32.

Jenkins, T., & Walton, C. (2005). Connecting culturally specific approaches to advising practices: A quick model for student affairs practice. *ACPA Interchange, 34*(2), 7–9.

Jenkins, T., & Walton, C. (2006). Setting the stage for character development through culturally specific advising practices. *Journal of College & Character, 2*(2), 1–6.

Jenkins, T., & Walton, C. (2008). Student affairs and cultural practice: A framework for implementing culture outside the classroom. In S. Harper (Ed.), *Creating inclusive campus environments for cross-cultural learning and student engagement* (pp. 87–101). Washington, DC: NASPA.

Karenga, M. (1997). African culture and the ongoing quest for excellence: Dialogue, principles, practice. *The Black Collegian,* pp. 160–163.

Kotler, P., & Armstrong, G. (1996). *Marketing: An introduction* (4th ed.). Upper Saddle River, NJ: Prentice Hall.

Milem, J., & Hakuta, K. (2000). The benefits of racial and ethnic diversity in higher education. In D. Wilds (Ed.), *Minorities in higher education, 1999–2000: Seventeenth annual status report* (pp. 39–67). Washington, DC: American Council on Education.

Noriega, C. (2001). Getting personal. *Aztlan: A Journal of Chicano Studies, 26*(2), 1–30

Strauss, W., & Howe, N. (2000). *Millennials rising: The next great generation.* New York: Vintage Books.

Take back the music campaign. (2007). *Essence Magazine.* Retrieved from http://www.essence.com/essence/takebackthemusic/about.html

9

CAMPUS CULTURE CENTER DIRECTORS' PERSPECTIVES ON ADVANCEMENT, CURRENT ISSUES, AND FUTURE DIRECTIONS

E. Michael Sutton and Phyllis McCluskey-Titus

Desmond Franklin currently serves as the associate dean of students and director of multicultural affairs at a predominantly White midsize institution in the Southeast. Although his professional title is associate dean of students, the majority of his time and effort is directed toward the academic and social success of ethnic/racial minority students at the institution. In particular, Desmond expends most of his energy ensuring the success of the culture centers on campus. Desmond's previous position as dean of students at a small historically Black institution in the Southeast provided him with some student affairs leadership experience in the areas of budgeting, supervision, and program development, but he felt his chances of securing a senior-level management position would be greater if he accepted the position as associate dean and director of multicultural affairs.

Prior to accepting the position, Desmond expressed to the vice-chancellor for student affairs his desire to enlarge his administrative responsibilities beyond the scope of ethnic/racial minority student concerns and programming, which would prepare him for a senior-level student affairs position. The vice-chancellor agreed to provide Desmond with additional responsibilities that not only would enhance his administrative skills in the areas of finance and supervision but would increase his visibility as a promising administrator in areas beyond the domain of multicultural services.

Although Desmond has provided outstanding service as director of multicultural affairs, he fears that the primary responsibilities of the position—namely, ethnic/racial minority student advising, programming, and recruitment—are not preparing him for his next student affairs position. He is afraid that if he continues in his current position another year, he will become professionally typecast in multicultural affairs and will be unable to transition to a senior-level generalist position.

As ethnic/racial minority student populations continue to increase on predominantly White and historically Black campuses, multicultural affairs and culture center (MACC) professionals are often perceived solely as advocates for racial and cultural parity. These professionals are responsible for educating the campus about the issues of underrepresented students through programming and research (Association of College Unions International, 2008; Birmingham-Southern College, 2006; HigherEdJobs .com, 2008). Professionals in MACCs help recruit and retain students from underrepresented backgrounds, help resolve and manage conflict, and serve as resources and consultants on matters related to underrepresented students (Birmingham-Southern College, 2006; HigherEdJobs.com, 2008). In addition, these professionals also serve as mentors and advocates for underrepresented students by offering leadership training and personal and career counseling, and by advising student affinity groups (HigherEdJobs.com, 2008; Western Michigan University, n.d.).

The first MACC professionals helped African American students adjust academically and socially on predominantly White campuses (Pounds, 1987; Siggelkow, 1991). As African American student enrollment increased on predominantly White campuses during the late sixties and early seventies, these professionals became responsible for serving racial and ethnic minority student groups (Latinas/os, Asian Americans, Native Americans) and for handling issues such as recruitment and retention and advising related affinity groups (Palmer & Shuford, 1996, p. 233). This resulted in marginal interaction between multicultural affairs professional staff (who may or may not be members of ethnic/racial minority groups themselves) and the non-minority student population. Furthermore, these circumscribed responsibilities provided little or no opportunity for MACC professionals to gain budgetary, planning, and supervisory experience, which is essential to securing middle and senior management positions in student affairs. In essence, the premier factor resulting in career typecasting of MACC directors is the accentuation of departmental rather than division-wide administrative experience. This chapter describes the valuable and beneficial services that individuals in this position provide and how, in spite of this, these professionals are often unable to secure more senior-level generalist positions in student affairs administration as a result of career typecasting. In addition, the chapter addresses how factors such as covert institutional racism and lack of investment in career development exacerbate the professional development of these individuals. The chapter concludes with practical strategies for minimizing this phenomenon among multicultural affairs professionals.

Benefits Provided by Multicultural Affairs Professionals

Ethnic/racial minority students attending predominantly White institutions greatly benefit from the presence of MACC professionals. In addition to serving as mentors and advocates for their student constituents, these individuals also assist in ethnic/racial minority student recruitment and retention initiatives, ensure ideas are brought forward for consideration when policy or hiring decisions are made, and help sustain the integrity of the academic experience for underrepresented students (Hefner, 2002). In conjunction with their advocacy role, these professionals provide initial leadership experiences for ethnic/racial minority students outside traditional campus organizations. According to Sutton and Terrell (1997), campus organizations that are advised by multicultural affairs professionals, such as Black student unions, Latina/o business associations, and gospel choirs, develop ethnic/racial minority students' organizational and planning skills, allowing them to assume leadership roles in other traditional campus organizations. As campus populations have diversified, so have the roles of MACC professionals. Now many offices offer support not only to ethnic/racial minority groups but also to lesbian, gay, bisexual, and transgender students, women, students with disabilities, and international students. This gives professionals in multicultural affairs the opportunity to interact with a variety of students considered to be members of underrepresented or marginalized student groups on predominantly White campuses.

Career Typecasting of Multicultural Affairs Professionals

Career typecasting occurs when promotional opportunities are not provided to an employee because the employee is perceived as having the ability to perform only the job for which he or she was hired or does the job so well that it would be a major loss to the campus should he or she decide to move on. The MACC professional becomes an invaluable resource that the institution is unwilling to replace. This phenomenon is typified by four definitive factors: (1) extremely specialized job responsibilities, (2) an organization's overdependency on an employee's skills, (3) pigeonholing of the employee, or perceptions that the employee is only capable of performing the job for which he or she was hired, and (4) career plateauing (Mainiero, 1990).

Extremely Specialized Job Responsibilities

The narrow and specialized functions of MACC offices such as retention and recruitment of ethnic/racial minority students, minority programming, and diversity education (outlined in Table 9.1) often marginalize these professionals and prevent them from developing other administrative skills beyond those that relate primarily to diversity issues or concerns. Carreathers (1996) suggested that these responsibilities limit interactions with non-minority students, which can be seen as a limitation when these professionals try to obtain higher-level more generalist positions.

TABLE 9.1
Major Potential Functions of a Multicultural Affairs Office

Function	Percentage of multicultural offices responsible for this function
Retention of ethnic/racial minority students	43
Programming	42
Diversity education	29
Leadership development	29
Ethnic/racial minority student recruitment	14

These findings were validated by Sagaria and Johnsrud (1991) and Mainiero (1990), who indicated that the responsibilities of MACC professionals are extremely specialized to a specific student population, which exacerbates career typecasting of these professionals. While the lack of varied administrative responsibilities may be the primary element contributing to career typecasting of MACC professionals, this phenomenon can be exacerbated when an institution relies heavily on the skills of these employees.

Overdependence on the Skills of the Multicultural Affairs Professional

A perception held by most campus administrators is that the concerns of ethnic/racial minority students should be the sole responsibility of the MACC professional. Such an expectation, according to Spotts (1991), not only reinforces career typecasting of these professionals but also, and more importantly, releases other campus administrators from their responsibility to work closely with ethnic/racial minority students. Although MACC professionals' positions cause them to assume institutional leadership for achieving ethnic/racial minority student retention goals, for instance, caution should be exercised to prevent other institutional staff from ignoring their professional responsibilities to underrepresented students. When this occurs, the institution develops an even greater dependency on MACC professionals for the implementation of these and other university goals regarding underrepresented students.

Although institutional personnel may unconsciously expect MACC professionals to resolve issues and concerns related to ethnic/racial minority students, it is apparent that campus administrators at all levels rely heavily upon the liaison role of these professionals when ethnic/racial minority students express dissatisfaction with institutional issues or during incidents of racial tension on campus. According to Sutton (1998), this was the primary role of many MACC professionals during the late 1960s. However, as the MACC director position has evolved, these professionals now not only manage sensitive racial issues but have gained enormous power with both student and professional constituencies. For example, multicultural professionals' referent power is often a result of the position's close identification with the president of the institution or the endorsement and support of the community's ethnic/racial minority political organizations such as the NAACP or Urban League. On the other hand, multicultural professionals' expert power is largely attributed to their knowledge of their student constituency and the trust established between university colleagues and the underrepresented student community on campus. Despite these attributes, some members of the campus community perceive MACC professionals as confrontational, biased, and not invested in the overall goals of the institution. This was evident at Cleveland State University, where the strategies and methods used by the director of multicultural affairs were characterized as being too antagonistic and hostile when he attempted to achieve the institution's diversity objectives (Leatherman, 1990).

Despite their ability to encourage cultural understanding and ease racial misunderstanding, it is possible for the careers of multicultural affairs professionals to plateau as a result of their success, and also because others lack skill or interest in performing their position responsibilities. When this occurs, multicultural affairs staff are forced to move laterally into other MACC positions rather than into higher-level senior staff positions in student affairs.

The concept of plateauing is commonly viewed as a result of the hierarchical structure found in most higher education organizations. For example Allen, Poteet, and Russell (1998) and Tan and Salomone (1994) suggested that the hierarchical design of many organizations, along with specialized job functions, inhibits vertical advancement for many staff members. Bardwick (1986) stated that job plateauing often occurs when an individual is no longer challenged by his or her job responsibilities. Even more relevant to this chapter are the findings of Greenhaus, Parasuraman, and Wormley (as cited in Allen et al., 1998), who suggested that African Americans are likely to plateau earlier in their careers than their White counterparts. Although it is unlikely that the hierarchical organizational structure of most student affairs organizations will change, presidents or chancellors and senior student affairs officers can ensure that these MACC positions are elevated within the administrative hierarchy and that their responsibilities are expanded so they can have an impact on institutional policies addressing equity and compliance, multiculturalism, and academic diversity concerns (Banerji, 2005). Engagement in a broader spectrum of institution-wide job functions such as policy development, planning, and fund-raising, as well as supervision of other professionals, can help MACC directors broaden their impact and develop skills allowing them to advance within the institutional hierarchy.

Traits Perceived by the Employer as Important to the Position

Career typecasting is also likely to occur when a candidate possesses traits that a supervisor perceives to be important or critical to the position or to the campus, or when the applicant has held similar responsibilities in previous positions. Hiring officials should be aware of possible biases against individuals with more specific or focused job skills, such as MACC directors, rather than broader generalist experiences when considering applicants for senior-level positions in student affairs. Employment based on completion of the responsibilities of the higher-level position does not necessarily provide opportunities for a candidate's professional development and may result in stagnation.

Conversely, career typecasting minimizes the creative insights that could be brought to the position by a different type of person with less experience in the new job. Innovative hiring for senior student affairs officers on campus without prior generalist responsibilities may initially require more direction and training from the president, but the payoff may be an invigorated work environment (Dunham & Freeman, 2000). While professional typecasting is a factor that can impede career advancement among MACC professionals, it is one of several salient components of institutional racism that contribute to the glass ceiling effect perceived by professionals in MACC positions.

Institutional Racism as a Factor in the Typecasting of Multicultural Affairs Professionals

Professional typecasting among MACC professionals can be attributed to minimal opportunities for career advancement resulting from the expertise demonstrated in the position, desire not to lose the campus expert on issues related to underrepresented students, or the perception that this person's skills are not broad enough for senior-level student affairs positions; however, the problem is exacerbated by institutional racism. Gill (1989) stated that race-based discrimination occurs as a result of prejudice, lack of information, and power. Whether real or perceived, racism as well as affirmative action legislation may be perceived as real barriers to the career advancement of MACC professionals who are members of ethnic/racial minority groups (Luzzo & McWhirter, 2001).

According to Johnson (1997), some campus administrators fail to promote ethnic/racial minority professionals to higher senior-level positions because of the perception that these individuals were hired only as a result of affirmative action legislation and are therefore unqualified. These organizations, according to Corsun and Costen (2001), have chosen to take an assimilationist position: the number of ethnic/racial minority staff on campus is important, but the organization does not truly value the multiple perspectives brought to the workplace by persons with different cultural backgrounds and life experiences. Although having an underrepresented professional in a position requiring him or her to work with ethnic/racial minority students is acceptable, and in some cases expected, hiring a senior-level staff member of color may not be.

Other organizations have adopted more of an access-and-legitimacy paradigm, in which individual differences are accepted and celebrated because of the diversity of the population of students served on campus (Thomas & Ely, 1996). These institutions hire professionals whose backgrounds mirror the racial/ethnic backgrounds of the campus community. In this case, affirmative action is supported because qualified staff members who look like the students on campus are hired and the institutional culture supports their value and worth. Although this may be a valid perception, Schmidt (2006) and Fleming (1984) advised that ethnic/racial minority professionals can reduce the impact of institutional racism by actively serving and providing leadership in various capacities throughout the institution. It is highly unlikely that ethnic/racial minority professionals will advance beyond traditional roles in the absence of a commitment to ethnic and cultural diversity by the institution's senior administrators and governing board that is reflected in institutional policies (Auletta & Jones, 1990; Banerji, 2005; Michael & Thompson, 1995; Ponterotto, 1990). Such policies are reflective of a society that is educated on the issues of race and ethnicity and does not blatantly or openly discriminate but still practices a subtle form of racism where equity and equality appear to exist, but discrimination is still prevalent (Brief & Buttram, 1997).

This covert racism can manifest itself in the unconscious segregation of ethnic/racial minority employees, with ethnic/racial minority supervisors in MACC positions, and with vague justifications for poor evaluations or failure to achieve promotions because of a lack of fit, or the absence of specific traits or attributes such as the ability to adjust, type of work ethic, or discomfort around ethnic/racial minority students or staff members (Brief & Buttram, 1997). Barnard, as early as 1938, found that this informal and sometimes unconscious discrimination occurs because companies select and promote people who are compatible with or like those already in management positions (p. 225). Despite the fact that institutional change occurs slowly, senior administrators can break the cycle of oppression by providing MACC professionals with opportunities for valuable learning experiences that will help them successfully make the transition to senior-level student affairs positions.

While institutional racism is a factor in multicultural professionals' inability to attain significant administrative positions, it is an issue that can be overcome through mentoring by seasoned professionals. In addition, methods unfamiliar to higher education such as job enlargement and enrichment may also provide solutions to assist these professionals in obtaining the skills needed to advance in their student affairs careers.

Lessening the Effect of Career Typecasting of Multicultural Affairs Professionals: Recommendations for Practice

A variety of different career development activities can help MACC professionals avoid being typecast or pigeonholed in roles as the campus experts and advocates for ethnic/racial minority students and can help them move into senior-level student affairs positions. These activities include mentoring by senior-level professionals, enhancement of skills that are not necessarily developed by individuals in MACC positions, job enlargement techniques, professional development activities, roles at the campus level that involve increased decision making, and the solicitation of feedback.

Mentoring

The process of mentoring is complex and involves a senior-level mentor providing support, assistance, and guidance to a protégé (Bey & Holmes, 1992). Howard-Hamilton (1990), Williams (1989–1990), and Fleming (as cited in Weber, 1992) suggested that mentoring and role modeling are frequently discussed in relation to career mobility among MACC professionals. The opportunity to share common interests with colleagues and build networks outside issues of multiculturalism (Cooper & Miller, 1998) can certainly help transform their professional image of specialist to that of generalist, thus creating greater opportunities to procure more senior-level administrative positions in student affairs.

In the optimal relationship, mentoring can be highly rewarding and satisfying. Hunt and Michael (1983) stated that "professionals who were mentored themselves are likely to become mentors of succeeding generations of professionals" (p. 12). This is often the case in relationships between MACC professionals and ethnic/racial minority students, who expect these professionals not only to be empathetic to their academic and cultural issues but also, more importantly, to provide them with emotional and moral support during their college years. Unfortunately, mentoring ethnic/racial minority students usually falls to the MACC professional as a result of the paucity of ethnic/racial minority faculty and staff mentors. This can become extremely time consuming, presenting yet another professional development challenge. As a result, MACC professionals are often placed in positions requiring them to give of themselves but fail to receive the valuable professional or personal mentoring needed for their own career advancement.

A lack of mentoring may be one of the reasons there are fewer advancement opportunities for minority affairs professionals. Johnson (1997) indicated that mentors can help new professionals feel comfortable in senior-level positions by socializing them to the culture. Because there are fewer minority affairs professionals in higher-level positions and their access to resources and career advancement opportunities is limited, opportunities to mentor other staff may also be limited (Corsun & Costen, 2001; Kanter, 1979). Therefore it is likely that ethnic/racial minorities or professionals with minority affairs work experience would not serve as mentors for minority affairs professionals. In fact, because non-minority professionals with other types of student affairs backgrounds serve as the gatekeepers in many selection processes, it might be most beneficial to choose a mentor who is not a member of an ethnic/racial minority group (Johnson, 1997) or one who has not served in an MACC position. This proves difficult, however, as the overall context of social and professional behavior is different for ethnic/racial minorities and has an impact on how professionals who are members of underrepresented groups use networks and the value they accord them (Ibarra, 1993). For instance, ethnic/racial minority professionals are less likely than Whites to belong to professional associations and organizations that offer job placement or information about positions (Edley, 1996; Mosely, 1996).

Desmond recognizes the value of having a strong mentor and believes
that the skills and reputation of the vice-chancellor for student affairs

can help him advance professionally. He has already had conversations with his vice-chancellor about his desire to be a senior student affairs officer, and so he asks if she would be willing to serve as a mentor to him.

Skill Development

Aside from the issue of mentoring, the staffing patterns of many MACC offices usually require these professionals to juggle various roles, including those of administrator, advisor, programmer, assessment expert, and campus consultant. As a result, these individuals are called upon to assume more responsibilities and tasks related to ethnic/racial minority student issues, whereas other generalist office skills such as supervision and managing budgetary issues are more likely to enhance potential for promotion. Carreathers (1996) found that 25% of the MACC offices affiliated with SACSA (Southern Association for College Student Affairs organization) were staffed by only one person. One solution could be to divide office responsibilities among a group of other student affairs professionals or delegate specific tasks to a wider range of staff members throughout the student affairs division. This not only will provide the MACC professional with an opportunity to broaden his her administrative experiences and offer needed assistance to one-person MACC offices but will offer opportunities for other student affairs staff to work with ethnic/racial minority students and get away from the mind-set that only MACC professionals can support or advise underrepresented students (Johnson, 1997).

> *Desmond recognizes that he cannot effectively manage his office and obtain the skills he needs to be selected as a senior student affairs officer. He approaches the director of residential life to propose that the five hall directors each provide leadership for the programming during one of the cultural heritage months (Hispanic Heritage, Black History, Women's Herstory, Native American Culture, Asian Awareness). This will give the housing staff some additional programming and advising experience and offer them the opportunity to work with a more racially diverse group of students.*

Job Enlargement

Job enlargement describes how one employee's responsibilities can be expanded to include tasks performed previously by others (Grensing, 1996;

Moorehead & Griffin, 1989). When other staff members are working cooper-atively with MACC professionals to assist in that office, this allows the MACC director the opportunity to become involved in other areas of stu-dent affairs. The MACC professional's tasks can be expanded horizontally to include supervision of professionals in other areas, budget responsibility, and policy making. For example, the responsibility for ethnic/racial minority recruitment and retention is commonly associated with MACC profession-als. Enlarging that responsibility to include other student subcultures such as first-generation students, nontraditional-age students, and transfer students can offer the MACC professional a broader look at the recruitment and retention functions of campus administrators. If senior administrators wish to use this method to broaden the careers of MACC professionals, it is imperative that the reassigned responsibilities enlarge employees' perspec-tives of the institution beyond the scope of multiculturalism. In other words, job enlargement should never be a means to an end of broadening a staff member's career without enlarging his or her perspective of the larger mis-sion and goals of the institution. For example, senior student affairs adminis-trators were challenged by Patten (1977) to make the responsibilities of MACC professionals more psychologically attractive in order to help these staff members develop a variety of skills, resulting in increased expertise in many areas. Moreover, developing a variety of skills and performing a variety of tasks outside multicultural affairs can enrich and broaden the profession-al's perspective and keep him or her from becoming typecast in a single staff role. Donaldson (1975) suggested that changing the content of professional responsibilities to optimize organizational effectiveness can prevent monot-ony and burnout.

> *The vice-chancellor for student affairs, in her role as mentor, recognizes Desmond's abilities in managing his small programming budget. She invites Desmond to work with her in the divisional budget process so he can see a more macro-level perspective on budgeting. In addition, she recommends that he assist the new director of service and leadership in preparing her budget request for the next year.*

Job Enrichment

Unlike job enlargement, which expands a person's role into related areas, job enrichment focuses on increasing the minority affairs professional's influence over how tasks are completed rather than adding tasks to his or her workload (Hackman & Oldham, 1975). This process of enrichment commonly involves encouraging employees to utilize their own judgment in making decisions about their work, receiving regular evaluations or feedback concerning their performance, and participating in the planning, goal-setting, and problem-solving processes of the division or the institution with their supervisor. The literature provides some valuable insight into how job enrichment can enhance the careers of professionals such as multicultural affairs directors. For example, Niehoff, Moorman, Blakely, and Fuller (2001) attributed employee loyalty to job enrichment, particularly in times of institutional downsizing. They suggested that staff members are less likely to leave their positions in times of economic hardship when their supervisors entrust them to exert control in their job settings.

Staff members who feel that they have more autonomy to make decisions perform at higher levels than those who do not perceive that they have as much autonomy. Catanzaro (1997) suggested that the elements of job enrichment (increased variety of tasks, increased autonomy, and feedback) are beneficial in motivating students to learn. When the supervisory role is viewed as a teacher-student relationship, staff motivation through job enrichment is validated. Similar to Catanzaro's study, the results of a study by Frase (1989) revealed that the intrinsic reward of professional travel resulted in greater teacher motivation than the extrinsic motivator of higher salaries. One should not misinterpret this as meaning that intrinsic rewards alone should compensate for inadequate employee compensation but rather this should suggest that when the nature of the job encourages minority affairs staff to expand their influence and direction within the institution, compensation alone is not a major factor in their doing so. Moreover, intrinsic rewards such as responsibility for decision making and autonomy in doing so also strengthen employees' confidence to assume broader and more challenging responsibilities, which ultimately improves their performance (Barling & Beattie, 1983). Supervisors may find it helpful to keep this in mind as they strive to prepare staff in MACC positions to assume senior-level staff roles in student affairs.

The principles of job enrichment and job enlargement certainly serve to prepare MACC professionals for higher-level positions in colleges and universities. Engaging in these activities is one way to discredit the practice of career typecasting, because it allows employees to develop the specific job skills that they need to advance, but more important, campus administrators must recognize the complete potential of these professionals and invest in their career development.

> *Desmond has traditionally worked closely with the dean of students on the planning and execution of the recruitment weekend for underrepresented students admitted to the university. After a discussion with the vice-chancellor, the dean allows Desmond to assume full responsibility for the weekend activities and the associated budget. This enhanced responsibility allows Desmond to be more visible to senior-level staff on campus and to develop stronger working relationships across campus than his position in multicultural affairs allowed him.*

Feedback

It is important that the supervisor provide the MACC director with timely and specific feedback when he or she assumes challenging and unfamiliar tasks, as with job enrichment or enlargement, and to remember that feedback does not need to be positive in order to be effective. In fact, constructive feedback can be motivating, as it challenges the staff person to reach his or her maximum potential. Furthermore, appropriate feedback indicates not only that a supervisor is attentive to the MACC director's performance but that he or she is committed to the professional growth and advancement of that staff member. By incorporating the objectives of job enlargement, supervisors and MACC professionals alike can modify tasks that are monotonous or unfulfilling as well as increase the visibility and validation of the position beyond the current scope. Lastly, job enrichment empowers the professional with the authority to evaluate his or her own professional and career objectives and further develop skills in areas where he or she has less expertise.

Investing in the Career Development of Multicultural Affairs Professionals

Institutional professional development sessions provide employees with an opportunity not only to enhance their skills but also to become knowledgeable about contemporary professional issues. Staff members who are satisfied with their work will help the institution meet higher-level goals when they are encouraged to participate in professional development activities (Zeiss, 1990). Although many student affairs professionals are cognizant of the benefits of in-service workshops and conference attendance, their demanding administrative and student advisory responsibilities may limit their participation. If short-term training workshops and conference attendance are not serving as professional career enhancement for MACC professionals, how can promotional opportunities for these professionals be structured? There are three methods of career enhancement that may be effective with MACC professionals whose jobs do not allow them sufficient time to engage in necessary in-service training: internships, sabbaticals, and continuing education. All three of these enhancements are longer and may be more conducive to a multicultural professional's unique career development needs than short-term one-time training sessions.

Internships are extended opportunities for professionals to obtain new skills and develop expertise in other administrative areas of the university. A semester- or yearlong internship with the student affairs vice president or other senior-level staff member can help an MACC professional develop significant and relevant competencies in areas such as supervision, university politics, fund-raising, and research. The decision to work in another office on campus also affords different mentoring and networking opportunities and a chance to get a new perspective on the needs of ethnic/racial minority students from the vantage point of others. Working in another office or at another campus can serve as a "vacation" and offer a different perspective, as well as a sense of accomplishment.

In addition to internships, sabbaticals are another professional career development option for MACC professionals. Although sabbaticals are generally associated with faculty, administrative staff can use the semester or academic year to conduct research, travel, write for publication, and take advantage of targeted workshops or conferences to sharpen or build needed skills. Time away from the job on a sabbatical should be carefully planned so that career development goals can be realized, but this is an effective and refreshing opportunity to prepare oneself for career advancement. Particularly when paired with strong mentoring, these longer-term learning opportunities can offer substantial growth experience for the MACC professional.

Finally, continuing education culminating in a terminal degree or an additional degree or certificate supporting an individual's career goals can enhance the MACC professional's chances of being promoted. A terminal, advanced, or professional degree in a different area of specialization such as finance, management, or law might be worth the investment of time and energy. Academic programs can be a very rewarding method of career development for four reasons. First, the subject matter can be stimulating and challenging. It can be satisfying to return to the classroom and be inspired by a whole new academic program and way of looking at the world of student affairs. Second, the other students in the program can provide new resources and support. Hearing about the backgrounds and work experiences of other students can introduce a variety of options for practice on a college campus. In addition, these new student colleagues may be able to provide assistance with programs, serve as mentors for students, or be a source of funding, if needed. Third, the class material may provide a different perspective allowing the MACC professional to resolve old problems or situations. Examining a retention problem using a marketing approach or a legal approach may provide insight never before imagined. Fourth, one gains the skills necessary to advance to a higher-level position while in the academic program. Every class taken or new degree earned will provide one less obstacle toward attainment of a more senior position in student affairs.

> *Desmond, in one of his mentoring meetings with the vice-chancellor, asked about what would happen when the associate vice-chancellor was away on maternity leave during the summer. Because the summer semester was a time when there were fewer students on campus, and much of the summer was devoted to planning, he and the vice-chancellor worked out an arrangement whereby Desmond would work mornings in the vice-chancellor's office, and the director of career services would work afternoons. Between the two of them, they assumed responsibility for the associate vice-chancellor's supervisory and planning duties, as well as campus crisis on-call duty, and each was able to gain valuable experience that would assist them in moving to more senior-level positions.*

Conclusion

While the phenomenon of typecasting is commonly associated with professional actors, the concept has serious implications for MACC professionals, whose responsibilities are viewed as narrowly focused and specialized. Despite the rhetoric of campus administrators regarding the desire to increase underrepresented staff in positions of influence and authority, the fact remains that MACC professionals hold mid-level positions that service a unique student population. Job enlargement and enrichment will be necessary for MACC professionals to successfully procure and advance to senior-level managerial roles within the student affairs profession. It is likely that employees' skills and career options will be strengthened as a result of intentionally planned job enrichment and professional development activities. Such experiences not only expand the breadth and depth of employees' understanding of the organization but also are likely to heighten their self-efficacy to seek career options outside MACC offices. While internships, sabbaticals, and continuing education are not frequently utilized in the arena of higher education, they can be quite valuable in eradicating career typecasting of multicultural professionals.

The research conducted by Reesor (1998) also suggested that mentoring benefits young professionals in the area of career advancement. These informal networks provide the mid-level professional with valuable skills and knowledge that an actual job rarely provides. Because the success of mentoring depends largely on the willing participation of a seasoned professional, it is likely that some MACC professionals may have to identify alternative options to avoid becoming victims of typecasting or pigeonholing. In essence, MACC professionals are ultimately responsible for their own professional development and should not become dependent on other campus administrators to prevent typecasting from occurring.

References

Allen, T. D., Poteet, M. L., & Russell, J. E. A. (1998). Attitudes of managers who are more or less career plateaued. *Career Development Quarterly, 47*(2), 159–172.

Association of College Unions International. (2008). *Job description: Assistant director for diversity and multicultural affairs.* Retrieved from http://www.acui.org/content.aspx?menu_id = 188&id = 3202

Auletta, G. S., & Jones, T. (1990). Reconstituting the inner circle. *American Behavioral Scientist, 34*(2), 137–152.

Banerji, S. (2005). Diversity officers—Coming to a campus near you? *Diverse: Issues in Higher Education, 22*(20), 1–5.

Bardwick, J. M. (1986). The plateauing trap, part 2: Setting employees free. *Personnel, 63*(11), 35–40.

Barling, J., & Beattie, R. (1983). Self-efficacy beliefs and sales performance. *Journal of Organizational Behavior Management, 5,* 41–51.

Barnard, C. (1938). *The functions of the executive.* Cambridge, MA: Harvard University Press.

Bey, T. M., & Holmes, C. T. (Eds.). (1992). *Mentoring: Contemporary principles and issues.* Reston, VA: Association of Teacher Educators.

Birmingham-Southern College. (2006). *Director of multicultural affairs.* Retrieved from http://www.bsc.edu/administration/humanresources/performanceevaluation/eval/job-descriptions/Student-Affairs/Multicultural%20Affairs/Dir-Multicultural%20Aff airs.pdf

Brief, A. P., & Buttram, R. T. (1997). Beyond good intentions: The next steps toward racial equality in the American workplace. *Academy of Management Executive, 11*(4), 59–73.

Carreathers, K. (1996, November). *Exploring the need to establish professional standards for the minority affairs profession.* Paper presented at the meeting of the Southern Association of College Student Affairs, Mobile, AL.

Catanzaro, D. (1997). Course enrichment and the job characteristics model. *Teaching of Psychology, 24*(2), 85–87.

Cooper, D., & Miller, T. (1998). Influence and impact: Professional development in student affairs. In W. A. Bryan & R. A. Schwartz (Eds.), *Personal and professional development in the 21st century* (New Directions for Student Services No. 84, pp. 55–69). San Francisco: Jossey-Bass.

Corsun, D. L., & Costen, W. M. (2001). Is the glass ceiling unbreakable? Habitus, fields, and the stalling of women and minorities in management. *Journal of Management Inquiry, 10*(1), 16–26.

Donaldson, L. (1975). Job enlargement: A multidimensional process. *Human Relations, 28*(7), 593–610.

Dunham, L., & Freeman, R. E. (2000). Leadership lessons from the theatre. *Organizational Dynamics, 29*(2), 108–123.

Edley, C. (1996). *Not all Black and White: Affirmative action, race, and American values.* New York: Hill and Wang.

Fleming, J. (1984). *Blacks in college: A comparative study of students' success in Black and in White institutions.* San Francisco: Jossey-Bass.

Frase, L. E. (1989). Effects of teacher rewards and recognition and job enrichment. *Journal of Educational Research, 83*(1), 52–56.

Gill, A. M. (1989). The role of discrimination in determining occupational structure. *Industrial and Labor Relations Review, 42*(4), 610–623.

Grensing, L. (1996). When the carrot can't be cash. *Security Management, 40*(12), 25–27.

Hackman, J. R., & Oldham, G. R. (1975). Development of the job diagnostic survey. *Journal of Applied Psychology, 60*, 159–170.

Hefner, D. (2002). Black cultural centers: Standing on shaky ground? *Black Issues in Higher Education, 18*(26), 22–29.

HigherEdJobs.com (2008). Retrieved from http://www.higheredjobs.com/admin/details.cfm?JobCode = 175293529

Howard-Hamilton, M. (1990). Ten tenets I would impart to African-American scholars. In C. A. Taylor (Ed.), *The second handbook of minority student services* (pp. 161–166). Madison, WI: Praxis.

Hunt, D. M., & Michael, C. (1983). Mentorship: A training and development tool. *Academy of Management Review, 8*(3), 475–485.

Ibarra, H. (1993). Personal networks of women and minorities in management: A conceptual framework. *Academy of Management Review, 18*(1), 56–87.

Johnson, W. J. (1997). Minority faculty: Are we welcome on campus? *Thought and Action, 13*(2), 113–124.

Kanter, R. M. (1979). Differential access to opportunity and power. In R. Alvarez (Ed.), *Discrimination in organizations: Using social indicators to manage social change* (pp. 52–68). San Francisco: Jossey-Bass.

Leatherman, C. (1990, September 12). Turmoil at Cleveland State over Black administrator's departure focuses attention on issues facing minority-affairs officials. *The Chronicle of Higher Education*, pp. A17–A18.

Luzzo, D. A., & McWhirter, E. H. (2001). Sex and ethnic differences in the perception of educational and career-related barriers and levels of coping efficacy. *Journal of Counseling & Development, 79*(1), 61–67.

Mainiero, L. A. (1990). The typecasting trap. *Training & Development Journal, 44*(3), 83–86.

Michael, S. O., & Thompson, M. D. (1995). Multiculturalism in higher education: Transcending the familiar zone. *Journal for Higher Education Management, 11*(1), 31–49.

Moorehead, G., & Griffin, R. W. (1989). *Organizational behavior.* Boston: Houghton Mifflin.

Moseley, A. (1996). Affirmative action: Pro. In A. Mosley & N. Capaldi (Eds.), *Affirmative action: Social justice or unfair preference?* (pp. 1–64). Lanham, MD: Rowman & Littlefield.

Niehoff, B. P., Moorman, R. H., Blakely, G., & Fuller, J. (2001). The influence of empowerment and job enrichment on employee loyalty in a downsizing environment. *Group & Organization Management, 26*(1), 93–113.

Palmer, C. J., & Shuford, B. C. (1996). Multicultural affairs. In A. L. Rentz & Associates (Eds.), *Student affairs practice in higher education* (2nd ed., pp. 214–237). Springfield, IL: Charles C Thomas.

Patten, T. H., Jr. (1977). Job evaluation and job enlargement: A collision course? *Human Resource Management, 16*(4), 2–8.

Ponterotto, J. G. (1990). Racial/ethnic minority and women administrators and faculty in higher education: A status report. In J. G. Ponterotto, D. E. Lewis, & R. Bullington (Eds.), *Affirmative action on campus* (pp. 61–72). San Francisco: Jossey-Bass.

Pounds, A. W. (1987). Black students' needs on predominantly White campuses. In D. W. Wright (Ed.), *Responding to the needs of today's minority students* (New Directions for Student Services No. 52, pp. 23–38). San Francisco: Jossey-Bass.

Reesor, L. M. (1998). Making professional connections. In M. J. Amey & L. M. Reesor (Eds.), *Beginning your journey: A guide for new professionals in student affairs* (pp. 53–65). Washington, DC: NASPA.

Sagaria, M., & Johnsrud, L. K. (1991). Recruiting, advancing, and retaining minorities in student affairs: Moving from rhetoric to results. *NASPA Journal, 28*(2), 105–120.

Schmidt, P. (2006, February 3). From minority to diversity. *The Chronicle of Higher Education*, p. A24.

Siggelkow, R. A. (1991). Racism in higher education. *NASPA Journal, 28*(2), 98–104.

Spotts, B. L. (1991). Creating a successful minority affairs position. *Journal of College Admission, 3*, 4–9.

Sutton, E. M. (1998). The role of the office of minority affairs in fostering cultural diversity. *College Student Affairs Journal, 18*(1), 33–35.

Sutton, E. M., & Terrell, M. (1997). Identifying and developing leadership opportunities for African American men. In M. J. Cuyjet (Ed.), *Helping African American men succeed in college* (pp. 55–64). San Francisco: Jossey-Bass.

Tan, C. S., & Salomone, P. R. (1994). Understanding career plateauing: Implications for counseling. *Career Development Quarterly, 42*(4), 291–301.

Thomas, D. A., & Ely, R. J. (1996). Making differences matter: A new paradigm for managing diversity. *Harvard Business Review, 74*(5), 79–80.

Weber, J. (1992). Creating the environment for minority student success: An interview with Jacqueline Fleming. *Journal of Developmental Education, 16*(2), 20–24.

Western Michigan University. (n.d.). Retrieved from http://www.studentworld .wmich.edu/StudentAffairsAssistantships.pdf

Williams, C. (1989–1990). Broadening access for Black students. *Community, Technical & Junior College Journal, 60*(3), 14–17.

Zeiss, T. (1990). Employee retention. *Community, Technical & Junior College Journal, 60*(4), 34–37.

PROMOTING STUDENT ENGAGEMENT

Administrative Considerations for Current
and Future Planning of Culture Center
Programming and Outreach

Salvador B. Mena

M ulticultural and identity-based centers (MIBCs) on college and
university campuses across the country have common roots;
none of the centers was created overnight, and their creation,
development, and preservation are grounded in the histories and contemporary contexts of their respective campuses. This chapter provides insight into
the contextual and administrative considerations that influence institutional
decision making regarding the establishment of MIBCs.

A quick scan of the higher education landscape offers insights about the
institutional contexts that led to the establishment of MIBCs on various college and university campuses. El Centro Chicano was established at the University of Southern California (n.d.) in 1972 as the result of a large
population of people of Mexican origin in the community, an increase in
the number of Chicana/o students seeking admission to USC, and campus
activism led by Chicana/o faculty, staff, and students demanding direct services and better representation in the university. Since 1972, many other
institutions have created centers that focus on the diverse experiences of
Latina/o groups from around the country, including Indiana University at
Bloomington, the University of Connecticut, the University of Illinois at
Urbana-Champaign, and Massachusetts Institute of Technology.

The University of Virginia experienced years of racial segregation and challenges accompanying the integration of African American students on campus. This situation ultimately led to the establishment of the Office of African-American Affairs (and Black Cultural Center) in the mid-1970s to meet the demands of African American students (Jordan, 2006). Many of the Black culture centers (BCCs) on campuses across the country date back to the early 1970s. The missions of these centers vary, but all strive to promote and preserve African American history and culture while exploring the experiences of members of the African diaspora. BCCs are located on a variety of campuses, both private and public, including Ohio State University, Swarthmore College in Pennsylvania, the University of Maryland–College Park, the University of Pennsylvania, and Virginia Polytechnic Institute and State University.

In addition to Latina/o and African American culture centers, culture centers that focus on the experiences of Asian American and Native American students are hosted on many campuses. The first two Native American students at Stanford University enrolled in 1894, which marked the beginning of a prolonged period of difficulty for the few Native American students who enrolled thereafter (Stanford Native American Cultural Center, n.d.). In 1974, Stanford opened the Native American Cultural Center in response to a needs assessment conducted by Native American students and the administration that revealed that the institution was not meeting the needs of Native American students. Other institutions with Native American culture centers include Portland State University in Oregon, San Juan College in New Mexico, and the University of South Dakota. More recently, the significant presence of Asian American students, faculty, and staff at the University of Illinois at Chicago led to the creation of the Asian American Resource and Cultural Center in 2005; the center was realized as a result of the tenacity of Asian American students, who pressed their case for institutional validation (University of Illinois at Chicago Asian American Resource and Cultural Center., n.d.). Other institutions with centers focusing on the experiences of students of Asian descent include California State Polytechnic University, Pomona; the University of Iowa; and Washington State University.

Some campuses host identity-based centers that provide outreach to specific ethnic or racial groups, and other campuses host ALANA/AHANA

(African, Latino/Hispanic, Asian American, and Native American), multi-cultural, intercultural, or unity centers with various missions to serve broader audiences. In 1989, Williams College in Massachusetts established a multi-cultural center as the result of a protest by a broad coalition of individuals who challenged the college's lack of support for ethnic minority students (Williams Multicultural Center, n.d.). Similarly, a multicultural center was created at Elon University (n.d.) in North Carolina after a group of concerned students submitted a proposal for an African American resource room, which resulted in the creation of a multicultural center with a specific emphasis on the success and development of African American students. Although multicultural centers are common on many campuses, they assume a variety of shapes and sizes. Institutions such as Boston College, Colgate University in New York, Grinnell College in Iowa, Humboldt State University in California, and the University of Maine have inclusive multicultural centers that share similar yet unique missions, with varying levels of staffing and resources.

As demographic trends shift across the country, some institutions are paying attention to emerging campus populations. Brown University (n.d.), in Rhode Island, has an active multicultural student center yet recently established a Muslim Student Center to provide space for a growing segment of the student body to conduct daily prayers and host other gatherings. At the University of North Carolina at Chapel Hill, a task force was appointed to examine emerging populations—in particular Latina/o students, who reflect the fastest-growing population in the state. Also, with the desire to increase the number of international students on campus, as well as the number of domestic students who study abroad (while accounting for the transitional experiences of both groups), institutions are increasing resources for international student centers. The International Student Center at San Diego State University (n.d.) in California focuses on the experiences of international students on campus as well as American students who study abroad.

Colleges and universities also recognize the importance of providing learning, reflecting, and connecting spaces for lesbian, gay, bisexual, and transgender (LGBT) students and for women, two groups who have been historically marginalized in society and in higher education. The University of California Santa Cruz (Lionel Cantú Gay, Lesbian, Bisexual, Transgender, Intersex Resource Center, n.d.) and University of Hawaii (University of

Hawaii Women's Center, n.d.) are examples of institutions that host LGBT and women's centers that often collaborate on issues of mutual interest.

Administrative Considerations

For an outsider looking in, it is easy to develop a romanticized view of the campus histories that led to the establishment of MIBCs. For instance, when reviewing the public history of a center, one might find references to the sustained activism of a group of students, the long-term leadership of a faculty member for diversity efforts on campus, or the collectivist spirit of a cross-section of individuals responsible for championing a campus culture center. Individuals with firsthand knowledge of the processes that led to the establishment of MIBCs often provide alternative stories to the well-known public histories. The full histories often involve multiple stakeholders and complex administrative considerations. An exhaustive overview of each administrative consideration is beyond the scope of this chapter; however, Figure 10.1 lists such considerations for individuals charged with envisioning, planning, and/or coordinating efforts to establish MIBCs.

Students

Historically, college students have been at the forefront of change in higher education. As illustrated by the previous examples, students played pivotal roles in the establishment of MIBCs on college and university campuses across the country. Students' perspectives and roles must be considered when MIBCs are created. Questions to consider include, Are students responsible for (i.e., the driving force for) presenting the proposal for a culture center? How long have students been asking for a center? How have students experienced the campus climate over time? Are there tensions or trust issues between students and the administration? What are students really asking for in their request for a culture center—do additional unmet needs or issues exist that are not being discussed? Do administrative leaders view students as partners in the creation of a culture center? What will be the institutional "line in the sand" when a compromise with student leaders on the establishment of a center is sought?

An example of a line in the sand when students demand that a culture center be established and a longtime advisor be hired as the inaugural director is campus administrators' agreement to support the creation of the center, accompanied by insistence that the inaugural director be a new hire. The

FIGURE 10.1
Considerations for Individuals Charged With Envisioning, Planning, and/or
Coordinating Efforts to Establish MIBCs

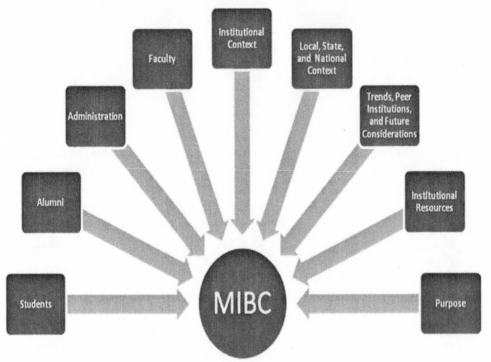

longtime advisor may have earned the respect and admiration of students but may not have the preferred academic qualifications or experience for the position. Or political issues—of which the students are unaware—may keep their beloved advisor from being appointed to the position. These types of issues reflect a fundamental need to anticipate, identify, and discuss institutional and student perspectives regarding the establishment of an MIBC before the process is initiated.

Alumni

Programs and buildings are not created overnight and often take years to establish. Alumni often pave the way for establishment of MIBCs, serve as bridges to the past, and prove instrumental in facilitating connections between students and administrators. Alumni serve as sources of financial support for the construction of new centers or the renovation of existing facilities. Moreover, alumni are often willing to serve on exploratory, implementation, and advisory committees and lend their expertise where needed (e.g., fund-raising and friend raising).

It is important to realize that alumni can work against institutional interests when at odds with their alma maters over a host of different issues. This often occurs when there are adversarial relationships between underrepresented students and institutional leaders regarding unaddressed issues of campus climate and long-standing inequities. In these situations, administrators are seen as part of the problem rather than the solution. Such alumni could be vocal critics of their alma maters on issues of diversity, pass on legacies of activism to current students that prolong adversarial relationships with their institutions, or refuse to support fund-raising campaigns for the establishment or enhancement of MIBCs. Despite the possibility that they may be operating at odds, alumni should be considered partners in these processes, as they provide invaluable perspectives and service.

Administrators

College and university administrators are charged with maintaining the well-being of their institutions and often have to consider multiple perspectives in their decision-making processes. A new proposal for an MIBC is brought to the attention of an institution's president, provost, and chief student affairs officer and leads to discussions by the president's cabinet and the institution's senior staff. In addition to understanding the student perspective, it is important that anyone charged with leading efforts related to the establishment of a culture center understand where key administrators stand on such an initiative, particularly the administrator who is responsible for green lighting the project. For example, an institution's chief executive officer may publicly support the creation of a multicultural center, but are there issues that are nonnegotiable for him or her? He or she may prefer for an existing space to be used for a new MIBC as opposed to the construction of a new facility. Or he or she may request that the new center receive a small operating budget in order to avoid straining limited resources during a difficult budget year. It is essential that the individual appointed to lead efforts toward the creation of an MIBC engage in frank conversation with key institutional leaders to gain clarity upfront and minimize questions later.

In considering the creation of an MIBC, it is also critical to identify points of tension or disagreement between the chief academic and chief student affairs officers. Are they in agreement about which division should house a new center? Will the operating budget be split between academic and student affairs, or will it be in one division's budget? If a new center is housed in an existing facility, who will control the space? Will the center's focus be the production of interdisciplinary research on the experiences of a group of people (e.g., Asian Americans), will it strictly serve as a student center (e.g., for Asian American students), or will it be a hybrid of the two (i.e., a center that generates knowledge and provides student services)?

In addition to the chief executive officer, chief student affairs officer, and chief academic officer, are there other administrators who, by virtue of their positions, have influence in the decision-making process regarding creation of an MIBC (e.g., chief financial officer or chief diversity officer)? Are there administrators who, as a result of their personalities or legacies as longtime members of the campus community, have opinions that should be considered in the establishment of a campus culture center (e.g., director of community service)? From an institutional perspective, deciding who chairs and serves on a culture center implementation committee is an important decision that will have ramifications for how the administrative perspective is represented with the ultimate outcomes associated with the future of the MIBC.

Faculty

Like students, faculty members have historically been at the forefront of advocating institutional change in higher education. As such, there are faculty members who have interest in the establishment of MIBCs. Faculty members with such an interest may be divided into three categories: (1) faculty members whose scholarship connects with the mission of the center, (2) faculty members who have a personal interest in campus diversity issues, and (3) faculty members who represent a hybrid of the two perspectives and wish to pursue their academic disciplines and social justice interests through participation in the creation of an MIBC. It is also common for faculty members to serve as advisors to multicultural and ethnic student organizations and to provide visible and vocal leadership when diversity-related issues arise on campus (e.g., bias incidents). Centers affiliated with academic programs—and therefore with the mission of generating knowledge—have different types of faculty engagement than do traditional culture centers. Regardless of the type of center one is interested in establishing, key faculty members can play active roles on exploratory or implementation committees and represent the institution, the students, and their academic and personal interests.

Institutional Context

In addition to identifying the institutional players who will be involved in the formation of an MIBC, knowledge of an institution's history in terms of race relations, issues of access, gender equity, workers' rights, town-gown relations, and the establishment of other campus centers should serve as the framework for the process and related conversations. Such issues or incidents could be the root cause or relevant context for a proposal to establish an MIBC.

Along with accounting for any long-standing historical perspectives, it is important to examine contemporary issues that might fuel or inform the need for the creation of a new culture center or modification of an existing one. Has there been steady growth of students from a particular ethnic or racial group? Are students demanding that the existing center connect with their interests in the community or aid in the recruitment of underrepresented students? Have there been significant incidents of bias or hate on campus in the last several years, or are administrators eager to focus on issues of identity development for students who are not members of an ethnic minority group? These questions represent the types of issues that institutions may face when considering the establishment of an MIBC. Additionally, factors such as institutional type (e.g., predominantly White institutions, Hispanic-serving institutions, historically Black colleges and universities, small liberal arts colleges, public colleges, private colleges), compositional diversity (e.g., racial and ethnic diversity of faculty, staff, and students), campus politics and climate, and any internal fears regarding the establishment of an MIBC should be considered in the decision-making and planning process.

Context: Local Community and Beyond

When an institution seeks to establish an MIBC, consideration should be given to the context beyond the campus borders. Every institution is located in a unique community. For example, while one school might be situated close to a growing and underserved primarily Southeast Asian community in an urban environment, another campus might be located in a small predominantly White town. These examples highlight the opportunities and challenges faced in the planning process for an MIBC. In the first example, the institution and students might envision a new center where outreach happens in the local community (e.g., working with Southeast Asian high school students on applying to college), whereas the center of a university situated in the small town could serve to improve town-gown relations (e.g., with cultural shows, diversity forums). MIBCs have the potential to reflect the values of their institutions and address the issues about which students care by serving as natural conduits between campuses and the communities in which they are located. As such, MIBCs contribute immensely to student development, the overall educational experience, and local communities.

The questions that frame the establishment of MIBCs on individual college campuses must also be asked at state and national levels. For example, are there hot-button issues at the state level that provide broader contexts for the creation of MIBCs at particular institutions? Questions related to context at the national level may also inform decision-making processes related to MIBCs. For example, in this post–September 11 era, individuals who appear to be of Middle Eastern descent are prejudicially targeted throughout the United States, and many Americans do not understand that Islam is a religion and have misinformation about what it means to be Muslim. As such, the experience of Muslim students on American college campuses provides a foundation for the creation of MIBCs that help campuses meet their needs.

Trends, Peer Institutions, and Future Considerations

Decisions regarding the establishment of a cultural center should be made with consideration of recent or ongoing trends related to MIBCs in general and MIBCs at peer institutions. Examination of the latest trends allows campus administrators to determine if they are heading in the right direction or if they need to reconsider their thinking about the missions and purposes of new and existing centers. In addition to site visits to MIBCs at other institutions, campus diversity professionals, diversity-related associations, and higher education diversity consultants are wonderful resources and can share information about how MIBCs evolve. Furthermore, establishment of new centers, or the renovation and/or reorganization of existing centers, provides opportunities to develop facilities that are national models of best practice and enticing to prospective students.

In addition to considering best practices and the activities of peer institutions, MIBC planning groups should also think about how new campus centers will remain relevant in the future. Issues such as shifting national, state, and local demographics (e.g., increases in biracial students), changing cultures in the United States (e.g., the "browning" of America), globalization, and the evolving political landscape should inform conversations about the relevance of culture centers now and in the future.

Institutional Resources

MIBCs receive various levels of financial support. The context and administrative considerations for funding vary from campus to campus. A culture center on one campus may have a sizable operating budget, several levels of staffing, and a state-of-the-art facility, whereas a center at a different institution may receive minimal budgetary support, be located on the outskirts of campus in a facility in need of repair, and be staffed by one entry-level professional who serves as director. Different levels of support reflect a wide variety of factors. For example, an institution that has long had a harsh campus climate for underrepresented students may now infuse resources into a culture center and other programs to address past inequities. On the other hand, another institution may view a culture center simply as a means to retain historically underrepresented students.

Regardless of the type of institution and level of campus commitment to a center, consideration should be given to the starting operating budget, level of staffing, and physical space allocation early in the planning process in order for a center to fulfill its mission. When a center's charge is to engage both a target population and a broader campus constituency around a set of outcomes, potential mishaps can occur as a result of inadequate funding. Questions regarding the level of funding needed to support the center's mission, desired experience and education of center staff who will carry out the mission, and physical space needed to support the work of the center should also be addressed early on.

Furthermore, decisions about the allocation of resources for a new center should be made with reliable assessment and evaluative data. Quantitative and qualitative data provide valuable information at each step of the planning process, including discussions related to budget, personnel, and space. For instance, data on the number of students involved in diversity-related organizations and activities on campus can provide insight into potential student interest in the establishment of a certain type of culture center on campus.

Allocation of center resources should be based upon new and existing campus resources. For example, would it make sense to relocate an existing campus program to a new center? Are there administrative staff and faculty members who could be affiliated with a new center? Are there administrative or academic programs with which a new center can be aligned in order to strengthen its capacity to fulfill its mission? Questions such as these will challenge decision makers and exploratory, planning, and implementation groups to think beyond the apparent available resources and to consider existing resources that can contribute to the success of an MIBC. Lastly, consideration should be given to attracting the interest of potential donors in the establishment or revamping of an MIBC, whether those donors are alumni, parents, or other friends of the institution (e.g., a company or major donor in the community).

Purpose

As noted earlier, many MIBCs on college and university campuses across the country were created as a result of students' demands to have their lived experiences validated and to receive institutional support to ensure their overall success. Similar circumstances may still drive the revamping or establishment of culture centers today, but additional consideration should be given to the opportunities and benefits a center provides for the entire campus community.

The current college-bound population has had more exposure to diversity than generations in past, and it has become ever so important for institutions to justify the existence and establishment of culture centers on campus.

Furthermore, with the globalization of society and institutions of higher education looking to extend their classrooms beyond campus borders, establishing a culture center should no longer be discussed from a deficit perspective (e.g., as a means of retaining students, keeping students happy). Instead, the conversation should be framed in terms of the benefits the center provides to the campus community, even if those benefits contribute to the aforementioned outcomes. By doing so, an institution is giving itself permission to define what a center will mean to the entire community while underscoring why the center is vital to the educational mission of the institution and beyond. As a result, an MIBC becomes a place where members of the campus community can learn about themselves in relation to others, actively engage across differences, and participate in learning opportunities to which they have not been previously exposed (e.g., learning how to be an ally to a marginalized group in society, or developing cross-cultural competencies) even as the center acts as a place where students can be validated, feel safe, and be supported.

The quality of the programs and services associated with the center will ultimately serve to solidify the center's reputation and demonstrate whether it is fulfilling its purpose. In addition to examining the activity of MIBCs at peer institutions, reviewing relevant benchmarks, and identifying notable programs, the Council for the Advancement of Standards in Higher Education (CAS) provides invaluable resources for institutions considering establishing MIBCs. Specifically, CAS provides guidelines for developing and assessing multicultural student programs and services. For more information, visit the CAS website (www.cas.edu).

References

Brown University. (n.d.). *Brown Muslim students association.* Retrieved from http://www.brown.edu/Students/Muslim_Students/

Elon University. (n.d.). *Multicultural center: About.* Retrieved from http://www.elon.edu/e-web/students/multicultural_resources/history.xhtml

Jordan, E. L., Jr. (2006). *The first generation: Thirty years of the Office of African-American Affairs at the University of Virginia.* Retrieved from http://www.virginia.edu/oaaa/Jordan.OAAA.lecture.2006.doc

Lionel Cantú Gay, Lesbian, Bisexual, Transgender, Intersex Resource Center. (n.d.). *Services and programs.* Retrieved from http://queer.ucsc.edu/about/services.shtml

San Diego State University. (n.d.). *International student center: About us.* Retrieved from http://www.isc.sdsu.edu/iscabout.html

Stanford Native American Cultural Center. (n.d.). *Native American history at Stanford: California history timeline.* Retrieved from http://nacc.stanford.edu/timeline.html

University of Hawaii Women's Center. (n.d.). *Programs we support.* Retrieved from http://www.hawaii.edu/womenscenter/programs.html

University of Illinois at Chicago Asian American Resource and Cultural Center. (n.d.). *AARCC mission.* Retrieved from http://www.uic.edu/depts/oaa/AARCC/mission.html

University of Southern California. (n.d.). *El Centro's history: Establishing El Centro Chicano.* Retrieved from http://www.usc.edu/student-affairs/elcentro/history_establishing.htm

Williams Multicultural Center. (n.d.). *The MCC.* Retrieved from http://mcc.williams.edu/?page_id = 190

MULTICULTURAL/ INTERCULTURAL CENTERS

The Paul Robeson Cultural Center (PRCC)
Rutgers University—New Brunswick, NJ
Established 1967

The Student Cultural Center
Colorado College—Colorado Springs, CO
Established 1969

Multicultural Center
Illinois Wesleyan University—Bloomington, IL
Established 1970

Carl A. Fields Center for Equality and Cultural Understanding
Princeton University—Princeton, NJ
Established 1971

Paul Robeson Cultural Center
Pennsylvania State University—University Park, PA
Established 1971

Ethnic Cultural Center/Theatre
University of Washington—Seattle, WA
Established 1972

The Slater International Center
Wellesley College—Wellesley, MA
Established 1972

ALANA Center
Vassar College—Poughkeepsie, NY
Established 1976

Era Bell Thompson Cultural Center
University of North Dakota—Grand Forks, ND
Established 1976

ALANA Student Center
University of Vermont—Burlington, VT
Established 1978

Romeo B. Garrett Cultural Center
Bradley University—Peoria, IL
Established 1978

The William Monroe Trotter Multicultural Center
University of Michigan—Ann Arbor, MI
Established 1981

Multicultural Center
Utah Valley University—Orem, UT
Established 1985

Multicultural Center
University of California Santa Barbara—Santa Barbara, CA
Established 1987

Multicultural Student Center
University of Wisconsin—Madison, WI
Established 1988

The Williams Multicultural Center
Williams College—Williamstown, MA
Established 1989

Multicultural Center
Ohio Northern University—Ada, OH
Established 1991

Multicultural Center
Southern Connecticut State University—New Haven, CT
Established 1991

Multicultural Center
Portland State University—Portland, OR
Established 1992

Snowden Multicultural Center
Kenyon College—Gambier, OH
Established 1992

Multicultural Center
California State University Dominguez Hills—Dominguez Hills, CA
Established 1994

The Ledonia Wright Cultural Center
East Carolina University—Greenville, NC
Established 1995

Bridges Multicultural Resource Center
University of California—Berkeley, CA
Established 1996

Multicultural Resource Center
University of North Carolina Charlotte—Charlotte, NC
Established 1996

The United Front Multicultural Center
University of San Diego—San Diego, CA
Established 1997

ALANA Student Center
University of Vermont—Burlington, VT
Established 1998

Multicultural Center
Michigan State University—East Lansing, MI
Established 1999

Multicultural Center
Ohio State University—Columbus, OH
Established 2001

Intercultural Relations/Cross-Cultural Center
San Diego State University—San Diego, CA
Established 2003

Cultural Center
University of Louisville—Louisville, KY
Established 2008

Multicultural Center
Iowa State University—Ames, IA
Established 2009

TRANSFORMING FOR THE 21ST CENTURY

Best Practices for Examining and Evaluating Campus
Culture Centers and Multicultural Affairs Offices

Lori D. Patton

All culture centers should conduct regular audits to learn more about their strengths as well as opportunities to enhance programs and services. While conducting an audit requires a significant investment of time, effort, and energy, engaging in the audit process promotes organizational learning and reveals areas needing improvement. Rather than perceiving the audit process as cumbersome and time-consuming, culture center directors are encouraged to imagine it as the route to discovery. Kuh, Schuh, Whitt and Associates (1991) emphasized, "This terminology implies that the discovery process requires a systematic (yet open-ended) effort, and reflects the depth and breadth of scrutiny required to understand a college or university" (p. 264). Kuh et al. created the Involving College Audit Protocol (ICAP) to assist educational leaders in assessing college and university environments. While the ICAP stems from their groundbreaking work on Involving Colleges, many of its components are relevant for transforming culture centers for the 21st century. Here I offer a customized list of considerations to assist culture center leaders with the process of conducting an audit. The audit components noted are partially influenced by the ICAP, feedback from culture center directors, and my own experiences as a consultant and researcher in the area of campus culture centers and multicultural affairs.

The beginning of a successful audit includes getting members of the campus involved in the process. A culture center audit team should comprise culture center staff, students, faculty, and other members of the campus with a vested interest in the campus. These individuals should serve as members of the internal audit team. In addition to the internal audit team, an external audit team representing individuals who are highly familiar with culture centers should be invited to participate in the audit.

Whether the audit is conducted in an effort to maintain quality, assess resources, or as part of a strategic planning agenda, the following aspects should always be addressed in some capacity. The responses to these components will serve as a necessary framework toward any present and future plans of the culture center. Each area should be addressed during the audit process and recorded in written form. In addition, a final audit should be accompanied with supporting documents and a rationale to substantiate any plans or recommendations that stem from the audit.

Mission and Philosophy

- What is the mission of the culture center?
  - Does the culture center have a clearly articulated mission and vision?
  - Does the mission align with the university or division-wide mission? To what extent?
  - In what ways is the mission evident? (website, brochures, etc.)
  - How is the mission communicated and to whom is it communicated?
  - How is the mission used to guide the programmatic thrusts of the center?
  - To what extent does the mission address student learning and education?
- How do campus constituents describe the culture center mission?
  - What are the shared understandings of the culture center mission?
  - Is there consensus among the descriptions?
  - Does the consensus reflect the mission?
  - Is there disagreement among the descriptions?
  - What aspects of these descriptions align with the mission? Which do not?
  - In what ways do (or could) these perceptions affect student experiences?
- How are student learning outcomes reflected in the mission?
  - Does the culture center have student learning outcomes?
  - To what extent are these outcomes consistent with the culture center mission?

- o How are the student learning outcomes theoretically, conceptually, and/or philosophically grounded?
- o How are students engaged in fulfilling the culture center mission?
- o To what extent do students feel engaged in the decisions that affect the culture center?
- What is the history of the culture center?
  - o To what extent does the mission reflect the history of the culture center?
  - o Is the history of the culture center carefully documented?
  - o How is the history of the culture center communicated?

Students

- How does the culture center define the characteristics of the students served?
- Does the culture center maintain pertinent information regarding diverse student populations on campus?
- How is information maintained with regard to which student populations use the culture center or attend its programs?
  - o To what extent is the knowledge gained from this information used to influence policies and practices of the culture center?
- How does who the center serves affect programming and services?
- If the culture center is race-specific, how are other students invited to engage within the culture center space?
- To what extent do students view the culture center as a space for seeking assistance?
  - o How are students in difficult situations noticed and assisted?
  - o What resources are available to assist students in need?
  - o How are relationships with students fostered by culture center staff?
- Does the culture center promote belongingness and community?
  - o To what extent does the culture center encourage students to practice agency as members of the campus community?
  - o How does the culture center identify students who may not have established a sense of belongingness and community on campus?
  - o What strategies does the culture center implement to help students establish a sense of belongingness and community?

- How is cross-cultural learning and engagement promoted through the culture center?
  - To what extent is cross-cultural learning and engagement reflected in the mission?
  - How are differences among diverse student populations acknowledged?
  - In what ways does the culture center promote collaborative learning opportunities for students?
  - How are students from diverse cultures and backgrounds engaged in celebratory opportunities?
  - How are students from diverse cultures and background engaged in educational opportunities?

Climate and Culture

- What is the overall culture of the campus for diverse student populations?
  - What strategies or resources are offered through the culture center to better understand the campus climate and culture?
  - What aspects of the campus climate or culture make students feel excluded?
  - What traditions or events make the campus less welcoming for students of color?
- How is the culture center positioned within the university's organizational structure?
  - What expectations are placed upon the culture center to address issues of campus climate and culture?
  - To what extent is the culture center represented in institutional decision making with regard to addressing issues of campus climate and culture?
- How does the culture center address what may be perceived as a chilly or unwelcoming climate for students it serves?
- To what extent do the programs and services of the center challenge negative campus racial climates?
- In what ways is the culture center complicit in maintaining a chilly campus climate or unwelcoming culture?
- How do students affiliated with the culture center learn about expectations for contributing toward the maintenance of a welcoming campus climate?

- What is the culture of the center?
  - Is the center frequented mainly by one or two student populations?
  - Is the center frequented by a wide-range of students representing diverse populations?
  - To what extent does the culture reflect the mission of the culture center?
- What symbols or messages are used to make students feel welcome and comfortable?
- What symbols or messages are used to communicate the value of student learning?
- How do prospective students or visitors to the campus learn about the culture center?
- What makes the culture center unique?
  - What does the center do well?
  - What opportunities are available to students? faculty? and staff?
  - How do campus constituents take advantage of these opportunities?
  - How are opportunities connected to student learning and life-long learning?
- Is the culture center aesthetically attractive?
  - Is the center easy to locate for campus visitors and prospective students?
  - How accessible are the facilities? (e.g., hours of operation, ease of use, conveniently located)
  - What resources are available for use? (e.g., books, computers, kitchen, programming space)
  - What arkwork, displays, or decor make the center visually appealing and attractive?
- Is the culture center staff friendly?
  - Does the culture center staff provide relevant and pertinent information to students?
  - Does the culture center staff project a welcoming demeanor?
  - Does the culture center staff address students by name?
  - To what extent is the culture center staff available and able to respond to student inquiries and requests?
  - To what extent has the culture center staff fostered an environment where students can challenge and support one another?

Programs and Services

- What are the programmatic goals of the culture center?
- How do these goals align with the mission?
- Does the culture center offer academic, social, or cultural programming? A combination?
- What is the programming curriculum of the culture center?
  - In what ways are student learning and engagement intentionally fostered through the culture center curriculum?
- How is culture center space used for programming initiatives?
- How is culture center space used specifically for educational purposes?
- Is programming at an appropriate level?
  - Does the culture center do too much programming? Too little?
  - Does the culture center focus too much on social programming?
- To what extent do culture center programs prepare students to do the following:
  - Engage in difficult dialogues, about race and racism in particular?
  - Recognize and disrupt oppressive behaviors and attitudes?
  - Engage in identity exploration and intersections of identity?
- To what extent is the programming curriculum designed to promote cross-cultural interactions among students from diverse backgrounds?
  - How easy is it for students to become involved with the culture center?
  - How often do cross-cultural interactions occur in the culture center?
  - What consistent evidence is available to demonstrate cross-cultural interactions?
- To what extent is the communication and marketing of the culture center and its programs thorough, appealing, and current?
  - What types of communication are used for marketing purposes? (e.g., e-mail listserves, website, newsletters, calendars, flyers, word of mouth)?
  - To what extent is technology used to promote culture center programs and services? (e.g., social networking via Facebook, Twitter, etc., text messages)
- To what extent is ongoing assessment and evaluation of programs and services conducted?

- Does the culture center work collaboratively with campus organizations and offices to implement overall mission and goals?
- Which agents within and beyond the institution does the culture center collaborate?
  - To what extent is community outreach addressed in culture center programs?
  - In what ways are alumni involved in culture centers programs?

Policies and Staffing

- Is the staffing structure sufficient to carry out the mission of the culture center?
  - Is staff qualified with necessary educational credentials?
  - Is the number of staff appropriate for the culture center to meet institutional expectations?
  - To what extent do culture center staff engage in professional development opportunities to enhance the effectiveness of the culture center?
- Does the culture center have sufficient financial resources to carry forth its mission?
  - Are monetary resources effectively used to address the needs of respective populations?
- Are resources prioritized and allocated according to the mission, goals and student learning outcomes of the culture center?
- Does the culture center have a policy manual?
  - Are policies appropriately aligned with the mission?
  - In what ways are the culture center policies made evident for members of the university community?
- How are decisions made regarding resource allocation?
  - To what extent is this process transparent and open to members of the university community?
  - To what extent are student voices involved in the resource allocation process?

Reference

Kuh, G. D., Schuh, J. H., Whitt, E. J., & Associates (1991). *Involving colleges: Successful approaches to fostering student learning and development outside the classroom.* San Francisco: Jossey-Bass.

ABOUT THE EDITOR

Lori D. Patton is an assistant professor in the Department of Educational Leadership and Policy Studies at Iowa State University. She earned her Ph.D. in higher education from Indiana University, M.A. in college student personnel at Bowling Green State University, and B.S. in speech communication at Southern Illinois University, as well as a graduate certificate in African and African American studies at Indiana State University. Much of her research introspectively examines issues of access, equity, and evidence of racial injustice in the academy, with a particular focus on gender, sexuality, and the engagement of Black college students. Dr. Patton contributed to the first volume published about BCCs and has published articles in *About Campus* and *The Journal of College Student Development*. Dr. Patton was recognized by the American College Personnel Association as an emerging scholar in 2004 and received the Association for the Study of Higher Education Council on Ethnic Participation–Mildred E. Garcia Award for Exemplary Scholarship in 2009. In addition, the Iowa State University College of Human Sciences has recognized her for early achievement in research.

CONTRIBUTORS

Michael Benitez Jr. completed both his bachelor of science and master of education at Pennsylvania State University and is currently a doctoral student at Iowa State University, where he focuses on educational leadership and policy studies with an emphasis on social justice in higher education. Prior to returning to school, he served for 7 years as a student affairs and equity practitioner in intercultural development, diversity, and social justice education at multiple higher education institutions. He is coeditor of the anthology *Crash Course: Reflections on the Film "Crash" for Critical Dialogues About Race, Power and Privilege*.

Rosa Cintrón is associate professor of higher education and policy studies at the University of Central Florida. She is coeditor of *College Student Death: Guidance for a Caring Campus, Building a Working Policy for Distance Education,* and *Issues in Higher Education: Enduring Enigmas in American Colleges and Universities*.

Michael J. Cuyjet is an associate professor in the College of Education and Human Development at the University of Louisville in Kentucky, where he has taught in the College Student Personnel Program and mentored master's and doctoral students since 1993. Prior to that, he served for more than 20 years as a student affairs practitioner at Northern Illinois University and at the University of Maryland–College Park. During his time at Louisville he has also served as associate dean of the graduate school and acting associate provost for student life and development. He received a bachelor's degree in speech communications from Bradley University and a master's degree in counseling and a doctorate in counselor education from Northern Illinois University.

Kandace G. Hinton is an associate professor in the Department of Educational Leadership, Administration, and Foundations' Higher Education Leadership Program at Indiana State University. Dr. Hinton holds a master's and Ph.D. in higher education administration from Indiana University Bloomington and a bachelor of arts from Jackson State University, Mississippi. Dr. Hinton has created a theoretical model that describes African American women's professional development. Dr. Hinton teaches in the areas of the history of higher education, foundations of education, academic leadership, ethics, and college student development and diversity. She is the coeditor of *Unleashing Suppressed Voices on College Campuses: Diversity Issues in Higher Education and Student Affairs* (Peter Lang, 2007) and contributed to *Exercising Power With Wisdom* (College Administration Publications, 2006), by James Lancaster and associates. Other publications include *Using Entertainment Media in Student Affairs Teaching and Practice* (Jossey-Bass, 2004) and *Meeting the Needs of African American Women in Higher Education* (Jossey-Bass, 2003). Dr. Hinton won the Holmstedt Dissertation Award in 2001 and is a member of the American College Personnel Association, the American Educational Research Association, NASPA, the Association for the Study of Higher Education, and Delta Sigma Theta.

Mary F. Howard-Hamilton is professor in the Department of Educational Leadership, Administration, and Foundations' Higher Education Program at Indiana State University. She received her B.A. and M.A. from the University of Iowa and a doctorate of education from North Carolina State

University. Dr. Howard-Hamilton has worked in higher education administration as well as academic affairs. She has published over 80 articles and
book chapters and coauthored three books. Dr. Howard-Hamilton received
the Robert S. Shaffer Award for Academic Excellence as a Graduate Faculty
Member from NASPA and the Albert Hood Distinguished Alumni Award
from the University of Iowa. She received the Monroe County (Indiana) Big
Brothers Big Sisters Mentor of the Year Award in 2006.

Robin L. Hughes is an assistant professor in the Department of Educational
Leadership and Policy Studies' Higher Education Student Affairs Program
at Indiana University Indianapolis. She is an adjunct professor in the Department of African American and African Diaspora Studies in Bloomington and
Indianapolis. Her research focuses on the development of student athletes
who participate in revenue-generating sports. In addition, she explores issues
of race and how those issues affect faculty and students of color in higher
education. She received a master of science and a doctoral degree in higher
educational administration from Texas A&M University.

Toby S. Jenkins holds a joint appointment as an assistant professor in the
Integrative Studies Program in the New Century College and the Higher
Education Program at George Mason University. Dr. Jenkins has close to 10
years of experience in administrative leadership of university culture centers.
Her work focuses on cultural and community leadership, the cultural arts
and social transformation, and the contemporary ideologies of culture
among young adults.

Sunny Lee is currently the director of the Office of Student Life and Cultural Centers at California State Polytechnic University, Pomona. She previously worked at the Cross-Cultural Center at the University of California,
Irvine, and Pomona College's Asian American Resource Center. She earned
her master's degree in college student personnel from the University of
Maryland and is currently a Ph.D. candidate in higher education at Claremont Graduate University. She is the coeditor of *Working With Asian American College Students*.

William Ming Liu is professor and program coordinator of counseling psychology at the University of Iowa. He received his doctorate in counseling

psychology from the University of Maryland. His research interests are social class and classism, men and masculinity, and multicultural competencies. He has received the Emerging Leader Award from the American Psychological Association's Committee on Socioeconomic Status (2008), the Emerging Young Professional Award (Division 45), and the Researcher of the Year Award (Division 51). He is associate editor of *Psychology of Men and Masculinity* and has served on the editorial boards of *The Counseling Psychologists, Cultural Diversity and Ethnic Minority Psychology, The Journal of Multicultural Counseling and Development*, and *Clinician's Research Digest*. He is one of the editors of the *Handbook of Multicultural Competencies in Counseling and Psychology* (Sage, 2003), an editor of the forthcoming *Culturally Responsive Counseling With Asian American Men* (Routledge), the author of the forthcoming *Social Class and Classism in the Helping Professions: Research, Theory, and Practice* (Sage), and the editor of the forthcoming *Handbook of Social Class in Counseling Psychology* (Oxford).

Corina Benavides Lopez is a Ph.D. candidate in race and ethnic studies in education at the University of California, Los Angeles, Graduate School of Education and Information Studies. Her research focuses on how immigration status and racialization processes affect the educational experiences and trajectories of (undocumented) Chicana/o immigrants and their families. She has several years of experience in higher education student affairs. She earned her B.A. in Chicana/o studies and women's studies with a specialization in education at UCLA and her M.A. in education at Stanford University.

Adele Lozano is assistant dean of students and director of La Casa Cultural Latina at the University of Illinois at Urbana-Champaign. She received her undergraduate degree and master's degree in student affairs at the University of Northern Iowa. She is currently pursuing a doctorate of education in educational organization and leadership at the University of Illinois, and conducting research on Latina/o culture centers in the Midwest.

Phyllis McCluskey-Titus is an associate professor in educational administration and foundations and coordinator of the master's program in college student personnel administration at Illinois State University. She holds a bachelor of arts and a master of science from Western Illinois University and a doctoral degree in higher education administration from Florida State University. Prior to assuming her faculty position, she worked as a student affairs practitioner for 18 years at Syracuse University, Indiana University of Pennsylvania, and Florida State University.

Salvador B. Mena currently serves as the assistant to the vice chancellor for student affairs at University of North Carolina at Chapel Hill. He is pursuing a doctorate in college student personnel from the University of Maryland at College Park. He recently served as the associate dean of community living and multicultural affairs at Goucher College in Baltimore, Maryland. He has a particular interest in diversity in higher education along with the experiences of historically underrepresented students at colleges and universities.

Heather J. Shotton is a member of the Wichita and Affiliated Tribes, and of Kiowa and Cheyenne descent. She is currently an assistant visiting professor in Native American studies at the University of Oklahoma.

E. Michael Sutton is associate professor of education at Winston-Salem State University. He received his bachelor of arts from Winston-Salem State University, a master of science from Southern Illinois University, and the doctorate of philosophy from Iowa State University. His research interests include multicultural issues in higher education, African American males, and Black Greek-letter organizations.

Star Yellowfish is the director of Native American student services for the Oklahoma City public schools. She is a member of the United Keetoowah Band of Cherokee. Dr. Yellowfish received her Ph.D. in adult and higher education from the University of Oklahoma in 2008 and has worked in various areas of Indian education for over 8 years. Her research focuses on Native American peer mentoring and retention, as well as Native college student success.

Tara J. Yosso is an associate professor in the Department of Chicana and Chicano Studies at the University of California, Santa Barbara. Dr. Yosso's teaching and research apply the frameworks of critical race theory and critical media literacy to examine educational access and equity, emphasizing the community cultural wealth that students of color take to school. The American Educational Studies Association selected Dr. Yosso's book *Critical Race Counterstories Along the Chicana/Chicano Educational Pipeline* (Routledge) for the 2008 Critics' Choice Book Award. Her research has been published in journals such as *Race Ethnicity and Education, Qualitative Inquiry,* and *The Journal of Popular Film and Television.*

Also available from Stylus

Becoming Socialized in Student Affairs Administration
A Guide for New Professionals and Their Supervisors
Edited by Ashley Tull, Joan B. Hirt, and Sue Saunders

"The authors use socialization theory as an overarching framework to examine the changing contexts of student affairs across institution types, the students we serve, and key transition issues facing new professionals in the field. The authors describe factors affecting many aspects of socialization including orientation, mentoring, staff-peer relationships, and professional associations. Individual and institutional strategies are provided to assist those entering student affairs, and for graduate preparation program faculty and student affairs practitioners invested in the success of new professionals. An important resource for new professionals."—*Marilyn J. Amey*, *Professor and Chairperson, Department of Educational Administration, Michigan State University*

Reframing Campus Conflict
Student Conduct Practice Through a Social Justice Lens
Edited by Jennifer Meyer Schrage and Nancy Geist Giacomini
Foreword by Edward Stoner

Social justice theory provides the lens for expanding our conception of student conduct administration, and the foundation for considering systemic changes in practice—changes that are vital to address the concerns and issues raised by an increasingly diverse student population.

"This publication is endorsed by ASCA as a collaborative, collegial new lens through which to consider how social justice practices and student conduct administration can come together to inform best practices in conduct and conflict management on college and university campuses. This approach serves to enhance the student's ability to fully comprehend the seriousness of the conduct, appreciate the people, community, or institutions affected by their conduct, restore the people, communities, and institutions affected, and hopefully eliminate a repeat of inappropriate behavior. When a student comprehends the impact of their behavior on others; this truly allows the student to participate in not only an educational but transformative process."—*Tamara J. King*, *J.D., 2009 President, Association for Student Conduct Administration*

A Day in the Life of a College Student Leader
Case Studies for Undergraduate Leaders
Sarah M. Marshall and Anne M. Hornak
Foreword by Susan R. Komives

"A litany of case studies designed to generate meaningful dialogue and critical analysis of realistic campus-based student experiences with leadership. In sum, the specificity and flexibility of this book make it a valuable contribution to faculty and administrators seeking to help students wrestle with the nexus of leadership theory and practice. It offers a much-needed contribution to the student leadership literature, is informed by and true to contemporary college student experiences, and useful across multiple educational contexts."—*Journal of College Student Development*

22883 Quicksilver Drive
Sterling, VA 20166-2102

Subscribe to our e-mail alerts: www.Styluspub.com